Helping Pastors Cope

A psycho-social
support system
for pastors

Benjamin D. Schoun, D.Min.

Andrews University Press, Berrien Springs, Michigan

Published December 1982 by
Andrews University Press
Berrien Springs, MI 49104

ISBN 0-943872-86-3

TABLE OF CONTENTS

PART I
EVALUATION OF THE NEED FOR A PSYCHO-SOCIAL SUPPORT SYSTEM

Chapter

iii

Chapter

PART II
DESIGNS FOR A POTENTIAL PSYCHO-SOCIAL
SUPPORT SYSTEM

Chapter

LIST OF TABLES

Table

ACKNOWLEDGMENT

Recognition and thanks are generously given to the many who helped to bring this project into being. There are the colleagues in ministry who shared their experiences informally, some who completed the pretest of the questionnaire, and those who willingly participated in the main survey. A number of denominational officials from both Seventh-day Adventist and non-Seventh-day Adventist Churches took time to respond to my inquiry for information. The Institute of Church Ministry and the personnel of the Andrews University Computing Center willingly assisted in making easier the work with the questionnaire. The editorial suggestions of Joyce Jones, the Andrews University dissertation secretary, and the skilled typing of Joyce Campbell were greatly appreciated. Spending much time and having a great influence on the thoughts in this paper are the members of the project committee: Arnold Kurtz, chairman, Roger Dudley, and Larry Geraty. These individuals as well as other faculty members who read or heard these ideas and responded with insights and evaluations, were most helpful. Finally, the greatest gratitude is expressed to my own family. My wife, Carol, whom I consider a partner in ministry and my best human support person, always listened and responded helpfully to my developing ideas. She and other members of the family helped with much of the busy work and waited patiently for me to finish.

INTRODUCTION

Beginnings

In my first assignment in the ministry I encountered a relatively young man who not long before had been a minister himself, but was one no longer. I spent considerable time listening to the details of his unfortunate experiences. We discussed the difficulties of ministry and shared idealism for its betterment. The impact of this relationship began to etch in my mind an image which now is being filled in with some detail in this project.

Following this initial experience I began to observe and encounter others, both present and former ministers, who struggled with problems related to ministry. I watched older men who were tired and wondering if their work had accomplished something significant. I came across individuals who were having family problems, career stress, and personal insecurity. I saw younger men, some of my friends, leaving the local parish to get advanced degrees and go into another career. Circumstances, providence, or whatever it might have been, led me to what seems to be a higher-than-usual number of opportunities to interact with these people. I began to study not only the problems of ministers but also the resources that might enable a minister to have a rewarding career.

Though these observations were valuable, it was my own

years of ministry that really gave me the feel for the demands and pressures as well as the joys and rewards of ministry. I was allowed to understand what a very bad experience can be when I struggled in a pilgrimage through two traumatic years of conflict and personal self-doubt. Fortunately, I found some resources that enabled me to recover my outlook and my energy. I am committed to ministry. I believe in the centrality of the work of the local church pastor. This is where the action is because it is where the people are. Ministry will never be without its trials. But it need not be without strengths as well. There are resources that can provide support to ministers in their work.

It is my contention that by becoming more intentional about providing and using support resources as needed, ministers will have a healthier, happier, and more effective approach to their ministry. Their influence will improve the quality and increase the growth of the church. We will also, I believe, conserve the investment made in ministerial training in that fewer ministers might drop out, change careers, or use some unacceptable method to cope with stress preventing their continuation in ministry. Some extra help from another person during a time of crisis might make the difference that enables a talented, otherwise strong pastor to adapt effectively. And indeed, supporting one another partakes of the very essence of Christianity.

While the concept of support for ministers has been receiving more and more attention in the general literature within the last twenty years, it has not received much systematic recognition in the Seventh-day Adventist (SDA) Church. In 1978 a Doctor of Ministry project[1] investigated some of the needs of pastors in relationship to the work of the conference ministerial secretaries. The Institute of Church Ministry (ICM)[2] has surveyed the personal and family situation of the Adventist ministry in North America in relationship to its church growth study. A small sprinkling of articles in Ministry, the denomination's publication for ministers, have dealt with such topics as burn-out, self-actualization, the mid-life crisis, and the benefits of closer clergy-lay relationships.[3] A few attempts are being made by local conferences to provide more systematic help to ministers who are facing encumbering stress.[4] Beyond this, there has been no comprehensive investigation or design of a support system for SDA ministers. The mission to spiritual brothers and sisters has a strong theological mandate just as does the mission to the unsaved. This leads me now to the purpose for this project.

---

[1] William Hinton McVay, "An Analysis and Role Description of the Seventh-day Adventist Conference Ministerial Secretary in North America" (D.Min. project, Andrews University, 1978).

[2] The Institute of Church Ministry (ICM) is an extension organization of the Seventh-day Adventist Theological Seminary, Andrews University, Berrien Springs, Michigan. The Institute contracts to do research for various organizations of the church. Further references to their studies are made in chapter 3.

[3] I.e., Jeffrey L. Cohen, "Male Metapause," Ministry, January 1978, pp. 18-20; Ron Flowers, "Journey Toward Intimacy," Ministry, April 1981, pp. 12-13; Mitchell F. Henson, "How to Be Yourself and a Pastor," Ministry, October 1979, p. 11; Kevin J. Howse, "When the Pastor Burns Out," Ministry, April 1981, pp. 28-29; William Rabior, "Ministerial Burnout," Ministry, March 1979, p. 25.

[4] These are explained in chapter 4. Local conferences constitute the organizational level in the SDA Church which relates most directly to churches and pastors. In most cases their territory covers one or two states. The organizational structure also includes union conferences (uniting several local conferences), divisions, and the general conference world headquarters.

Preview

The intent here is to investigate the needs of ministers in
the area of career adjustment and personal satisfaction, and then
to suggest a variety of resources that can help deal with these
needs. Formally stated, the task is to design a psycho-social
support system based upon an evaluation of the needs and potentially
applicable to the local pastor of the SDA Church in North America.[1]
The thesis claims that an evaluation of the current situation of
the local pastor in the SDA Church in North America will indicate
a need for an improved psycho-social support system for him.

The project is divided into two parts. First is the
evaluation of the need for such a support system. Chapter 1 reviews the literature which investigates the common situations of
human development that cause vulnerability to breakdown, or
create non-optimal functioning; it reviews the factors in the
career of ministry that establish a unique pattern of vulnerability for the minister; and it discusses how the need for a
support system is tied to these factors. Chapter 2 reflects on
the theological implications of the concept of support against
the background of the Scriptures by looking at the nature of man
and God's chosen methods for helping people, particularly his ministers. Chapter 3 reports on a survey conducted of a random sample
of SDA pastors throughout North America. The survey measures the

---

[1]In this project the phrase "psycho-social support system"
refers to the network of various resources that a person might draw
upon from both himself (psycho) and from people around him (social)
which could help him to relate positively to his life and career. A
more detailed definition and description of this concept is found in
the latter part of chapter 1.

availability, the use, the effectiveness, the dynamics involved, and the interest in using each of several types of support resources.

Part 2, which includes chapters 4 and 5, turns to the solution as it seeks to suggest designs for a potentially effective psycho-social support system. Chapter 4 reveals methods that individuals or organizations have already tried in the support of ministers or those in parallel situations. Chapter 5 concludes the project with a constructive design for a support system potentially applicable for the SDA Church in North America. It outlines a host of support resources which individual pastors or church organizations could use, according to their situations.

Limitations

This project is written to apply specifically to the SDA Church in North America. The same principles might apply in other countries, but that would need to be assessed separately. The general literature makes evident the cross-denominational similarities in the needs of pastors. But many of the resources and methods of support are tied to unique denominational situations.

It should be noted that this project is descriptive and prescriptive in its research. Its suggestions, although tried by others, for the most part have not been tested personally in actual practice. Further research could be done with a more developmental approach in which a person in a conference could actually have opportunity to implement an intentional support system, measuring attitudes before and after to check its actual effectiveness.

There may be other factors that function as support resources for some individuals than are treated in this project. Our lives and relationships are very complex. I have attempted to present the major ones, particularly those that can be initiated by individuals or organizations intentionally. Furthermore, support resources may vary with changing times. Consequently there is a continuing need for updating the support system as situations change.

It is hoped that this project may offer a possible plan to follow, and may serve as a catalyst for implementation of an intentional support system by SDA conferences in North America. It would also be gratifying if the ideas presented here might enable individual pastors to increase their self-awareness of the dynamics operating in their lives and to take steps to prevent crises. But its effectiveness is limited according to the initiative that individuals or organizations take to implement such ideas for themselves.

PART I

EVALUATION OF THE NEED FOR A PSYCHO-
SOCIAL SUPPORT SYSTEM

CHAPTER I

THE PSYCHO-SOCIAL NEED FOR A SUPPORT SYSTEM

General Vulnerability in Common
Situations of Human Life

Ministers are human too. Like everyone else they pass
through the various stages of development; they face the crises
which are part of earthly life; they have personal characteristics
that determine tendencies for various types of needs. Certain
factors may exist in their lives that make them vulnerable to
unhappiness, unfulfillment, maladjustment, poor functioning, or
total breakdown, affecting their physical, mental, social, or
spiritual health. In this first part of Chapter 1 we will look
at several of these factors that are not tied to one's role, but
simply to the fact that one is human. Then the second and third
main sections of this chapter will deal with the unique vulnerability of a career in ministry, and the concept of a support
system.

Transitions in Adult Development

Since the middle 1970s, several researchers have reported
new findings in the area of adult development.[1] Two professors of

---

[1]Several of the most significant of these studies include
Daniel J. Levinson, The Seasons of a Man's Life (New York:
Ballentine Books, 1978); George E. Vaillant, Adaptation to Life
(Boston: Little, Brown, 1977); Roger L. Gould, Transformations:

social work, Eileen M. Brennan and Ann Weick, have summarized the
common elements of these studies into five basic assumptions.

Assumption 1. Humans continue to develop throughout life.
Assumption 2. Life unfolds in stages during the course of
adulthood.
Assumption 3. The stages are divided by transition periods that
are sometimes punctuated with crises.
Assumption 4. Transitions provide opportunities for growth.
Assumption 5. Adulthood is to be examined in terms of the underlying health and strength people have to cope
with change.[1]

Daniel J. Levinson has produced possibly the most comprehensive
theory of adult development. He says that the life cycle involves
a series of alternating stable periods and transitional periods.
What he calls early and middle adulthood is illustrated in figure 1.
Each period has certain tasks that must be accomplished. A stable
period is a time to "make firm choices, rebuild the life structure
and enhance one's life within it." A transitional period is a time
to "question and reappraise the existing structure, to search for
new possibilities in self and world, and to modify the present
structure enough so that a new one can be formed."[2] Human potential
has more possibilities than can be encompassed in any life structure
at one particular time. Transitional periods allow for changes and
adjustments enabling a person to fulfill the neglected parts of the

---

Growth and Change in Adult Life (New York: Simon and Schuster,
1978); Gail Sheehy popularized much of this material in her best
selling book Passages: Predictable Crises of Adult Life (New York:
E. P. Dutton, 1974; Bantam Books, 1976).

[1] "Theories of Adult Development: Creating a Context for
Practice," Social Casework: The Journal of Contemporary Social
Work 62 (January 1981):16.

[2] Levinson, p. 53.

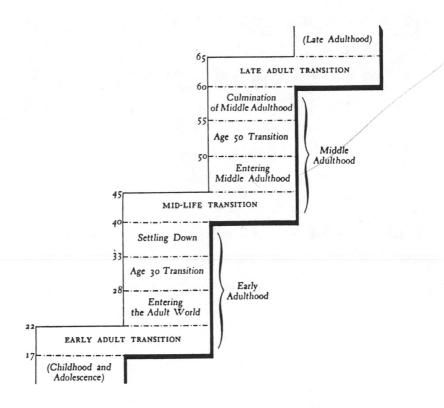

Fig. 1. Developmental periods in early and middle adulthood.[1]

self. This is often called "self-actualization."[2] It is also a time to deal with new circumstances of passing age.

In the age thirty transition a person works on the flaws and limitations of his current life structure. This person feels the press of making changes before it is too late. He may not yet have gotten into the career of his choice. He may feel dissatisfied

---

[1]Levinson, p. 57.

[2]Hanna Zacks, "Self-Actualization: A Midlife Problem," Social Casework: The Journal of Contemporary Social Work 61 (April 1980):223-33.

with his social status. He may feel unfulfilled or frustrated by
current home or work circumstances.[1]

The transition about which most is written is the one in
mid-life, often called "the mid-life crisis."[2] A person's values
and the meaning of life are central issues. He may feel unfulfilled, disillusioned, bored, or fatigued. He may question his
accomplishments, begin to value other things, and yet feel trapped.
His marriage may be disenchanting. There may be loneliness from
the emancipation of children. He may sense physical changes in
his body, the tendency to illnesses, or a reduced sex drive. He
senses that he is being rejected in favor of younger people. He
begins to face the prospect of dying. Ministers face these things
too, albeit in their own unique situation.[3] Whoever one is, there
commonly are drastic changes in personality, habits, career, and

------

[1]The reader may note that masculine pronouns are sometimes
used. This is not because the author refuses to recognize women.
However, men predominately fill the roles under study in this project, at least in the SDA Church. Furthermore, the writer feels
that there is a legitimate, non-demeaning place for the use of
generic pronouns. These are used occasionally.

[2]Several publications dealing with the mid-life crisis include Nancy Mayer, Male Mid-Life Crisis (Garden City, NY: Doubleday,
1978); Jim Conway, Men in Mid-Life Crisis (Elgin, IL: David C.
Cook Publishing Co., 1978); William E. Hulme, Mid-Life Crises,
Christian Care Books, no. 7 (Philadelphia: Westminster Press, 1980).
The latter two books are written from a Christian perspective. See
also Cohen's "Male Metaphase."

[3]See Ray W. Ragsdale, The Mid-Life Crises of a Minister
(Waco, TX: Word Books, 1978). A book that deals with the whole
career cycle of a minister is Cecil R. Paul, Passages of a Pastor
(Grand Rapids: Zondervan Publishing House, 1981). A sample of
articles include Robert M. Collie, "Counseling the Middle-yeared
Pastor," Pastoral Psychology 22 (March 1971):50-53; Thomas E. Brown,
"Vocational Crises and Occupational Satisfaction among Ministers,"
Princeton Seminary Bulletin 63 (December 1970):52-62.

relationships with family and friends. Levinson says, "All men make some changes during this period, so that the life structure at its end is necessarily different, for better or worse, from that at the start."[1]

Although there are individuals who seem to pass through these transitions with stability and continuity in their lives, the majority have quite an upheaval. In Levinson's study, 62 percent had a moderate or severe crisis in their age-thirty transition, and about 80 percent had such in their mid-life transition.[2] Too often people react with actions that are contrary to Christian principles or are hurtful to other people. But this need not be. The transition can be an opportunity for positive growth. The determining factor is whether the person has adequate coping resources to use in adapting and changing.

Regarding such crises Brennan and Weick say, "The goal of intervention is not to remediate the crisis but to strengthen coping skills through the ever-present structure of social groups." Good coping and problem-solving skills are not automatically maintained throughout one's lifetime. They are "time- and situation-linked."

> Not even a "normal" childhood guarantees the emotional psychological tools that will carry one throughout life. No matter how successfully we have gained skills in our first physical and social interactions with our environment, those skills must be constantly improved and expanded.[3]

Although the transitions of adult development make one vulnerable

---

[1]Levinson, p. 85.　　　　[2]Ibid., pp. 87, 199.

[3]Brennan and Weick, pp. 18-19.

to psycho-social dysfunctions, the coping resources available can make the difference between growth and decline.

Stress and Crises

Besides the normal developmental stages which challenge a person, there are also those occasions of stress and crisis that can arise at any time, to which we are all vulnerable. For instance, we all eventually face the death of people who are close to us. Sometimes we have accidents or get sick. Occasionally there may be conflicts at home or at work.

These things exert pressure on us and cause a bodily response called stress.[1] Stress can have a positive or negative effect. If its effect is negative, it is called "distress," according to the father of stress studies, Hans Selye.[2] A crisis is a severe distress that requires a decision, adaptation, or change. If too many crises occur together, severe health consequences can result. Morse and Furst list a wide range of stress-related problems. Physiological conditions include cardiovascular diseases, cancer, depression, headaches, backaches, ulcers, diabetes, allergies, rheumatoid arthritis, warts, gout, dental caries, graying of hair, dandruff, etc. Stress-related disorders can result in alcoholism, obesity, smoking, caffeinism, drug addiction, accidents,

---

[1] Donald Ray Morse and M. Lawrence Furst, Stress for Success (New York: Van Nostrand Reinhold Company, 1979), pp. 5-9; Karl Albrecht, Stress and the Manager (Englewood Cliffs, NJ: Prentice-Hall, Inc., 1979), pp. 47-48.

[2] Stress Without Distress (Philadelphia: J. B. Lippincott Co., 1974, p. 31.

divorce, business break-up, and suicide. Stress also leads to pre-mature aging.[1]

Thomas J. Holmes and Richard H. Rahe have assigned a value that each of forty-three life events (sometimes called stressors) has in producing stress. The death of a spouse ranks highest with a value of one hundred. Other examples include divorce (seventy-three), personal injury or illness (fifty-three), retirement (forty-five), change to a different line of work (thirty-six), change in residence (twenty), and a minor violation of the law (eleven).[2] A person may test himself by adding up the values for each of the life events he has faced within one year. In their survey work, Holmes and Rahe found that 80 percent of those whose scores were three hundred or above had become severely depressed, had heart attacks, or developed other serious ailments. Of those whose scores were between one hundred fifty and three hundred, 53 percent were similarly af-fected, as were 33 percent of those scoring up to one hundred fifty.

The Research Center in Religion and Society of Lancaster Theological Seminary surveyed a group of ministers to find out what stress-producing life events they were encountering. They concluded that "clergy experience life stresses about as often

---

[1]Morse and Furst, pp. 119-20, 134, 146. An experiment in the Navy reported by Stuart G. Leyden indicates that men who had recently been under much stress were the ones who turned up at the ship's bay most frequently and for the longest periods of time. The conclusion: "People under stress are more susceptible to whatever illness is on the prowl." See "Coping With Stress," Church Management: The Clergy Journal, January 1981, pp. 14-15.

[2]Thomas H. Holmes and Richard H. Rahe, "The Social Read-justment Scale," Journal of Psychosomatic Research 11 (1967):213-18, cited by Morse and Furst, pp. 87-88. See appendix A for a special adaptation of this scale for ministers, plus several other measures of stress.

and in the same way anyone else does."[1]

The fact that stressors often produce these negative consequences does not mean that they are inevitable. There are many
people who live highly stressed lives and do not get sick. What
distinguishes the people who stay healthy from those who do not?
William A. Miller has isolated several attitudes and behaviors that
are similar among those who do break down (he is thinking particularly of mental break-down):

1. For one reason or another they are generally afraid to
   express their real feelings.
2. They didn't have an opportunity to "talk through" their
   conflicts and stresses. They were unable to find a
   "listening ear."
3. The people with whom they did talk didn't really hear what
   they were saying.
4. They generally felt that sheer will power could overcome
   their problem, even though they really didn't understand
   it.
5. They denied reality and moved into their own world which
   was less painful, less confusing, less demanding and had
   fewer responsibilities to meet and decisions to make.[2]

On the other side, Maya Pines presents a complementary
theme regarding those who stay healthy. The social resources available to a person are a significant factor in protecting people from
the ill-effects of stress. In one study, ten thousand men in Israel
who were forty years of age or older were followed for five years
to assess their tendency to angina pectoris, a form of heart disease.
Among high risk men, fewer developed this problem who had loving and
supportive wives than those whose wives were cold. A nine-year

---

[1] Loyde H. Hartley, A Study of Clergy Morale (Lancaster, PA:
Research Center in Religion and Society, Lancaster Theological
Seminary, 1980), appendix, pp. 5-7.

[2] Why Do Christians Break Down? (Minneapolis: Augsburg
Publishing House, 1973), pp. 111-12.

study of seven thousand persons in Alameda County, California, showed that men in their fifties who were in a high risk category due to their low socioeconomic status, but who scored high on an index of social networks, actually lived longer than men of higher status, but who had low social-network scores.[1]

The stressors and crises of life are common to us all. But the fact that we are vulnerable does not mean that we need to be overcome. A variety of coping resources of both a psychological and social nature can enable a person to handle these life events in a constructive way.

Personal Characteristics

Some people, just because of their unique makeup, need more or want more help than others. Morse and Furst explain several genetic factors that make a person vulnerable to stress. For example, sympathicotonics are people whose bodies release too much adrenaline and noradrenaline, causing them to have extreme reactions to stress and to easily develop high blood pressure and related diseases.[2] A person's physical condition and mental state can affect the need for help. Some believe that the body operates by biorhythms. On bad days a person would be particularly vulnerable. Past experiences, especially from childhood, can affect the present ability to cope.[3] The number of behavioral skills a

[1]Maya Pines, "Psychological Hardiness: The Role of Challenge in Health," Psychology Today, December 1980, pp. 34-44; Aaron Antonovsky, Health, Stress, and Coping (San Francisco: Jossey-Bass, 1979, pp. 163-65.

[2]Morse and Furst, pp. 33-39.

[3]Selye, pp. 39-40, 74, 93-99; Ronald J. Burke and Tamara

person has learned, such as assertiveness, problem-solving, and conflict resolution, is also a factor.

Then there are the various personality traits. Meyer Friedman and Ray H. Rosenman have made popular the Type A personality--the hard-driving, competitive achiever, who also is prone to suffer stress-related diseases. In contrast is the Type B personality who is passive, restrained, not overly ambitious, but also without the tendency to suffer from stress.[1]

David C. McClelland has typed people according to motivations that they have. Some have the need for power and prestige, and some for friendship and affiliation. Those who have a strong drive for power, but are inhibited about expressing it, will suffer the most when they are subjected to the kind of stressor that threatens that motivation. A person who is motivated by the need for affiliation, on the other hand, will not suffer illness resulting from the pressure of a stressor that threatens power. McClelland concluded, "Generally speaking, when the stress is related to the dominant motive disposition in the individual, it is more likely to be associated with illness."[2]

Pines has reported the research of Suzanne C. Kobasa and Salvatore R. Maddi who have found that stress-resistant people are

---

Weir, "Coping with the Stress of Managerial Occupations," in Current Concerns in Occupational Stress, eds. Cary L. Cooper and Roy Payne (New York: John Wiley & Sons, 1980), p. 326.

[1]Meyer Friedman and Ray H. Rosenman, Type A Behavior and Your Heart (New York: Alfred A. Knopf, 1974); Mayer, pp. 46-51.

[2]David C. McClelland, "Sources of Stress in the Drive for Power," in Psychopathology of Human Adaptation, ed. George Serban (New York: Plenum Press, 1976), cited by Pines, p. 44.

those who have a specific set of attitudes toward life. They have an openness to change, a feeling of involvement in whatever they are doing, and a sense of control over events. "They score high on 'challenge' (viewing change as a challenge rather than a threat), 'commitment' (the opposite of alienation), and 'control' (the opposite of powerlessness)." Those who appraise stressful situations in these terms seem to remain healthy despite the pressure. Those who do not, often malfunction in some way. These researchers believe that by re-educating people in their attitude toward stressors, they will be striking at the basic cause of stress reactions and will be creating psychological hardiness.[1]

There are many personality traits. In Raymond B. Cattell's personality inventory, "Sixteen Personality Factor Questionnaire" (16 PF), sixteen primary personality factors and eight secondary factors are measured. There are seemingly infinite combinations as these factors are integrated with one another. For instance, people with a low "C" factor are less emotionally stable and may need more reassurance. People with a high "I" seem to have many personal and attention needs that must be met by others. Those with a low "Q_2" enjoy the presence of other people and desire their approval and advice.[2] This illustrates how a person's needs for help may be determined by his personal characteristics.

---

[1]Suzanne C. Kobasa, Robert R. J. Hilker, and Salvatore R. Maddi, "Who Stays Healthy under Stress?" Journal of Occupational Medicine 21 (1979):595-98, cited in Pines, pp. 34ff.

[2]Raymond B. Cattell, Herbert W. Eber, and Maurice M. Tatsuoka, Handbook for the Sixteen Personality Factor Questionnaire (Champaign, IL: Institute for Personality and Ability Testing, 1970), pp. 77-120.

Besides the general vulnerabilities that are common to the human experience, there are unique aspects of the career of ministry that may threaten the minister's well-being. That will be the topic of the next main section.

Unique Vulnerability in the Career of Ministry

Perspective

In describing the career of ministry there are those who speak in inflated ways about the glories, challenges, and successes of their ministry. There are also those who get caught in a melancholic lament of all the frustrations, hardships, and the "why-I-left-the-ministry" talk. James D. Glasse says that either of these extremes keep ministers and others from facing reality and taking responsibility for their situations.[1] Some may question whether the career of ministry does in fact have any unique challenges which justify separate attention. After all, every other person in his own career can report difficulties that he or she is facing. Peter Drucker, a prolific writer in the field of business management, has emphasized this very point in his somewhat satirical article entitled "Martyrs Unlimited":

> There is not one occupation, trade or profession in this country that is not misunderstood, neglected, underrated, unloved and rejected. No group that is not steadily slipping in popular esteem and in ability to attract the young. . . . Two-thirds of the dentists do not want their children to become dentists, one survey shows. Other surveys give similarly alarming figures for a lawyer and banker, plumber and nurse. Science as a career "has very little attraction for young Americans today," concluded Margaret Mead in the survey cited earlier: "the best

---

[1] James D. Glasse, _Putting It Together in the Parish_ (Nashville: Abingdon Press, 1972), pp. 19-20, 69-71.

young men go into government rather than into business,"
every conference of personnel vice presidents is told. The
government agencies, on the other hand, have figures that prove
conclusively that good young men don't seek government jobs
but go into business instead. The engineers complain that the
ablest of the young fall for the glamour of pure science; the
teachers, that the ablest of the young want to go into research; the researchers, that the ablest of the young lust for
the fleshpots of industry. I am sure that portentous reports
are presented at the board meetings of the Mafia warning that
the ablest young Sicilians no longer want to make a career
in dope peddling.[1]

To this Drucker says "hogwash." On a more serious note he con-

cludes, "No one occupation or profession is persecuted, misunder-

stood, or rejected in this country. . . . We suffer from an in-

dulgence in self-pity of epidemic proportions."[2]

The intent of this study is not to beg any special prefer-

ence; it is not to encourage ministers to feel sorry for themselves.

It is not seeking ministerial coddling. But just as each profession

has its uniquenesses, the ministry has a certain configuration of

structures and dynamics with resulting pressures which can legiti-

mately be studied. If each profession, and ultimately each person,

deliberately ignores taking responsibility to humanize its situation,

there will indeed be unnecessary martyrs. Jud, Mills, and Burch

place their study of ex-pastors in perspective like this:

The ministry is not, either to ex-pastors or to pastors, a
bundle of miseries or a vocational hair shirt--there are, of
course, a few exceptions. Most regard the ministry as a worthy
challenge with exciting possibilities and supremely important
goals. Our point in detailing the reasons for leaving is not
to tell sob stories about clergymen but to show that as an
occupation within a major social institution there are system
pressures and culture-wide trends which are reshaping the entire concept of ministry and the institutional patterns it will
follow in the future. It is possible to see beyond the

---

[1]Peter Drucker, "Martyrs Unlimited," Harper's Magazine,
July 1964, pp. 12-16.

[2]Ibid.

idiosyncratic accounts of each ex-pastor to the structural implications for the whole church.[1]

There are those who find it easy to write off the problems and the person of a pastor who has become discouraged or faced some crisis by making some demeaning comments about his inability to take the pressure, his lack of faith, or his undependability. And it has been done by fellow ministers. Such a reaction is often an unrealistic denial of their own vulnerability. John C. Harris has said pointedly, "Over-simple psychological explanations like 'troubled ministers are the neurotic ones' do not fit the facts." He says that there are cultural and institutional factors beyond the control of clergy themselves.[2] This does not mean that clergy are helpless. Some things may be nearly impossible to change, but there are ways of neutralizing the painful elements. But before these helps are shared, the situation in the career of ministry is described.

Clergy Morale and Demissions

Research studies do indicate that church pastors suffer from periods of low morale, and sometimes when the stress becomes too great they demit or resign their pastorates. The Research Center in Religion and Society at Lancaster Theological Seminary recently completed a study of clergy in the Penn Central Conference of the United Church of Christ. They defined low morale in these terms:

---

[1] Gerald Jud, Edgar W. Mills, and Genevieve Walters Burch, Ex-Pastors; Why Men Leave the Parish Ministry (Philadelphia: Pilgrim Press, 1970), p. 53.

[2] John C. Harris, "New Trends in Pastoral Care for Pastors," Pastoral Psychology 22 (March 1971):6.

> A low morale experience is any negative feeling or attitude
> clergy have which reduces their effectiveness or enthusiasm
> for their work as pastors. For example, a sense of losing hope,
> a feeling of being overwhelmed, a loss of direction, or an
> experience of futility in relation to the ministry would
> indicate low morale. A low morale experience may be a rela-
> tively brief episode, lasting a month or so, or it may be a
> chronic condition.[1]

Eighty-four percent of the respondents had such low morale ex-

periences. Furthermore, about two-thirds admitted to some diffi-

culty in openly discussing their low morale with others. It is

these individuals who have more frequent and longer lasting inci-

dents. They also tend to serve churches with declining memberships.

It was also found that low morale experiences were due primarily

to organizational stress in the church itself, rather than other

general life stressors.[2]

A study of stress in the ministry reported in 1971 by the

Ministry Studies Board was based on nearly five thousand Protestant

clergymen from twenty-one different denominations. Three-fourths

of these pastors had experienced periods of major stress in their

ministries. Two-thirds of these had more than one stressful time.

What was their stress like?

> As experienced by these ministers, it was unpleasant. Anguish,
> frustration, conflusion [sic], worry and bewilderment were
> mentioned by 49% of the men. Another 14% were depressed, sad,
> sorrowful or hurt, and 7% were fearful.
>   In addition to these generalized feelings of distress, one-
> fourth of the men reported doubts about their competence, feel-
> ings of helplessness or personal inadequacy. Another 4%
> described a sense of failure, defeat, shame or guilt. . . .

---

[1]Hartley, p. 3. The population for this study included all
198 pastors in the Penn Central Conference. Questionnaires were
sent and 75 percent (or 149) were returned and used in the analysis
reported. In addition twenty-five personal interviews were conducted.

[2]Ibid., pp. 10, 14. 18.

> Approximately one man out of four implied that his problems arose from others, producing feelings of rage, contempt, disgust, alienation, betrayal and the like.
> Only 8% reported physical symptoms such as illness, irritability or excessive fatigue.[1]

As in the previous study the source of the problem was predominately job-related--conflicts with parishioners of a personal or ideological nature, personality clashes, overwork, communication problems, work adjustment problems, a sense of frustration and lack of accomplishment.[2]

When these problems surpass the person's threshold of tolerance, many leave the local parish either to a totally new occupation or to a non-parish type of ministry, such as chaplaincy, teaching, or denominational positions. Jud, Mills, and Burch observed that pastors do not differ much from ex-pastors in attitudes, beliefs, job dissatisfaction, or role enjoyment. They are simply on opposite sides of a tipping point, a hope-frustration balance. Pastors are those who continue to hope for fulfillment. Ex-pastors are those for whom frustration has taken precedence. One percent of the active United Church of Christ clergy leave the ministry annually.[3] This is quite a modest figure. But it seems more serious when a minister leaves his position than when others change occupations because ordination is conceived as a life-long commitment.

Other researchers give higher percentages of dropouts.

---

[1]Edgar W. Mills and John P. Koval, Stress in the Ministry (Washington, D.C.: Ministries Studies Board, 1971), p. 9.

[2]Ibid., pp. 13, 22.

[3]Jud, Mills, and Burch, pp. 107, 58.

Marvin T. Judy followed up more than one thousand of his students at Perkins School of Theology. He found four categories among them. Forty-eight percent were classified as "pastoral-content." They were quite happy and content in their profession. Sixteen percent he called "pastoral-uneasy." They were discontented, restless, dissatisfied, or considering leaving. Another group consisted of those who still regarded themselves as ministers but served in related capacities such as teaching, chaplaincy, or denominational work. These he called "connectionals," and they made up 26 percent of his study. Finally, there were those who had surrendered their ministerial credentials and were no longer serving under a denominational authority, the "discontinued" group. Nine percent were in this category.[1] Another study checked persistence in the ministry of 572 seminary graduates from fourteen schools, fifteen years after graduation. Nearly 8 percent were not in any ministry-related position.[2]

This sampling of research is enough to convey the message that a significant number of ministers are troubled for periods of time, whether short or long. The ICM study of SDA ministers in North America indicates that "the overall morale of most pastors is high, but a substantial minority struggle with some doubts and discouragements concerning their calling."[3] What are some of the main problems

---

[1] Marvin T. Judy, "Professional Ministry: The Call, Performance, Morale, and Authority," Perkins School of Theology Journal 30 (Winter 1977):16-18.

[2] Sue Webb Cardwell and Richard A. Hunt, "Persistence in Seminary and Ministry," Pastoral Psychology 28 (Winter 1979):120-21.

[3] Roger L. Dudley, Des Cummings, Jr., and Greg Clark, "The Pastor as Person and Husband: A Study of Pastoral Morale," The

they face? That is what we consider in the next few sections.

Role Conflicts

It was Samuel W. Blizzard whose research first noted the effects of contemporary society on the career of ministry and sparked the movement for the care of pastors. What he discovered and reported in the mid-1950s was that ministers were caught in a conflict of roles.[1] Blizzard reduced the many tasks of a minister to six basic roles: preacher, pastor, priest, teacher, organizer, and administrator. And this order reflected the priority that ministers placed on these roles as influenced by their seminary training, their theology, and their own convictions. But the actual time demand for each role determined quite a different order. Administration took the most time. No matter how different ministers wished it to be, found Blizzard, they all ended up doing about the same thing. They had to do most what they felt was least important. Furthermore, the church-at-large had not pro-vided the minister an adequate theological justification or practical training to do this work. That, Blizzard said, was "the minister's dilemma."

Since Blizzard's report, studies in role conflicts in the ministry have multiplied and become quite sophisticated in their analysis.[2] We know, for instance, that "role senders" are

Institute of Church Ministry, Berrien Springs, Michigan, May 1981. (Photocopied).

[1]Samuel W. Blizzard, "The Minister's Dilemma," The Christian Century, April 25, 1956, pp. 508-10.

[2]One of the best resources is Donald P. Smith, Clergy in the Cross Fire (Philadelphia: Westminster Press, 1973). See also

individuals who expect something from a focal person, in this case,
the minister. The minister is a "role receiver." The role senders
or groups of senders, all those who relate to the role player in
that role, make up the "role set." These include the members of
the congregation, the church officers, fellow ministers, denominational leaders, community leaders, etc. The desires of the role
senders are actually "role pressures," since the sender is trying
to influence the receiver to conform to his expectations. The
minister's ability to move quickly and efficiently from one role to
another is "role flexibility." If the expectations of role senders
are unclear or confusing, the role receiver experiences "role
ambiguity." When two or more role expectations interfere with
each other or contradict one another altogether, there is "role
conflict."

Role conflicts may come about in three ways.[1] There is
"external" role conflict where the senders may disagree with each
other over the expectations for the minister. For instance, some
church members may feel that the pastor should be out at the

"Role Conflict among Clergy," Ministry Studies 2 (December 1968):
13-82; this contains a series of articles which are procedings of
the Research Conference on Ministry, Racine, Wisconsin, October
18-20, 1968. From a sociological perspective are these resources:
R. L. Kahn, D. M. Wolfe, R. P. Quinn, J. D. Snoek, and R. A.
Rosenthal, Organizational Stress: Studies in Role Conflict and
Ambiguity (New York: John Wiley & Sons, Inc., 1964); Daniel Katz
and Robert L. Kahn, The Social Psychology of Organizations (New
York: John Wiley & Sons, Inc., 1966; William Scott and Terence R.
Mitchell, Organization Theory (Homewood, IL: Dorsey Press, 1972).

[1]Edgar W. Mills, "Types of Role Conflict among Clergymen,"
Ministry Studies 2 (December 1968):13; John Craig Forney, "Tran-
sitions: A Study of United Methodist Clergy of the Southern
California-Arizona Conference Who Have Left the Parish Ministry"
(Rel.D. dissertation, School of Theology at Claremont, 1975),
pp. 83-110.

building site directing construction; others may think that the pastor's work is to be visiting the members in their homes; the denominational officials may expect him to be engaged in evangelism.

Second, there is "internal-external" role conflict where a person's self-understanding and values are in conflict with the role he is required to play by others. The conflicting feelings regarding administrative tasks as reported by Blizzard fit into this category. The ICM study found this same conflict operating among SDA ministers. The greatest areas of frustration and disappointment were motivation of laity, administrative work, dealing with members' problems, and board, business, and committee meetings. The sources of greatest satisfaction were preaching, personal evangelism, visiting people, and public evangelism.[1] There are situations where a minister feels convicted to take a stand on certain moral issues, but the congregation opts for the quiet status quo.[2] The pastor's approach in counseling and in the way he assists church organizations often conflicts with the expectations of the congregation. Lay people seem to want a more superficial involvement of the pastor. They want him to do things for them, whereas the pastor seeks a deeper role of enabling them to be better able to do things for themselves.[3] Internal-external role conflict may also exist between the minister and denominational

---

[1]Dudley, Cummings, and Clark, pp. 13, 15.

[2]Jeffrey K. Hadden, "Role Conflict and Crisis in the Churches," Ministry Studies 2 (December 1968):19-21.

[3]James Dittes, "Why Conflicts?" in Growth in Ministry, ed. Thomas E. Kadel (Philadelphia: Fortress Press, 1979), pp. 52-53.

officials, peers, or community people. It can be quite threatening
when both his own values and the external expectations are strong.
He wants to be a man of integrity and yet responsible and responsive
to his public.

Third, some role conflict is "internal." A minister may
impose upon himself, and internalize, conflicting expectations. He
may be torn between two equally high values, such as his church
ministries and his family.

There is yet another situation which is understood as a type
of role conflict. A person may feel the pressure, put upon him by
others or by his own conscience, to complete more tasks than can
possibly be accomplished within his available time or energy.
This is called "role overload." If a minister tries to keep up
with the many and varied demands placed upon him, he may, and
often does, fall into the pattern of a workaholic. In a study of
ministers in the Minneapolis, Minnesota area, 85 percent of them
had problems with overwork.[1] Only about 4 percent of the ministers
have had specific training in time management.[2] Overwork can cause
physical illness and mental imbalance. It can hinder the minister
in developing his spiritual life and can negatively affect his
family.

Other occupations face role conflicts also. But ministry

---

[1]Paul D. Robbins, "The Ministers of Minneapolis: A Study
in Paradox," Leadership 1 (Winter 1980):121.

[2]Richard Daniel Paul, "An Investigation and an Analysis,
Leading to a Reassessment of the Minister's Attitudes Toward and
Time Spent in Leisure Activities" (D.Min. dissertation, Drew Uni-
versity, 1980), pp. 117-21.

certainly is one career with characteristics that set it up for

high vulnerability to this pressure. Speed Leas has listed some

of these:

> They structure their own time.
> They do not have a supervisor closely observing what they do.
> There is a list of unwritten expectations that they are supposed
> to know but have not agreed, in a contract, as to what
> their job is.
> They are expected to perform a wide variety of job skills
> competently, from preaching and teaching to counseling and
> organizational administration.
> They usually work alone in the performance of ministry and do
> not work with partners or peers collaborating with them or
> observing what they do.
> They are not clear about the separation between work, family,
> recreation, and personal privacy.
> They have very few things they can measure at the end of the
> day to be sure of their accomplishments.
> Their job is not universally understood, and they are sometimes
> asked questions like, What do you do between Sundays?[1]

Some role conflict is to be expected and is healthy in the

prophetic task of ministry. But much of it is unnecessary, a

hindrance to the progress of the church, and a drain on the

minister's energy and happiness. Donald Smith, in enumerating the

pressures, put it like this:

> It is not that the clergyman is caught in the cross fire from
> several snipers with high-powered rifles. A more apt analogy
> may be that of machine guns, grenades, and booby traps going
> off around him all at once.[2]

Such a situation warrants the investment in resources that

strengthen the pastor to deal with these things wholesomely.

---

[1]Speed B. Leas, Time Management (Nashville: Abingdon,
1978), pp. 56-57; see also pp. 26-30.

[2]Smith, p. 74.

Pastoral Pedestal

The mystique surrounding the "call" of God, the "set-apartness" that comes with ordination, and the symbolic nature of a minister's position contribute to his being placed upon a pedestal above the ordinary person. Psychiatrist Louis McBurney lists the reasons why parishioners encourage the pedestal as

> . . . the need for an omnipotent, benevolent father; an expression of the all-American trait of hero worship; the desire for a personal high priest; and the all-too-frequent practice of commitment to Christ by proxy.[1]

Brooks Holifield maintains that people tend to establish heroes according to their underlying anxieties and needs.[2] They project upon the minister the ideals that they envision of a person without such problems and who can help them to that end. Oscar Eggers lists some of these ideals.

> Among the things that parishioners especially hope are for their minister to be doubt-free, tension-free, untroubled by the familial, the interpersonal, and the social problems of our time. Perceived public expectations perhaps include that he shall be a personal Rock of Gibraltar, on whom parishioners, family members, friends, and acquaintances may depend and look to for support.[3]

From the minister's perspective, he may encourage the pedestal because he may believe that becoming too close to his people erodes his authority and respect. There may be conflict or privileged information that keeps pastor and people from getting

---

[1]Louis McBurney, Every Pastor Needs a Pastor (Waco, TX: Word Books, 1977), p. 80.

[2]E. Brooks Holifield, "The Hero and the Minister in American Culture," Theology Today 33 (January 1977):371, 377-78.

[3]Oscar Eggers, "Seminar for Ministers: A University-Sponsored Approach to Self-exploration," Pastoral Psychology 23 (October 1972):19.

close. The minister may worry that he will be accused of playing
favorites or taking sides if he develops some closer friends. And,
as McBurney says, "It feels good. There is a nice safe buffer
zone between him and his people, and he can avoid facing his own
frustrations and failures."[1] Sometimes pastors seek and cherish
the pedestal as a defense mechanism against some unresolved
developmental needs, i.e., independence, authority, and control.[2]

Although there is value in the minister having high
standards, it is evident that there are some inherent problems with
the pedestal. There is the pressure to be perfect when the pastor
knows he has human weaknesses. This discrepancy often leads to
his wearing a facade, to his being unrealistic, and to denying
his limitations; or it may fuel feelings of inadequacy, poor
self-image, hypocrisy, and the fear of being discovered. This
pressure also extends to the minister's wife and children.
Preacher's "kids" are judged by a higher standard just because of
who they are. Ministers' wives are always expected to have clean
houses, pleasant dispositions, and eager hands. The prominence
of their position places them all in a fishbowl where everyone can
scrutinize their lives as though transparent. And if the halo
slips, there are plenty of voices ready to point it out.

Because the pedestal separates the people from the minister,
it brings to him loneliness and isolation. Dennis Doyle reports

---

[1]McBurney, p. 84.

[2]Irene Lovett, "Pastor on a Pedestal," in Growth in Ministry, ed. Thomas E. Kadel (Philadelphia: Fortress Press, 1980),
pp. 85-86; also McBurney, pp. 61-63.

that 93 percent of the ministers he surveyed had experienced these feelings,[1] as did 67 percent of the ministers of Minneapolis.[2] Fifty-eight percent of SDA ministers sometimes feel lonely and isolated.[3] Although the work of the clergyman appears to involve intimate relationships, Eggers points out that the minister actually is not given much opportunity to express "his own doubts and uncertainties, his own sense of bafflement, and the stresses and strains of endeavoring to be what others hope him to be."[4] Larry Graham, who wrote a dissertation on ministers and friendship, indicates that those in leadership roles are not usually approached for friendship or informal relationships, nor do leaders seek these relationships with their constituents.[5] Not only the pedestal but latent childhood developmental problems, time pressures, role conflicts, frequent moves, and other factors encourage superficial, guarded relationships. And depending on the height of the pedestal, people, and pastors themselves, may believe that ministers and their families either do not have human needs or that they mysteriously have power to minister to themselves. These things inhibit the care of pastors from happening in an unplanned or spontaneous way.

---

[1]Dennis Lee Doyle, "Annual Study Leave as a Means of Reducing Pastoral Dysfunction" (D.Min. dissertation, The Southern Baptist Theological Seminary, 1977), p. 26.

[2]Robbins, p. 121.

[3]Dudley, Cummings, and Clark, p. 5.   [4]Eggers, p. 19.

[5]Larry Kent Graham, "Ministers and Friendship: An Examination of the Friendships Established by a Selected Group of Protestant Parish Clergymen in the Light of a Working Understanding and Theological Analysis of the Nature of Friendship," 2 vols. (Ph.D. dissertation, Princeton Theological Seminary, 1978), p. 22.

Family Issues

The effects of role conflict and the pastoral pedestal spill over into the private life of the minister and his family. William Presnell, pastor, counselor, and pastoral supervisor, states:

> In no other profession are the philosophy and performance of the vocation so intimately entwined with the commitments, values, and behavior of one's private life, in the eyes of those who serve and those who are served.[1]

Seldom in another profession is the job threatened if a person has marriage problems, a divorce, or children in trouble or does some private indiscretion. Ministry so involves the whole family that wives find it difficult to be themselves--a wife of their husband rather than the minister's wife. There is a confusion of boundaries between public and private life, e.g., in the way the minister's home is sometimes treated as public domain. Usually the wife has received less specialized training for the roles expected of her, creating further anxiety.[2] One survey of Baptist ministers' families revealed that 85 percent felt that ministers' wives bore burdens never revealed to anyone. Seventy-six percent felt that members expected too much of pastors' wives.[3] The study of ex-pastors by Jud, Mills, and Burch showed that ministry is a strain

---

[1] William B. Presnell, "Minister's Own Marriage," Pastoral Psychology 25 (Summer 1977):272.

[2] Five such major issues are discussed by David Martin, "Forgotten Members: The Pastor's Family," in Growth in Ministry, ed. Thomas E. Kadel (Philadelphia: Fortress Press, 1980), pp. 141-42.

[3] Jerry Boyd Graham, "The Development of a Support Ministry for Ministers in the Susquehanna Baptist Association" (D.Min. dissertation, The Southern Baptist Theological Seminary, 1975), p. 37.

even on strong marriages. Ex-pastors who had happy marriages while
in the ministry reported greater relaxation and freedom after
leaving.[1]

In their book on clergy marriages, David and Vera Mace,
leaders in the field of marriage counseling and founders of the
Marriage Enrichment Program, present a summary of the disadvantages
of clergy marriage that they gleaned from surveys of ministers and
their wives. Below are listed the items in order, from those that
drew the most frequent responses to those that drew the least.

1. Marriage expected to be model of perfection
2. Time pressures due to husband's heavy schedule
3. Lack of family privacy--"goldfish bowl"
4. Financial stress-wife must seek job
5. No in-depth sharing with other church couples
6. Children expected to model church's expectations
7. Husband, serving others, neglects own family
8. Role expectations suppress "humanness" of pastor and wife
9. Wife's duties assigned by church: She feels exploited
10. Emotional stress caused by crisis situations
11. Unfair criticism from church members
12. Confusion about wife's identity and roles
13. Dissatisfaction with housing arrangements
14. Frequent moves: no permanent roots
15. Husband "on call" throughout 24 hours
16. Family "belongs" to congregation
17. Husband must work when others are free
18. Peer pressure to conform and compete
19. No one "ministers" to clergy family[2]

(Fortunately there is also a list of nineteen advantages of clergy
marriage.)

D. W. Holbrook, Director of Home and Family Service of the
General Conference of SDAs, conducted an informal telephone survey
of a dozen church administrators. One of the questions he asked

---

[1]Jud, Mills, and Burch, p. 100.

[2]David and Vera Mace, What's Happening to Clergy Marriages?
(Nashville: Abingdon, 1980), p. 37.

was, "Where do you spend most of your time?" The answer from all but one was "personnel problems involving a variety of difficulties with pastors, their wives and children." Holbrook says:

> We have identified as the number one problem among pastoral couples resentment and anger on the part of the wife because of the role she has to play and the difficulty the pastor has in understanding the problem.[1]

One of the best supports for the family is the presence of the husband/father, but family neglect is one of the greatest problems. John Koehler found that Baptist ministers spend less than a quarter of their waking hours at home. And those who had several children did not seem to spend any more time than those who did not. Over a four-week period only about half of the ministers had taken any time off at all, and only two out of 119 had taken a day off each week.[2] The minister's work, which demands evenings and week-ends, is out of phase with the times when his family is most available and when leisure activities are normally done. But even more than the small amount of time, ministers' wives are frustrated over the inability to count on agreed-upon time.

When the minister can be with his family, there are limits on his functioning as their pastor. Ministers are husbands to their wives first, and ministers to them only when possible. They are parents to their children first, and only secondarily ministers

---

[1] D. W. Holbrook, Director of Home and Family Service, General Conference of SDAs, personal letter, April 10, 1981.

[2] John G. Koehler, "The Minister as a Family Man," in The Minister's Own Mental Health, ed. Wayne E. Oates (Great Neck, NY: Channel Press, 1955; 1961), pp. 160-62, 165.

to them. In many instances, such as family conflicts, the primary
relationship precludes the possibility of the other relationship.[1]
The husband/father is not able to have ministerial objectivity.
Ministers' families need a pastor too.

Church Problems

Ministry is often like grief work, says James Dittes. He
refers not merely to the people's trials and sorrows that the
minister shares but also to the affronts that he bears. People
do not always act like a church. They often rebuff, repudiate,
or grieve the minister. But then, if the people were a church,
there would be no need of a ministry. So, Dittes says, we must
continue to work in the grief.[2] This is one of the vulnerabilities
of ministry.

Among the reasons some ministers have dropped out is "dis-
gust with the pettiness of the local church."[3] Seventy-one percent
of Graham's respondents admitted experiencing opposition during
the last year. Forty-five percent had difficulty in motivating
their congregations.[4] Besides the typical challenges of administering a large program, ministers face the problems of working with
a volunteer organization. They do not have the power to move

---

[1]Donald P. Troost, "The Minister's Family--People Without
a Pastor," Reformed Review 31 (Winter 1978):76.

[2]James E. Dittes, When the People Say No (San Francisco:
Harper & Row, Publishers, 1979), pp. 1-2.

[3]Arnold Aswell Coody, "Factors Motivating Established
Ministers of the Church of God (Anderson, Indiana) to Leave Its
Ministry" (Th.D. dissertation, Boston University School of Theology,
1974), p. 73.

[4]Jerry Graham, pp. 41-42.

decisively that a business executive might have because they do not
hire, fire, or pay church members. Church members are volunteers
who control their involvement of time, money, and other resources.
Consensus decision making is particularly important. Conversely,
the potential for conflict is also high. In fact, conflict
management has grown into its own field of study. Conflicts can
develop in the church over theological or ideological issues,
differing methods of doing things, or personality clashes and
struggles for power.

At times the minister feels the brunt of very traumatic
experiences. Harold Myra, publisher of _Leadership_, noticed the
frequent "horror stories" that were coming to his attention. So
the _Leadership_ staff did some research to find out what was
happening. Back came descriptions of a great variety of true-to-
life traumas. For instance:

> The associate pastor took advantage of discord over the build-
> ing project--he tried to get me fired and take my position.
> A hundred members followed him off to new work, rejecting me
> and the church. It was hard for me to believe a God-called
> man could split a church to further his own position.
>
> My wife was serving as minister of music; some choir members
> rebelled against her, and eventually half the choir went on
> strike. They stabbed her in the back, and I felt a lot of
> pain for my wife. I was crushed that Christians could be so
> antagonistic.
>
> I was humiliated by board members; they called me all kinds of
> names including liar. Two of them brought false accusations
> against me before the executive committee of the national
> board. I was totally rejected; even the man over me who should
> have helped was inclined to believe the false accusers.[1]

The _Leadership_ questionnaire found that 60 percent had experienced

---

[1]Harold L. Myra, "Trauma and Betrayal," _Leadership_ 2
(Winter 1981):44-48.

a very traumatic event in their professional lives. Of those,
85 percent had felt betrayed by persons they thought they could
trust. These situations disrupted the direction of the respondent's
career in almost 40 percent of the cases. It would almost seem
self-evident that those who face these things could use an advocate, some support, a way to spread the weight of these situations.

Personal Issues

Ministers are also vulnerable to a cluster of personal
issues with which they often struggle in the world of their own
minds. Others may never know of the back and forth turmoil that
may plague their lives. Thomas E. Brown, one of the pioneers of
the career development movement, lists seven crises of this kind.[1]
First is the crisis of _integrity_. There may be programs that the
minister dislikes, methods with which he disagrees, but he must
appear to support them and actively promote them. He may feel anger
and hostility toward people but must never express it. So his
feelings may be simply repressed or denied, and that, as McBurney
points out, is never permanently effective.[2] He may have theological doubts, as did 24 percent of the ministers in the Minneapolis
study,[3] and 19 percent in the study of SDA ministers.[4] Yet he feels
obligated to preach the expected theology. The saintliness that
others ascribe to him is not consistent with his spiritual weaknesses. An aside to this problem is the sexual attraction that a

---

[1] Brown, "Vocational Crises," pp. 53-60.

[2] McBurney, _Every Pastor_, pp. 65-66.   [3] Robbins, p. 121.

[4] Dudley, Cummings, and Clark, p. 5.

minister faces in counseling and working closely with women in the church. He may deny his sexuality but the temptations still lurk.[1] The crisis of integrity involves a discrepancy between a person's public role and his real self. How does a minister deal with guilt, the inner conflict, the drive to be authentic that this creates?

Next is the crisis of <u>power</u>. A minister may be struggling with the unfinished childhood developmental issue of personal security. Power is one way of seeking it.[2] Or he may simply feel the inability to have impact in the church and in the world. Will he run the program himself, or will he share power with others? How does he handle differences? Does he feel futility in trying to get things done? Is he tempted to think he would be more effective in secular work? These are some of the inner dynamics of this crisis.[3]

Third is the crisis of <u>capacity</u>. Partly because of the high standard always held up before them, partly to attain the virtue of humility, ministers may doubt their abilities and feel inadequate or inferior. They may need more training, but usually the problem centers around low self-esteem. Irene Lovett found that in intelligence testing clergy seriously underestimate themselves by consistently placing themselves at least two categories below

---

[1] Charles L. Rassieur has written a valuable book on this subject: <u>The Problem Clergymen Don't Talk About</u> (Philadelphia: Westminster Press, 1976).

[2] Louis McBurney, "A Psychiatrist Looks at Troubled Pastors," <u>Leadership</u> 1 (Spring 1980):111.

[3] John C. Harris, <u>Stress, Power and Ministry</u> (Washington, D.C.: Alban Institute, 1977), pp. 55-61.

where they actually ranked.[1] David Seamands describes how perfectionism is related to self-doubt.

> The perfectionist, with his oversensitive conscience, his low
> self-esteem, and false sense of guilt, is naturally very
> sensitive to what other people think about him. Since he
> does not like himself, does not approve of himself, and is
> quite unsure of God's approval, he desperately needs the
> approval of other people. He is easy prey to the opinions of
> other Christians. All the while the do's and the don'ts are
> piling up, because more and more people have to be pleased. His
> halo has to be adjusted for this person, and readjusted for
> that one. He keeps fitting it this way and that way, and be-
> fore he realizes what is happening, his halo has become what
> Paul called "a yoke of bondage."[2]

Closely related to the crisis of capacity is the crisis of

failure (or the problem of success). What is success in the

ministry? This is often mulled over in the minister's mind. One

option is to adopt the industrial model and play the statistical

game. However, that does not quite fit the spiritual principles

of the Scriptures. If he rejects it, he is without a clear measure

for success in a success-oriented society. If he is judged un-

successful, does that mean God is not with him or that he has

failed God? Doyle reports that all but 7 percent of those in his

survey experienced the fear of failure to some extent.[3]

The crisis of destination is the fifth crisis. Ministers

may spend considerable time wondering about their futures. Is

their present job secure? Maybe even more demanding than this is

the question, "Will I be satisfied in the parish the rest of my

---

[1]Lovett, p. 87.

[2]David A. Seamands, "Perfectionism: Fraught with Fruits of
Self-Destruction," Christianity Today, April 10, 1981, p. 25.

[3]Doyle, p. 19.

life? Am I looking forward to a bigger church, a 'promotion' to a denominational position, or do I want to get into another type of work?" Robbins found 28 percent of ministers questioning their calling.[1] The exact same percentage of SDA ministers sometimes want to leave pastoral ministry, and 33 percent have seriously considered transferring to another type of ministry.[2]

Next Brown mentions the crisis of role. We have already mentioned some of the personal struggles of ministers who try to sort out in their own minds the many tasks of their career.

Finally, the crisis of meaning penetrates and somewhat summarizes all the others. "Why am I doing what I am doing?" If a minister can keep in focus a clear meaning and strong purpose for his work, he can endure many trials, as a vibrant developing individual. If he loses this, he is a mere functionary, ready to leave. This is basically the struggle for self-actualization. It is particularly threatening if a person entered the ministry for the wrong reasons.

Denominational Circumstances

Most studies reveal that denominational organizations not only are inadequately supportive of their ministers but also are part of the cause of their pressures. In his study of the Mississippi Conference of The United Methodist Church, Thomas Burnett concluded that the central problem causing pastors to

---

[1]Robbins, p. 121.

[2]Dudley, Cummings, and Clark, p. 5.

leave was conflict with and restraints by the institutional leadership.[1] Forney studied the Southern California-Arizona Conference of the same denomination and found that conference administrator-pastor relationships were more influential in producing a desire to leave the parish ministry than minister-congregation relationships. Mentioned were role conflicts with the conference hierarchy, disagreement on the philosophy of parish priorities, and an ivory tower type of ignorance regarding the real situation of local churches.[2]

The Ohio Conference of SDAs had a professional management consultant team study the organization and management effectiveness of the conference. One of the main findings was that "pastors feel disenfranchised from the conference organization."[3] The ICM study found that 34 percent of SDA ministers are concerned about not meeting the approval of their superiors.[4]

Jud, Mills, and Burch found that in the case of both pastors and ex-pastors, the denominational official was less supportive than was desired. In fact, ex-pastors had had a greater desire for such support than pastors. But they also perceived that their denominational officials isolated them more than the

---

[1] Thomas Stevens Burnett, "Ministerial Roles and Institutional Restraints: The Mississippi Conference of The United Methodist Church" (D.Min. dissertation, The School of Theology at Claremont, 1976), pp. 48ff.

[2] Forney, p. 136.

[3] Paul W. Robberson, "Report on Organization and Management Effectiveness Study for the Ohio Conference of Seventh-day Adventists," Towers, Perrin, Forster, & Crosby, February 1981, p. 7.

[4] Dudley, Cummings, and Clark, p. 5.

pastors.[1] It is partly the same problem of role conflict once again, but this time in the person and function of the denominational official. He is responsible for financial matters, administrative decisions, and the promotion of programs and these organizational functions hinder his pastoral functions. Also time pressures and distance reduce his effectiveness in helping pastors. In most cases there is no separate support person in the denomination for the pastor.

Peer pastors within a denomination are isolated from each other by distance as well. It is not only the distance in miles that keeps them from friendship, fellowship, and support of one another, it is the competition that often exists between them. The pressure for reaching goals fuels this competition as each one seeks to protect his own success record.

Burn-out

Burn-out is a specialized consequence of some of the vulnerabilities we have discussed. In the last few years it has been investigated quite widely. It is a problem particularly of those in the helping professions where there is heavy involvement with people's problems.[2] Jerry Edelwich defines burn-out as

---

[1] Jud, Mills, and Burch, p. 182.

[2] Some of the best resources include Jerry Edelwich, with Archie Brodsky, Burn-out--Stages of Disillusionment in the Helping Professions (New York: Human Sciences Press, 1980); Ayala M. Pines, Elliot Aronson, with Ditsa Kafry, Burnout: From Tedium to Personal Growth (New York: Free Press, 1981); Herbert Freudenberger, with Geraldine Richelson, Burn-out: The High Cost of High Achievement (Garden City, NY: Doubleday & Company, Anchor Press edition, 1980); Kenneth E. Reid and Rebecca A. Quinlan, eds., "Burnout in the Helping Professions," papers presented at a symposium on burnout,

. . . a progressive loss of idealism, energy, and purpose experienced by people in the helping professions as a result of
the conditions of their work. Those conditions range from
insufficient training to client overload, from too many hours
to too little pay, from inadequate funding to ungrateful
clients, from bureaucratic or political constraints to the
inherent gap between aspiration and accomplishment.[1]

Herbert Freudenberger says,

A Burn-out is someone in a state of fatigue or frustration
brought about by devotion to a cause, way of life, or relationship that failed to produce the expected reward.
    Whenever the expectation level is dramatically opposed to
reality and the person persists in trying to reach that ex-
pectation, trouble is on the way.[2]

Edelwich identifies five stages in the burn-out process.[3]

First is enthusiasm, where the worker takes on a job with high

hopes, great energy, and some unrealistic expectations. He is

willing to overwork because he plans to make a real impact in

people's lives, in the church or society. He feels a certain sense

of omnipotence. But as time passes, the constant involvement with

people's problems becomes wearing. People are not changing as

quickly as he hoped, and so many of them regress it makes him

wonder if he is really accomplishing anything. He is not as

appreciated and his job is no longer as thrilling. Exhausted, he

---

Western Michigan University, Kalamazoo, MI, September 27-28, 1979.
Articles that deal with burn-out in relationship to ministers in-
clude H. Newton Malony and Donald Falkenberg, "Ministerial Burn Out,"
Leadership 1 (Fall 1980):71-74; Kevin J. Howse, "When the Pastor
Burns Out," Ministry, April 1981, pp. 28-29; William Rabior,
"Ministerial Burnout," Ministry, March 1979, p. 25; Gary R. Collins,
"Burn-out: The Hazard of Professional People-Helpers," Christianity
Today, April 1, 1977, pp. 12-14.

[1]Edelwich, p. 14.   [2]Freudenberger, p. 13.

[3]The reader can assess his vulnerability to burn-out by
responding to the series of inventories found in appendix A. These
were prepared by Roy M. Oswald of the Alban Institute, Washington,
D.C.

begins to feel the need and takes an interest in things for himself--
home, family, friends, money, car, leisure time. This person is in
the second stage called stagnation. As he enters the third stage,
frustration, he questions more seriously his effectiveness at work
and the value of the job itself. People do not respond. The
organizational bureaucracy is not helpful. Now the worker may
begin to suffer emotional, physical, or behavioral problems. The
fourth stage is apathy. The worker is totally frustrated, yet he
needs his job to survive. He puts in minimum time, detaches from
people and problems as much as possible, and does only those things
that are necessary for him to remain in good standing. The last
stage is intervention. It breaks the cycle. The person either
changes jobs or restructures his whole approach to his job. He
may get some continuing education and determine to balance his
life with appropriate leisure time.

Burn-out needs to be dealt with but not always in the way
people assume. Edelwich gives this pertinent advice:

> To the extent that individuals and institutions can recognize
> --better yet, anticipate--what Burn-out is and how, when, and
> where it occurs, they will be better prepared to resist the
> ineffectual, wishful remedies that are often practiced today
> and to seek more realistic antidotes. A positive approach
> to Burn-out will be based not on the hope of preventing it
> (which is virtually impossible), but on the realization that
> it will happen--perhaps repeatedly--in a person's career and
> must be dealt with on an ongoing basis. Burn-out can even be
> turned to advantage in that it can energize a person to break
> out of a rut. When frustration is used creatively, it becomes
> a stimulus to the kind of enthusiasm that it normally erodes.[1]

---

[1]Edelwich, pp. 14-15.

Initial Entry to Ministry

Developmentally, adolescence and the mid-life transition
are particular trouble spots. Looking at the career of ministry,
the initial entry period is the most crucial. Mills and Koval
found that 42 percent of all the stress periods reported in their
study occurred in the first five years. One-fourth of the ministers
reported that their first major stress period was in the first or
second year of their ministry.[1] The Alban Institute investigated
the dynamics of a pastor's move to a new parish. Although that is
a vulnerable time whenever it happens, the greatest difficulties
were found in crossing the boundary from seminary to the first
full-time parish ministry. They said, "Of all their career
transitions, this was the most traumatic and the most crucial."[2]
In the study of ex-pastors, Jud, Mills, and Burch discovered that
30 percent of those who dropped out did so in the first six years.[3]
The average time when pastors made the break to secular employment
was three years and eight months after seminary graduation,
according to Allen Wadsworth's inquiry.[4]

Joseph Wagner notes that some of these demittals are
appropriate because of clarified vocational abilities or other
situations; the individuals who make them should be encouraged and

---

[1]Mills and Koval, p. 11.

[2]Roy M. Oswald, Crossing the Boundary (Washington, D.C.:
Alban Institute, 1980), p. 1.

[3]Jud, Mills, and Burch, p. 47.

[4]Allen P. Wadsworth, Jr., "Drop-out from the Pastorate:
Why?" The Journal of Pastoral Care 25 (June 1971):124-27.

respected. But others are unnecessary consequences of the lack of
an effective system of support for the parish pastor.[1] Although
stress begins almost immediately, the first two years usually
carry enough enthusiasm and momentum from the seminary to offset
the negative forces. But by years three to five, something like
burn-out may have occurred.[2] One new book on this initial entry
time indentifies unique stresses to this period as the crisis of
competence, the clash of idealism and reality, the traumas of
cultural shock, and then the fears and frustrations related to
the issues previously discussed, which are high-lighted during
this time.[3] This period deserves special attention.

Retrospect

What has been said may seem to portray a bleak, pessimistic
picture. But let us remember that the purpose in this section is
to note the vulnerabilities that ministers could encounter. Not
all ministers face all of these problems. One should note that
a paradox often exists in their experiences. The same ministers
who are undergoing the stresses we have mentioned can also report
that they are "very satisfied" with their ministry--as 90 percent
of the ministers of the Minneapolis study attested.[4]

---

[1]Joseph M. Wagner, "Parish Dynamics; Stress as the Opportunity for Supportive Teamwork in the Congregation," Lutheran
Quarterly 23 (May 1971):166, 170.

[2]Mark A. Rouch, Competent Ministry (Nashville: Abingdon
Press, 1974), pp. 113-14.

[3]C. W. Brister, James L. Cooper, and J. David Fite,
Beginning Your Ministry (Nashville: Abingdon, 1981), pp. 68-84.

[4]Robbins, p. 119.

The Maces found nineteen advantages of a clergy marriage, besides the nineteen disadvantages, and others have also reported the satisfactions and rewards. Nevertheless, those stressful events do occur. When church members have a problem they can go to their pastor. Where can the pastor go? Who pastors the pastor? Maybe we can best punctuate this section of our study by considering the thoughts and challenge of Thomas Klink, a long-time leader in the field of pastoral care and supervision:

> Such troubles are not, in themselves, peculiar to the ministry. Other people in other vocations or professions have troubles, distresses of ordinary life. What is unique to the ministry is the deficiency of usable, available resources. We have no chaplain who can "punch our card," and it is next to impossible to share burdens with the laymen of the church. Wives are much used but, with all proper credit, as the least happy choice. There are denominational leaders, of course, but they are generally charged with pushing programs, too busy and, in any case they are also involved with the whole placement-pastoral-move-processes to be freely usable. Even where there are multiple staff ministries there are few which provide the pastoral support and assistance needed.
> Please note that I am not talking about complicated technical skills like psychotherapy or professional counseling, although such resources are important. I am noting only that we have few easily available opportunities in our immediate work environment to objectify an emotional relationship, test out our disquiet about a course of events, elicit concerned feedback about our work, think through a complicated problem, etc. Yet every analysis of preventive mental health care, every approach to enlightened personnel management, puts such resources highest on the list. It is a truism that the isolated person is more susceptible to exacerbation of his problems.
> We need to perfect systems of supervision which recognize responsibility to seek aid in professional learning as the highest expression of responsible freedom--not a compromise of it. We need to recognize the need for counsel/consultation resources close at hand. We need to find ways--in seminary and in continuing education--whereby we can be ministers one to another.[1]

The ministry to ministers for which Klink appeals is suggestive of

---

[1]Thomas W. Klink, "Ministry as Career and Crisis," Pastoral Psychology 20 (June 1969):18-19.

the concept of a support system, the subject of the third main section of this chapter.

The Concept of a Support System

Definitions

"No man is an island, entire of itself; every man is a piece of the continent," said John Donne, the sixteenth century writer.[1] This expresses a truth recognized by psychology and theology alike. Human beings are bound to one another by a variety of ties. They are social creatures. Psychiatrist Gerald Caplan makes explicit some of the social needs that people have:

> People have a variety of specific needs that demand satis-faction through enduring interpersonal relationships, such as for love and affection, for intimacy that provides the freedom to express feelings easily and unself-consciously, for vali-dation of personal identity and worth, for satisfaction of nurturance and dependency, for help with tasks, and for support in handling emotion and controlling impulses.[2]

Research by John C. Cassel makes evident that individuals need feed-back from their environment, messages that clarify expectations and report evaluations of their actions. If this feedback is not forth-coming, the person is unable to assess the friendliness or hostility of his environment; he is not able to feel safe and valued,

> . . . and his autonomic nervous system and hormonal mechanisms are continually in a state of emergency arousal, so that the resulting physiological depletion and fatigue increase his susceptibility to a wide range of physical and mental dis-orders.[3]

---

[1] John Donne, "Devotions upon Emergent Occasions," (1624), no. 17, in John Bartlett, Familiar Quotations, 15th ed., edited by Emily Morison Beck (Boston: Little, Brown and Company, 1980).

[2] Gerald Caplan, Support Systems and Community Mental Health (New York: Behavioral Publications, 1974), p. 5.

[3] Ibid., pp. 1-2.

Caplan's own study reinforces this finding. When a crisis places
a person in danger of responding maladaptively, the nature of the
stressor and the ego strength of the individual are overshadowed
by the "quality of the emotional support and task-oriented
assistance provided by the social network within which that individual grapples with the crisis event."[1] Social support acts as
a buffer between the vicissitudes of life and ill-health. It
enables a person to react in ways that are strengthening rather
than hurtful to his future.

What is the nature of social support? It has been
described as

>. . . information leading subjects to believe that they are
>cared for and loved, esteemed, and valued, and that they belong
>to a network of communication and mutual obligation.[2]

In the occupational setting it is

>. . . interaction between two or more people . . . [which]
>focuses on work-related concerns and provides emotional sup-
>port and encouragement, useful information and ideas, and/or
>constructive feedback and social comparison.[3]

Other authors have divided the functions of social support into six
basic categories: listening--the ability to hear what a person
says without making judgments or giving free advice; technical
appreciation--the affirmation of a person's competence by a
knowledgeable, trustworthy person; technical challenge--the encouragement to greater accomplishments by a resourceful person who

---

[1]Ibid., p. 4.   [2]Pines, Aronson, Kafry, p. 123.

[3]Cary Cherniss, "Institutional Barriers to Social Support
among Human Service Staff," in "Burnout in the Helping Professions,"
eds. Kenneth E. Reid, and Rebecca A. Quinlan, papers presented at a
symposium on burn-out, Western Michigan University, Kalamazoo, MI,
September 27-28, 1979, p. 1.

has one's best interest at heart; emotional support--to have someone on your side who cares about you as a person; emotional
challenge--the pointing out of personal defeating behaviors by
a concerned friend; sharing social reality--the opportunity to
check with others one's perceptions, e.g., "Did you hear that? I
guess I'm not going crazy after all!"[1] In essence it fulfills
those basic social needs mentioned by Caplan above.

Sometimes the word help or helping relationship is used
to describe such assistance. Carl R. Rogers, the leader of a
school of counseling, describes the helping relationship as one

> . . . in which at least one of the parties has the intent of
> promoting the growth, development, maturity, improved function-
> ing, improved coping with life of the other . . . that there
> should come about, in one or both parties, more appreciation
> of, more expression of, more functional use of the latent
> inner resources of the individual.[2]

A support system, with the emphasis on system, implies that there
is an interrelated/interdependent network of supportive or helping
relationships that operate in a continuous or intermittent pattern
over an enduring period of time.[3]

In this project the phrase psycho-social support system is
used. It is defined as the network of various resources that a
person might draw upon from both himself (psycho) and from people
around him (social) which could help him to relate positively to
his life and career. This definition broadens the scope of the

---

[1]Pines, Aronson, Kafry, pp. 124-29.

[2]Carl R. Rogers, On Becoming a Person (Boston: Houghton
Mifflin Company, 1961), p. 40.

[3]Caplan, Support Systems, p. 7.

help to include not just relationships but also resources of a
personal nature that can strengthen an individual. When an
individual helps himself it is sometimes called coping. Coping

> . . . refers to any attempts to deal with stressful situations
> which a person feels he must do something about, but which tax
> or exceed his existing adaptation response patterns. Coping
> behaviours can range from the most casual manoeuvres to compli-
> cated forms of problem-solving, from the most highly proactive
> behaviours, to the most pathologically reactive attempts, from
> the most rational to the most irrational efforts. Yet, all
> are undertaken with the same ultimate objectives--preventing,
> reducing or resolving the stress and its consequences.[1]

The resources that an individual uses to cope may be called coping
mechanisms or coping strategies. Examples include developing new
attitudes, making decisions, taking pills, reorganizing time,
prayer and meditation, physical exercise or diversion, sleep, and
many others. These psychological coping resources are greatly influenced by a person's social resources.

The social resources of the support system may include relationships that are natural or spontaneous, e.g., family and
friends. Or they may be organized with intentionality--appointed
or sought-out helpers, e.g., clubs and associations that have a
common interest. They may be professional care-givers or simply
fellow human beings. J. Lennart Cedarleaf makes the point that
touching the hem of the super-healer therapist's garment is not the
only way to obtain help. The more biblical and realistic way is to
help each other. "It is not perfection or status or training that
heals. It is open communication between people and a willingness

---

[1]Burke and Weir, p. 300.

to hang in that starts the flow of the healing spring."[1] Carl

Rogers intensifies this thought:

> I have had the strong conviction--some might say it was an
> obsession--that the therapeutic relationship is only a
> special instance of interpersonal relationships in general,[2]
> and that the same lawfulness governs all such relationships.

We need not depreciate the value of peer support.

A support system is not merely for crisis situations or

for the weak, psychological cripple. Says Caplan:

> The idea that a person receives support or is in need of
> support usually carries the connotation that he is weak, and
> from this point of view the term is unfortunate, because what
> we have in mind is not the propping up of someone who is in
> danger of falling down, but rather, the augmenting of a per-
> son's strengths to facilitate his mastery of a stress or a
> challenge.[3]

A minister needs support, he says, to maintain "his poise and

freshness of spirit" in his demanding task of continually helping

others. Speed Leas reminds us that support systems do not suddenly

appear in times of crisis. If we have not cultivated them all along

in the every-day give and take of life, there is no network of ties

to draw upon when the serious blows come.[4] Edward Wimberly likes

the concept of a support system particularly because it focuses on

"normal rather than pathological needs of persons." It deals with

prevention. It grew up in the field of community mental health and

---

[1]J. Lennart Cedarleaf, "Pastoral Care of Pastors," _Journal of Pastoral Care_ 27 (March 1973):33.

[2]Rogers, p. 39.

[3]Gerald Caplan, "Support Systems," in _Helping the Helpers to Help_, by Ruth B. Caplan (New York: Seabury Press, 1972), p. 193.

[4]Speed B. Leas, _Should the Pastor be Fired?_ (Washington, D.C.: Alban Institute, 1980), p. 20.

is an alternative to the one-to-one medical model of psychiatry. Support systems can help larger numbers of people and can focus on a wider range of environmental factors that affect them. He also adds that it is most compatible with the nature and mission of the church.[1]

History

Some may wonder why this big ado over support systems when ministers and others of the past seemed to have functioned without knowledge of it. Seemingly a recent development, why have we not heard about it before? Is our present day situation more aggravating? Are we just more sophisticated in our analysis of problems and solutions? Are we over-emphasizing our needs? Is it all really necessary?

Ministers of years ago did have similar needs. Jean Frederic Oberlin was a minister in the eighteenth century. He spent fifty years in a single parish in Europe. Note his frustration and stress as he describes it in his own words:

> The pastor of Waldbach, if he tries to be what he ought to be in this vast parish--is a poor dog, a beast of burden, a cart-horse. He must do everything, watch everything, provide for everything, answer for everything. Everything sits upon the pastor who meets everywhere nothing but hindrance, obstacles, delays, and red-tape; and not being able to please everybody must fight constantly with malevolence.[2]

[1] Edward P. Winberly, "Pastoral Care and Support Systems," Journal of the Interdenominational Theological Center 5 (Spring 1978):68-69.

[2] Robert G. Dickson, "Ministering to the Minister: Formulating a Program," Reformed Review 31 (Winter 1978):88. Other descriptions of the demands and frustrations of ministry years ago can be found in Wilhelm Pauck, "The Ministry in the Time of the Continental Reformation," in The Ministry in Historical Perspectives,

Richard Baxter, who served somewhat as a minister to ministers in the 1600s, recommended strongly that ministers not neglect communion among themselves. Ministers need mutual edification, he said.

> Ministers have need of one another. They can improve the gifts of God in one another. Even the most self-sufficient may be the most deficient, often being the proudest and most empty of men. Therefore some . . . do not come among the brethren, claiming that they desire to live privately. To these we say, Why do you not on the same grounds forbear going to church? Is not ministerial communion a duty as well as common Christian communion?[1]

Some suffered and died prematurely, as did James White, pioneer/founder of the SDA Church. He suffered from frequent depression, despondency, and overwork. His wife, Ellen, writes that he could have lived longer if others had supported him more adequately.[2] Many times these people of times past simply accepted their lot in life,[3] partly because they knew of no alternative (the understanding of health and illness was not as advanced) and partly because of the social structures which made them fear to change. Edelwich suggests that burn-out "undoubtedly has always occurred and will always occur," but it has been given a name in the 1970s.[4] And social support certainly has been functioning through the

---

eds. H. Richard Niebuhr and Daniel D. Williams (New York: Harper and Bros., 1956); Henry C. Mabie, "Pastoral Discouragements: How to Overcome Them," in The Young Pastor and His People: Bits of Practical Advice for Young Clergymen, ed. B. F. Liepsner (New York: N. Tibbols & Sons, 1878), pp. 137-38, quoted in Doyle, pp. 21-22; Holifield, pp. 371-77.

[1]Richard Baxter, The Reformed Pastor, ed. Jay Green (Marshallton, DE: National Foundation for Christian Education, n.d.), p. 63.

[2]Ellen G. White, Testimonies for the Church, 9 vols. (Mountain View, CA: Pacific Press Pub. Assn., 1948), 5:67; 3:16-17, 85-88, 495, 500-01.

[3]Freudenberger, p. 56.   [4]Edelwich, p. 33.

centuries without being named as such. In our time curious people
have reached for the ends in understanding the workings of our
lives.

Maybe the most important factor that presently draws us
to pay attention to these things is the fact that our modern
world is simply not fulfilling these needs. We can no longer
let social support go unnamed because its absence is so notice-
able. Our world has changed. Authors such as Alvin Toffler,
Harvey Cox, and Jeffrey Hadden portray the threats of our new
world.[1] The pace of our life is faster. Though we live more
congestedly in urban areas, we are more distant from each other.
Our lives are more complex; we meet more strangers. We move to new
places every few years. Though we have better ways of sending
messages, our means for interpreting them are confused.[2] Extended
families are no longer together; nuclear families are disinte-
grating. John Harris observes:

> The nomadic existence of our lives means that people leave be-
> hind networks of support (friends, family, clergy, teachers,
> relatives) and enter new cities as strangers without ties where
> the re-creation of community is a delicate problematic business.
> To a far greater extent than in past centuries, people are left
> to their own devices and with dwindling resources to make sense
> out of life.[3]

Ministers are also

---

[1]Alvin Toffler, Future Shock (New York: Random House,
1970; Bantom Edition, 1971); Harvey Cox, The Secular City (New York:
Macmillan Company, 1965); Jeffrey K. Hadden, The Gathering Storm
in the Churches (New York: Doubleday & Co., 1969).

[2]Gerald Caplan, Support Systems, p. 2.

[3]Harris, Stress, Power and Ministry, p. 38.

. . . caught in the maelstrom of cultural pressures that are
transforming all traditional institutions in our society. So
there is a sense in which clergy distress is a predictable
accompaniment of the Church's struggle to work out the nature
of its own contribution in a secular industrial country.[1]

As with others, the problems the minister faces have increased,

while at the same time his natural resources are not as effective.

Payne discusses the major support role that the family once played,

then comments: "It is perhaps because this traditional role is not

being adequately fulfilled that the question of organizationally

based support occurs at all."[2] If social support does not happen

spontaneously, we need to organize it intentionally. Toffler

calls for "stability zones" which can cushion and help people

through future shock and suggests a variety of resources.[3]

The phenomenon of social support is as old as the human

race. The terminology is quite recent. The degree of emphasis is

determined by the situation of our changing world. In our times it

needs special attention!

Benefits

An adequate support system for pastors benefits the church

organization. Some might fear that it would cost extra money, which

is always less in supply than in demand. However, many support

resources can be provided with almost no cost--only the intentional-

ity and effort to put them into practice. Business has found that

---

[1] Harris, "New Trends," p. 5.

[2] Roy Payne, "Organizational Stress and Social Support," in
Current Concerns in Occupational Stress, eds. Cary L. Cooper and
Roy Payne (New York: John Wiley & Sons, 1980), p. 282.

[3] Toffler, pp. 374-88.

even where there are costs, they are overshadowed by the savings
in less absenteeism, less turnover, better performance, fewer anti-
social acts, etc.[1] In the ministry this can be translated into
fewer unnecessary moves, fewer dropouts (thereby conserving the
cost of ministerial training), better interpersonal relationships,
greater church growth. Church-growth studies have been revealing
that such things as longer pastoral assignments and a positive attitude by the pastor are determining factors in growth.[2] The very
nature of the pastoral position causes the minister to influence
and affect many other people. He has a key position in the church
structure, for the local ministry is where the action happens, the
money is given, the programs are carried out, and the people are
baptized. He needs, by all means, to function at a high level of
effectiveness for the sake of the church.[3]

But preserving a successful organization is not the only
benefit from support of pastors. Though a pastor who has observ-
able problems or who drops out may be an embarrassment to the denomination, John Patton reports that many churches now are operating
from a higher motivation in the care of ministers--concern for the
pastors themselves.[4] Pastors as persons benefit from the support

---

[1]See Albrecht, pp. 128-33, for a calculation of the costs of
stress on a business and what is saved if some of it can be reduced.
Regarding the economics of a support system in the helping professions, see Edelwich, pp. 31-41.

[2]C. Peter Wagner, Your Church Can Grow (Glendale, CA: Regal
Books Division, G/L Publications, 1976), pp. 55-67; Roger L. Dudley,
"How Churches Grow," Ministry, July 1981, pp. 4-7.

[3]David K. Switzer, "Minister as Pastor and Person," Pastoral
Psychology 24 (Fall 1975):52-64.

[4]John Patton, "The Pastoral Care of Pastors," The Christian
Ministry 11 (July 1980):16.

structures in many ways. They are assisted in dealing with the struggles and stresses that they face from the long list that we have already outlined.

Kenneth Johnson investigated whether being in a growth group actually did any good. After administering batteries of psychological tests before and after such group experiences he concludes:

> Participation in a spiritual growth group for a minimum of twenty weeks does produce measurable changes in four indices of growth--(1) improved psychological functioning, (2) a more realistic and positive self concept, (3) a more open, flexible, and well differentiated religious sentiment, and (4) improved interpersonal attitudes and relationships.[1]

James Hunter says that his "ministry seminar," a regular peer-group meeting of ministers, fostered trust and understanding among them. They were able to share themselves, breaking out of their isolation. An openness and candor prevailed. It enabled the author to free himself from tendencies toward manipulation and misuse of the pastoral office. Servant ministry took on a renewed meaning in his own life.[2] Carlyle Marney and Mark Rouch maintain that continuing education can benefit a person's selfhood as much as it can increase his competence.[3] Russell Patrick described how an executive leadership course gave him the insight to be more honest

---

[1] Kenneth E. Johnson, "Personal Religious Growth through Small Group Participation: A Psychological Study of Personality Changes and Shifts in Religious Attitudes Which Result from Participation in a Spiritual Growth Group" (Th.D. dissertation, Pacific School of Religion, 1963), pp. 614-15.

[2] James Elmo Hunter, III, "Ministry Seminar" (D.Min dissertation, Emory University, 1975), pp. 76-77.

[3] Carlyle Marney and Mark Rouch, "Continuing Education: For Selfhood or Competence?" The Drew Gateway 47/1, 1976-77, p. 31.

with himself and others, to increase the number of significant
persons in his life, to engage in more meaningful play and relaxation, to increase his tolerance of pressure and conflict, to value
affirmation, to view himself more positively, and several other
benefits as well.[1] Richard Hester suggests that a peer support
group can help the minister become liberated from transference and
the temptation to heroism in his role as a counselor.[2] Roy Oswald
shows how a support consultant can help a minister in his termination in one parish and his start-up in another.[3] This is just a
sampling of testimonials.

Responsibility

Who is responsible to initiate support structures for
ministers? Robert Kemper says that ministers are responsible for
their own careers.[4] They usually find it easier to blame others
or to allow others to determine the course of their lives. But
ministers themselves can step out to create support agencies for
themselves and each other. Harris says that denominational offices
or judicatories are responsible.

I have observed a direct relationship between a judicatory's
ability to do these functions well and the satisfaction its

---

[1]Russell A. Patrick, "What the Executive Leadership Course
Did for Me," Church Administration, October 1976, pp. 10-12.

[2]Richard L. Hester, "Transference and Covenant in Pastoral
Care," Pastoral Psychology 28 (Summer 1980):230-31.

[3]Roy M. Oswald, Running through the Thistles (Washington,
D.C.: Alban Institute, 1978), p. 8; Roy M. Oswald, New Beginnings:
Pastorate Start Up Workbook (Washington, D.C.: Alban Institute,
1977; reprint, 1980), pp. 49-62.

[4]Robert G. Kemper, The New Shape of Ministry (Nashville:
Abingdon, 1979), pp. 40-41.

pastors find in their work. . . . We know that if the judicatory
leadership fails to care and work for intelligent placement
practices, pragmatic continuing education for clergy, career
guidance, strong peer bonds between clergy, competent parish
development consultation, then the consequence is likely to be
visible in the form of depressed, unproductive pastors and
apathetic churches. It is a matter of 'bad water, dead fish.'[1]

Robert Rasmussen really lays the burden on the church when he says,

"The church is morally irresponsible if it does not provide a sus-

tained support for persons in ministry from the point of enlistment

to the terminus of retirement."[2] Harris, however, suggests that

what is really needed is a "systems" approach which involves both

the institution and the individual in this task. Jud, Mills, and

Burch sum it up like this:

Pastors alone cannot solve the trouble in the church system
relative to church professionals. They cannot pull themselves
up by their bootstraps. Seminaries cannot solve it alone.
Judicatories and church executives cannot solve it alone. If
the problems are really going to be addressed and some solutions
found, every part of the system must work together in problem-
solving. This means that national and judicatory leaders,
seminary policy-makers, and the most creative leaders of the
local church must address the problems together and work out
solutions. In this crisis of identity the church has a right
to expect guidance from its leaders, and unilateral approaches
will never be able to cope with the massive problems with any
degree of effectiveness.[3]

The needs of ministers and a concept of how to meet these

needs have been described from a psychological perspective in this

chapter. But how does this information relate to theological

categories? Should ministers need support? How does human support

---

[1] Harris, "New Trends," p. 7.

[2] Robert D. Rasmussen, "Resources for Career Development,"
in The Continuing Quest, ed. James B. Hofrenning (Minneapolis:
Augsburg Publishing House, 1970), p. 125.

[3] Jud, Mills, and Burch, p. 119.

relate to God's help to individuals? Some possible objections to the concept of a support system may relate to a person's understanding of these theological issues. This is the subject of the next chapter.

CHAPTER II

THEOLOGICAL REFLECTIONS ON THE
CONCEPT OF SUPPORT

Support and the Doctrine of Man

Man in Perfection

Theological thinking about the concept of support suggests, first of all, that it is tied to the very nature of humankind. The biblical creation story recounts that though Adam, the first man, was in his pristine state of innocence, perfection, and strength, God still found it desirable to say, "It is not good that man should be alone; I will make him a helper fit for him" (Gen 2:18).[1] The evidence suggests that God intended for mankind to have inter-locking bonds of relationships.

Graham suggests that the doctrine of the Trinity, the pattern of interrelationships among the Father, Son, and Holy Spirit, is the ground and pattern also for human relationships.[2] The New Testament is quite explicit regarding the communion and mutual support that Jesus shares with his Father. Three times the audible voice of the Father was heard on earth confirming the life and work of Jesus Christ (Matt 3:16-17; 17:5; John 12:28). At

---

[1]All biblical references use the Revised Standard Version unless otherwise noted.

[2]Larry Graham, "Ministers and Friendship," p. 117.

Jesus' baptism the Spirit of God manifested himself with the same purpose in the form of a dove. Just before the final tumultuous events of Christ's life he said to his disciples, "The hour is coming, indeed it has come, when you will be scattered, every man to his home, and will leave me alone; yet I am not alone, for the Father is with me" (John 16:32). The prayer that Jesus spoke on this same occasion clearly conveyed the mutuality he had with the Father (John 17). Just a short time before, Jesus explained the role of the Comforter, the Spirit of God, describing the inter-relationship of the three (John 15:26). These descriptions take on even greater significance when we realize that man was made in the image of God (Gen 1:26). There is a correspondence between these beings. Graham says, "The essential nature of the human being as a creature in the image of God consists of the will to communion, the will to belong." The self is always seeking to discover where he or she is at home in the immense and threatening world of time, persons, social structure, and nature. "It is through the necessity of ongoing, life-long participation in the environment that the self begins to belong."[1] Graham concludes that friendship is one primary expression of this basic character-istic with which man was created.

Not only by the way the members of the Godhead interrelate are the intentions of God revealed but also by the efforts of God to be "with" man. The Genesis record relates that God sought occasions of walking and communing with the people he had made

---

[1]Ibid., p. 116.

(Gen 2:15; 3:8-9). The Sabbath was a special time for interaction (Gen 2:2-3; Exod 31:13; Lev 23:3; Ps 92, a song for the sabbath day; Isa 66:23). Mankind was separated from God at the entrance of sin, but God still desired to be with his people. Two of the most dramatic demonstrations of this were the presence of God in the Old Testament tabernacle and the incarnation of Jesus Christ in the New Testament. God desires to dwell with us still by means of the Holy Spirit taking up residence in our body temples. But this veiled communion will become visible and physical when the kingdom of God comes to this earth (Rev 21:3). The intelligent beings of this universe were created for each other.

Man in Sin

Sin broke these relationships. And sin is not merely an isolated problem of a few people. The theologian, Paul, tells us with the authority of an apostle that all people have sinned (Rom 3:23; 5:12). The effect of sin is not merely weakness, just as salvation is not obtained by giving man strength. There is something much more radical about sin that removes man's ability to save himself, even with help, and requires a total, substitutionary act in order to make justification and reconciliation possible. The immediate effect of sin could have been death. But the grace of God by means of his sustaining power has prevented that penalty from being immediate. Still the marks of sin are very evident. Sin not only breaks relationships, but it seems to intensify the need for such relationships because those who have sinned are suffering from the degenerative consequences that it carries. Sin has made us vulnerable to all kinds of physical disease, mental and emotional illness, social conflict, injustice, temptation, stress, and spiritual malaise.

Jesus acknowledged this when he spoke of his disciples who had not been able to watch with him in that last hour in Gethsemane, "the spirit indeed is willing, but the flesh is weak" (Matt 26:41). Paul addresses this issue when he says that "the Spirit helps us in our weaknesses" (Rom 8:26). The writer of Hebrews tells us that we have a high priest who is able to help us with our weaknesses (Heb 4:15). In Ps 103:14 we read that God "knows our frame; he remembers that we are dust." The Psalm further reminds us that the years of our life span shortened considerably as a result of sin (Ps 103:15-16). That frustrations would plague our work was the primary prediction in the original pronouncement of God to Adam at the time of the beginning of sin (Gen 3:17-19). The book of Ecclesiastes confirms the reality of this fact. It says that man's "days are full of pain, and his work is a vexation; even in the night his mind does not rest" (2:23). One author reports that "fifteen to twenty percent of the population of the United States have emotional difficulties (ranging from alcoholism to schizophrenia) that significantly interfere with their daily functioning."[1] Another study made in Canada, reported by the same author, reveals that 65 to 75 percent of the residents were unhappy and dissatisfied with their lives.

Even Christians who have accepted Jesus Christ and are

---

[1]Dan G. Blazer II, Healing the Emotions (Nashville: Broadman Press, 1979), p. 11.

justified by his blood continue to be vulnerable. They can become
"weary in well-doing" and even "lose heart" (Gal 6:9; 2 Thess 2:13;
2 Cor 4:1). They can "drift away" from what they have heard
(Heb 2:1; 6:4-6). Christians who are not continuing in deliberate
sinful acts, who no longer allow sin to reign in their lives, still
may suffer its results. They continue "groaning in travail,"
waiting for their full redemption (Rom 8:18-23). Their "thorns
in the flesh" may not be removed (2 Cor 12:7). The weaknesses are
still present. The devil is still bombarding every soul with
temptations (Rev 12:12; Eph 6:10-20). They may be "afflicted,"
"perplexed," "persecuted;" they may be "struck down," but with the
help of God they are not "crushed," "driven to despair," "forsaken,"
or "destroyed" (2 Cor 4:8-10). In fact, they can be "strong,"
but it is "in the Lord" (Eph 6:10). They can have "assurance," but
it is in a "hope" and "faith" in something beyond themselves
(Heb 6:11; 10:22). They can be "happy whose God is the Lord"
(Ps 144:15). This does not come about by means of people's natural
inherent resources. The nature of man as informed from theological
categories does point to the necessity of help.

Support and the Calling of Ministry

The Nature of Ministers

Wayne Oates has written:

Ever since the establishment of the posterity of Aaron as the
priesthood of Israel, men have--sometimes articulately and sometimes tacitly--expected that the minister of the Bread of Life
be "without blemish."[1]

---

[1] Wayne E. Oates, "The Healthy Minister," in The Minister's
Own Mental Health, ed. Wayne E. Oates (Great Neck, NY: Channel
Press, 1955; 1961), p. 3.

The Levitical law did prescribe that no blind, lame, brokenfooted, scabbed, or man with any other such blemish should approach the holy place of the tabernacle (Lev 21:16-24). It is true that in the New Testament the qualifications for those who were to serve as leaders were high (Titus 1:5-9; 1 Tim 3:1-7; 1 Pet 5:1-4). Larry Richards and Clyde Hoeldtke say in their new book, A Theology of Church Leadership:

> The spotlight is placed squarely on the character of leaders. Simply put, those recognized as leaders in the body of Christ are to be those whose lives publicly and visibly provide a Christlike example. Leaders are selected on the basis of the kind of model they are of what each Christian should become.[1]

The ministry is a calling of God. The ministers' work is accomplished by means of gifts of the Holy Spirit. Ministers have been ordained to fulfill this purpose.

These factors sometimes lead ministers to act as though they do not need help. They are the care-givers, not the receivers. They may be somehow endowed with strength to take care of themselves that others do not have. They may deny their vulnerabilities as though their position insulates them from those things, or they may simply pass off their sins as virtues, and, as Daniel Walker says, "sin piously."[2] Indeed there is the doctrine of perseverance. Jesus says that his sheep will not be snatched out of his hand (John 10:28-29), for he is able to keep his people from falling (Jude 24). But these expressions apply to all Christians, not just ministers. The human nature of ministers is

---

[1](Grand Rapids: Zondervan Publishing House, 1980), p. 117.

[2]Daniel D. Walker, The Human Problems of the Minister (New York: Harper & Brothers, 1960), p. 4.

not different from that of all other persons. They are basically
as weak as any other, while others can be as strong as the minister.
If someone has become a person of noble character, worthy of being
a shadowy example of what Christians might become, whether minister
or lay person, it is attained by means of help beyond one's self.

The human nature of ministers is illustrated many times in
the Scriptures. For instance, there is Isaiah the prophet who
readily acknowledged his weakness. Notice how he identifies with
the same condition as that of his people. "Woe is me! For I am
lost; for I am a man of unclean lips, and I dwell in the midst of
a people of unclean lips" (Isa 6:5). Jeremiah vividly expresses
his vulnerability to the mistreatment by his people. He becomes
discouraged, asking, "Why did I come forth from the womb to see
toil and sorrow, and spend my days in shame?" (Jer 20:18). On
several occasions the apostle Paul makes clear his humanity. In
their first visit to Lystra, Paul and Barnabas were worshipped as
gods because they had healed a cripple. But these men urgently
protested saying, "Men, why are you doing this? We also are men,
of like nature with you. . . ." (Acts 14:15). It was the divine
help that enabled them to do what they did and be what they were.
Their own natures were more transparent in the "sharp contention"
they had with each other over John Mark (Acts 15:36-39). Paul
calls himself the "foremost of sinners" (1 Tim 1:15). He describes
his vulnerability to spiritual struggles in his familiar Rom 7
passage (vss. 15-25). He is most explicit in 2 Cor 4:7 when he
says, "But we have this treasure in earthen vessels, to show that
the transcendent power belongs to God and not to us." Just as

today there are ministers who sometimes succomb to their vulnerabilities, the Old Testament had its Balaams (Num 22-24; 2 Pet 2:15)
and the New Testament its Demases (2 Tim 4:10).

Ministers and Laity

Hendrik Kraemer clarifies considerably the relationship between clergy and laity. He points out that in the New Testament,
"kleros" and "laos" refer to the same people. All Christians are
chosen by God and thereby belong to the "laos." But this same
group is a "body of men and women who share in God's gift of
redemption and glory, which is their 'inheritance' ("kleros"), because they are incorporated in the Son."[1] These terms were used
differently in the Graeco-Roman city-state. The "kleros" were the
magistrates and the "laos" were the common people, uneducated and
uncultured. As time passed, this type of relationship using this
terminology developed in the church. The clergy became a separate
body, higher in status, with greater powers than the laity. They
were two separate classes of Christians, ordination being the line
of demarcation. The clergy lived a sacred life (which led into
monasticism), the laity a secular or profane life. The clergy
dispensed and administered divine grace, the laity only received
what was conveyed to them.[2] Remnants of this dualism contribute
today to the unrealistic attributions of the pastoral pedestal.

Glasse brings to our attention another background factor

---

[1]Hendrik Kraemer, A Theology of the Laity (Philadelphia:
Westminster Press, 1958), pp. 49, 52.

[2]Ibid., pp. 49-55.

that contributes to our conception of ministry. If we believe

ordination to be a sacrament and that thereby the man of God is

infused with some supernatural elements, becoming in some real

sense a different order of human being, then we might be able to

justify that the minister is in a class by himself. Some groups

believe this, but as Glasse says, "for most of us it just won't

do."[1]

The basic equality among the people of God as evidenced

in the New Testament does not mean that the minister holds no

distinctive office. He has been called, given special gifts, and

ordained to a specific work. But his distinction is not of status

or of enjoying a different nature or exclusive relationship with

God. He is simply called to the special function of leadership,

a public ministry, a full-time work. Jesus did his best to try

to help his disciples understand that leadership does not mean

status (Mark 9:33-35). Leadership is a role that one among equals

fills for the sake of order and progress. Martin Luther put it

this way:

> There is, at bottom, really no other difference between lay-
> men, priests, princes, bishops, or between religious and
> secular, than that of office or occupation, and not that of
> Christian status.[2]

Since all Christians partake of the privilege and responsibility

of service and soul-winning, the minister, Frederic Greeves says,

---

[1] James D. Glasse, Profession: Minister (Nashville: Abingdon Press, 1968), p. 22.

[2] Martin Luther, "An Appeal to the Ruling Class of German Nobility as to the Amelioration of the State of Christendom," in Martin Luther: Selections from His Writings, ed. John Dillenberger (New York: Doubleday, 1961), p. 403.

is a pastor of pastors, a shepherd of shepherds.[1]

Vulnerability and the
Work of Ministry

If a minister admits his vulnerability and need for help,
there is a chance that he might hear the same chant that was repeated to Jesus: "He saved others; he cannot save himself"
(Matt 27:42). And there would be truth in it. Many times those
who have skillfully helped others would have been overcome themselves without some intervention in the times of their crisis.

But admitting vulnerability need not be feared for another
very important reason. The book of Hebrews tells us of the high
priest who "can deal gently with the ignorant and wayward, since
he himself is beset with weakness" (Heb 5:1-3). The Old Testament
priests had to offer sacrifices for their own sins as well as for
those of the people. Jesus Christ is our true high priest.
Though he lived without sin (Heb 4:15; 7:28), he voluntarily took
upon himself a position of weakness. He partook of the same nature
and was made like us in every respect (Heb 2:14, 17). He took the
form of a servant and was tempted in every point as we are (Phil
2:8; Heb 4:15). He made himself vulnerable. He did this to be
"able to help those who are tempted" (Heb 2:18).

Henri Nouwen suggests that the wounds we suffer can become
a resource for healing to others. Our wounds become helpful
teachers of our own and our neighbor's condition. The sharing of

---

[1]Frederic Greeves, Theology and the Cure of Souls
(Manhasset, NY: Channel Press, 1962), p. 155.

pain and the common search for life create a community of hope.
In a sense our wounds are gifts to us. We should not flaunt them
as a kind of spiritual exhibitionism. But even though we do not
talk about them, our accepting them prepares us for healing
service. Nouwen relates an old legend from the Talmud which
illustrates his thoughts vividly:

> Rabbi Yoshua ben Levi came upon Elijah the prophet while he
> was standing at the entrance of Rabbi Simeron ben Yohai's
> cave. . . . He asked Elijah, "When will the Messiah come?"
> Elijah replied, "Go and ask him yourself."
> "Where is he?"
> "Sitting at the gates of the city."
> "How shall I know him?"
> "He is sitting among the poor covered with wounds. The others
> unbind all their wounds at the same time and then bind them up
> again. But he unbinds one at a time and binds it up again,
> saying to himself, 'Perhaps I shall be needed: if so I must
> always be ready so as not to delay for a moment.'"[1]

Jesus is the wounded healer. It was by the wounds of his own
broken body that he brought healing, liberation, and new life. He
did not try to do it in strength, might, or power as others hoped
he would. Paul also reminds us that there can be strength in
weakness (2 Cor 12:9-10). In one place he describes what is very
suggestive of a wounded healer:

> He comforts us in all our troubles, so that we in turn may be
> able to comfort others in any trouble of theirs and to share
> with them the consolation we ourselves receive from God. As
> Christ's cup of suffering overflows, and we suffer with him,
> so also through Christ our consolation overflows. If distress
> be our lot, it is the price we pay for your consolation, for
> your salvation; if our lot be consolation, it is to help us
> to bring you comfort, and strength to face with fortitude the
> same sufferings we now endure. (2 Cor 1:4-6 NEB)

A minister need not fear his vulnerability. He need not shy away

---

[1]Henri J. M. Nouwen, The Wounded Healer (Garden City, NY:
Doubleday, 1972; Image Book edition, 1979), pp. 81-82.

from help for himself, for he is called to be a wounded healer.
He must look after his own wounds and also be prepared to heal the
wounds of others.

It is when a minister denies his limitations that he overworks, sets himself up with unrealistic expectations, neglects his
family, and gets discouraged, if not ill. Edelwich, who wrote on
burn-out, says that the danger of the enthusiasm stage is "an
'arrogant' or 'grandiose' view of oneself that covers up a superficial and inadequate knowledge of what one is doing."[1] Celia
Hahn suggests that a minister in this situation is assuming the
role of God's omnipotent helper, rather than having a healthy dependence upon him.[2] It is an insidious seduction for ministers,
and it is shocking and, of course, theologically condemned when it
is identified and named. No human should assume the capacity of
God. We demonstrate our creatureliness by living within the
limits of our humanity and accepting the help that our weaknesses
require.

Vulnerability and Responsibility

There are those who ignore the problems ministers face
and neglect any effort toward helping because they believe that
sacrifice is something that must be accepted as part of the
Christian life, particularly in the call of ministry. But this
attitude seems to be contrary to the New Testament spirit of

---

[1]Edelwich, p. 63.

[2]Celia Allison Hahn, "'The Madness of God'--is it Catching?"
Action Information, April 1980, p. 1.

sacrifice. The appeal coming to us is to present ourselves as "living sacrifices, holy and acceptable to God" (Rom 12:1). This implies that sacrifice is to have a constructive orientation. Its purpose is to build up what God values most--his people, including his ministers. It does not require needless neglect, especially of the very things that are its objective, e.g., health, a saved family, an active spiritual communion. Bennett Sims writes that sacrifice does not exclude self-realization:

> We know now that there is a self-destructive impulse deep in man that needs as much restraint as his self-indulgent drive. Self-realization is not antithetical to discipline and sacrifice, since self-realization requires the much resisted work of self-understanding and personal growth. Without these costly gains, unhealthy self-hatreds can be unconsciously nourished under a cloak of self-losing piety--like a vessel rusting itself full of holes beneath a fresh coat of battleship gray.[1]

Sacrifice needs to be governed by the principle of stewardship. Can more overall positive gains be realized by expending or conserving? A person who overworks and dies early, or who takes so little refreshment that his labors become inefficient and harmful, will not make as great a contribution as one who functions within the natural laws of human life, and fulfills God's ideal for self-development.

Counsel for ministers regarding the stewardship of their ministry is given by Ellen G. White, a woman SDAs believe had a special prophetic gift.[2] Apparently in the late nineteenth century

---

[1] Bennett J. Sims, "Continuing Education as a Peer Support in the Dynamics of Change," Pastoral Psychology 22 (March 1971):39.

[2] According to the article, "White, Ellen Gould (Harmon)," in the Seventh-day Adventist Encyclopedia, ed. Don F. Neufeld (Washington, D.C.: Review and Herald Pub. Assn., 1966), pp. 1406-1418, Mrs. White lived from 1827 to 1915. She is noted as a

she saw many ministers suffering from ill-health. She strongly
advises them to pay attention to their bodies for "nature will not
long suffer abuse without protesting."[1] She recognized the strain
and wear that comes with ministerial duties and mental labor, and
urged ministers to regularly relax and exercise physically.

> Some of our ministers feel that they must every day perform
> some labor that they can report to the conference, and as the
> result of trying to do this, their efforts are too often weak
> and inefficient. They should have periods of rest, of entire
> freedom from taxing labor. But these cannot take the place of
> daily physical exercise.
> Brethren, when you take time to cultivate your garden,
> thus gaining the exercise you need to keep the system in good
> working order, you are just as much doing the work of God as
> in holding meetings. God is our Father, He loves us, and He
> does not require any of His servants to abuse their bodies.[2]

She recommended studying the best authors in the field of health and
then living by those principles.[3] Quoting Jesus' command to come
apart and rest awhile, she in fact states that it is a duty to
rest.[4] We are not to try to crowd two days work into one. God does
not ask us "to pursue a course of action that will result in the
loss of physical health or the enfeebling of the mental powers."[5]
She rebukes ministers who work single-handedly, trying to embrace

---

cofounder of the SDA Church and writer, lecturer, and counselor to
it. She had visions and dreams which she and her followers be-
lieved carried the marks of divine origin. These informed her
literary output which consisted of well over 100,000 pages. SDAs
believe that the writings of Ellen G. White contain special insight
and authority.

[1]Ellen G. White, Counsels on Health (Mountain View, CA:
Pacific Press Pub. Assn., 1951), p. 563.

[2]Ibid., p. 564.   [3]Ibid., p. 566.

[4]Ellen G. White, Gospel Workers (Washington, D.C.: Review
and Herald Pub. Assn., 1948), p. 243.

[5]Ibid., p. 245.

the whole work in their arms.[1] But there are also those, she

points out, that take things too easily and are lazy. She chides

them to get busy and even out the inequities with which God is

displeased.[2] Church members, she instructs, must also play an im-

portant role in sharing the burdens,[3] and pastors must recognize

this interdependence of human beings upon one another.

> He who talks of independence, and shuts himself up to himself,
> is not filling the position that God designed he should. We
> are all children of God, mutually dependent upon one another
> for happiness.[4]

These are just a sampling of her thoughts.[5]

Support and God's Way of Helping

God's Help Directly

So far in this chapter we have found that the need for a

support system is indicated in basic human nature, whether in

original perfection or in the weakness of sin. We have also said

that the call of ministry does not place a person outside the pur-

view of those needs. But where can one confidently go for help?

The first thing many ministers say is that God alone is their helper.

---

[1]Ellen G. White, Evangelism (Washington, D.C.: Review and
Herald Pub. Assn., 1946), p. 113.

[2]White, Gospel Workers, p. 246; White, Testimonies for the
Church, 2:502-03.

[3]Ellen G. White, Christian Service (Washington, D.C.:
Home Missionary Department of the General Conference of Seventh-day
Adventists, 1947), pp. 68-69.

[4]Ellen G. White, "Christian Work," Review and Herald,
October 10, 1882, p. 625.

[5]The full text of a select number of these and other
counsels relating to support and ministers is found in appendix B.

He is the only one to whom they turn.[1] It is true that God is our supreme counselor and great burden-bearer. The weaknesses of mankind, which we have just established, preclude a human being from being the source of any ultimate power. We must never forget that support is never purely "psycho" or "social." It always finds its origin in God. Furthermore, God has sent and still does send his help directly to those in need.

Just before his ascension Jesus promised to be with us always, right to the close of the age (Matt 28:20). It gives great assurance to know that right now we have a high priest, "one who is seated at the right hand of the throne of the Majesty in heaven" (Heb 8:1-2). He is there ministering in our behalf, making it possible for us to come with confidence to this throne of grace, "that we may receive mercy and find grace to help in time of need" (Heb 4:16).

God's direct help comes to us by means of a second avenue as well. Jesus said, "I will not leave you desolate . . . I will pray the Father, and he will give you another Counselor, to be with you forever, even the Spirit of truth" (John 14:16-18, 26). Sometimes the Holy Spirit is called the Comforter. He teaches, guides, reproves, empowers; he "helps us in our weakness;" he intercedes in behalf of our feeble and inaccurate prayers (John 14:26; 16:8-13; Acts 2:8; Rom 8:26-27); and he gives gifts that are enabling to us (1 Cor 12:3-11). But maybe most meaningful of all,

---

[1]For a description of this typical attitude see Daniel Zeluff, There's Algae in the Baptismal 'Fount' (Nashville: Abingdon, 1978), pp. 38-39; McBurney, Every Pastor Needs a Pastor, pp. 90-91.

the Spirit dwells in our very bodies (1 Cor 6:19). We have ready access to him. The Christian can speak of those times of strength-obtaining communion, when through Bible study, prayer, or simply the meditation of the mind, he senses the actual communication passing back and forth. What a boon in the face of discouraging conflict or stressful frustration!

There are also the angels, "ministering spirits sent forth to serve, for the sake of those who are to obtain salvation" (Heb 1:14). Angels have been given "charge" over God's people to "guard" them in all their ways (Ps 91:11; also 34:7). Angels helped Jesus in times of his weakness--at the end of his forty-day temptation/fast and in his agony in Gethsemane (Matt 4:11; Luke 22:43). Angels helped Peter out of a threatening situation by bringing him out of prison (Acts 12:6-11). An angel brought hope to Paul and his terror-stricken cohorts in their storm-tossed ship near Malta (Acts 27:23-25). Many are the recorded occasions of angels assisting people in their times of extreme need. And with what wonderment we listen to modern-day stories that bear the un-mistakable evidence of the intervention of these special beings.

Finally, God helps directly by intervening in the events and circumstances of our lives by means of his overruling providence. Although he respects our choices, he also hears our petitions. He can and does direct the happenings of our lives, just as he over-sees the establishment of nations and the course of history (Rom 8:28; Dan 2:21). Ellen White wrote:

> Our heavenly Father has a thousand ways to provide for us of
> which we know nothing. Those who accept the one principle of

making the service of God supreme, will find perplexities
vanish, and a plain path before their feet.[1]

God's help is unfailing whereas human help is often wanting.
In Ps 142 there is an outcry to God in an instance when the author
had no other refuge. No fellow human seemed to notice or care.
Micah 7:5-7 describes a situation when friends, neighbors, and
even family cannot be trusted. The Lord is the only surety. Just
before Christ's second coming, in the time of tribulation and
trouble, God's people will be scattered, some imprisoned, some in
hiding (Matt 24:9-10; Isa 33:16; Jer 30:7). Many will be isolated
from supportive human contact. God's direct help will be all the
more precious (Ps 27:5; 91:3-10; 121:5-7; Isa 26:20-21). But
these are not the only methods God uses in helping.

God's Help Through Human Agencies

It has been God's choice throughout the history of this
world to use human agencies as his servants in accomplishing his
work in behalf of mankind. This is part of the doctrine of election.
Not only does God call people to be saved themselves, but he calls
them to be his "ambassadors," agents of reconciliation (2 Cor
5:18-20). Through the progeny of Abraham, God sought to bless the
world (Gen 12:1-3). He called Israel to be a whole kingdom of
priests, witnessing to the nations in his name (Exod 19:6;
Isa 2:1-4; 43:10; Mic 4; Zech 8:20-23). Every Christian is also in
some sense a priest ministering the benefits of God's goodness to
others (1 Pet 2:9-10). Note that human help in this sense is not

---

[1]Ellen G. White, The Ministry of Healing (Mountain View, CA:
Pacific Press Pub. Assn., 1905; 1942), p. 481.

merely human help. It is, as Paul puts it, "God making his appeal through us" (2 Cor 5:20); it is divine help coming through the human. It is "psycho-social resources" with a divine imprint and origin, for human help is not antithetical to divine help. It is not salvation by man versus salvation by God. It is one way that God has chosen to do his work. Note these statements from Ellen White:

> The Lord has need of you. He does not do His work without the co-operation of the human agent.[1]

> Angelic agencies, though invisible, are co-operating with visible human agencies, forming a relief-association with men. . . . Human agencies are the hands of the heavenly in-strumentalities; for heavenly angels employ human hands in practical ministry. Human agencies as hand-helpers are to work out the knowledge and use the facilities of heavenly beings. By uniting with these powers that are omnipotent, we are benefited by their higher education and experience. Thus, as we become partakers of the divine nature, and separate selfishness from our lives, special talents for helping one another are granted us. This is Heaven's way of administering saving power.[2]

> The Holy Spirit is to work through human agencies. A partner-ship between God and the workers must be maintained. Man works because God works in him; all the efficiency and power is of God. Yet God has so arranged that all the responsibility rests with the human instrument. These are the appointed conditions of partnership. Men are required to move among men, doing divine work.[3]

As beneficiaries we need to discern the work of God in the help of others. The Bible says, "Test the spirits to see whether they are of God" (1 John 4:1). And again, "Test everything; hold fast what is good" (1 Thess 5:21). But that is no reason to reject

---

[1]White, Testimonies for the Church, 6:40.

[2]Ellen G. White, "Help for Our Scandinavian Institutions," Review and Herald, March 19, 1901, p. 177.

[3]Ellen G. White, "If Ye Know These Things, Happy Are Ye If Ye Do Them," Review and Herald, November 4, 1902, p. 9.

human help. Ministers who limit themselves only to the direct help
of God are not receiving the full help of God, and often this limi-
tation is a sign that the person is somehow threatened by such human
relationships. The work of ministry, the things a pastor does
every day, testify to the need for human intervention. The minister
is in need of this same intervention. T. C. McGinnis says,

> All too often the clergyman functions as if he were an island
> unto himself. If he is joyous, he is happy by himself. If
> he is sad, he lives alone with his depression. If he has con-
> flicts, he uses his own psychological devices to cope with them.
> While every man must use his own resources and accept responsi-
> bility for himself and his actions, the clergyman's tendency
> toward rigidity of personality and isolation severely limit[s]
> continued emotional growth. Roy Pearson, in commenting on
> the role of the clergyman, stated: "We cannot be Christians
> by ourselves, nor can we stand alone and do the deeds which
> must be done if God's will in Christ is not to be rejected.
> Call the group (congregation) what you will. Christianity is
> impossible without the group.[1]

Those who spend their time counseling ministers have seen that
human problems can sometimes grow in magnitude until personal religious and devotional resources no longer seem adequate by themselves to help them cope.[2] Sometimes a human agent bringing
immediate and tangible help is necessary before the channel to
things spiritually discerned can be opened. Might it be that God

---

[1] T. C. McGinnis, "Clergymen in Conflict," Pastoral Psychology 20 (October 1969):17; the statement from Roy Pearson is
found in "Why I Quit the Ministry," The Christian Century,
December 1962, p. 1558.

[2] Gerald Caplan, "Support Systems," p. 194; Wilford Clinton
Manley, "Stress among Selected Pastors in Industrial Settings"
(D.Min. dissertation, The Southern Baptist Theological Seminary,
1974), p. 54. From his study of one hundred pastors around Green-
ville, South Carolina, Manley reports that spiritual and religious
things were adequate resources during times of moderate stress.
But when stress reached more dangerous levels, other resources became vitally important, and the spiritual less effective as a
major means of coping.

is waiting for his human partners to do that part of his work?

The mutual care of souls, each man his brother's keeper in spiritual fellowship, has been called the "priesthood of all believers." It has sometimes been misunderstood to imply that every individual is his own priest. No. The whole church is a holy priesthood. We are interdependent in this corporate body. Says Greeves:

> Thus, a great doctrine has been perverted in the interests of a purely individualistic conception of Christian life. None of us would have come to believe the gospel had not somebody "told" us; so, too, each of us is in debt to many who have helped to bring God to us and us to God. It is pride, not truly Protestant conviction, that causes us to forget our debt; and because we forget our debt, we fail to recognize our responsibility for each other.[1]

The Scriptures say: "Bear one another's burdens, and so fulfil the law of Christ" (Gal 6:2). "Confess your sins to one another, and pray for one another, that you may be healed" (Jas 5:16). "Rejoice with those who rejoice, weep with those who weep" (Rom 12:15). "We who are strong ought to bear with the failings of the weak" (Rom 15:1). "Let each of you look not only to his own interests, but also to the interests of others" (Phil 2:4). "Encourage one another and build one another up" (1 Thess 5:11). "Admonish the idle, encourage the faint-hearted, help the weak, be patient with them all" (1 Thess 5:14).

"Ministers" in Scripture were the recipients of support also--sometimes by means of God's direct help and sometimes by means of human agencies. Moses had a sabbatical on Mt. Sinai where he was strengthened by a direct encounter with God to face a

---

[1]Greeves, p. 145.

discouraging situation with his people. In fact he was gone so
long that the people thought he was not coming back (Exod 24:12-18;
32:1; 33:17-34:10). Yet when he faced burnout from overwork, it
was human help that enabled him to resolve his frustrations (Exod
18:13-20; Jethro, Moses' father-in-law, advises him to organize
assistants to relieve his heavy burden). On one occasion the
success of Israel in battle was determined by Moses holding high
his hands in an attitude of prayer. But due to his human weakness,
Aaron and Hur had to support Moses' hands in order to continue
progress (Exod 17:8-13). The SDA Bible Commentary suggests that
God permitted success to be tied to this circumstance to teach
both the importance of intercessory prayer and the need to support
God's chosen leaders.[1]

Elijah is an interesting case study of the need for support.
One of the most powerful spokesmen for God, he nevertheless got
discouraged and needed help. On the one hand God ministered to
him directly by sending the ravens to feed him. On the other hand
God ministered to him by the human instrumentality of the woman of
Zeraphath (1 Kgs 17). When he feared Jezebel and supposed that he
was the only one still faithful to God, God helped him directly by
sending an angel to feed him in the wilderness and by speaking to
him in a still small voice. God had to tell him that there were
still seven thousand faithful in Israel. In isolation Elijah had
gotten into trouble. But God helped him thereafter by giving him
Elisha as a constant companion, who "ministered to him" (1 Kgs 19).

---

[1]Francis D. Nichol, ed., The Seventh-day Adventist Bible
Commentary, 7 vols. (Washington, D.C.: Review and Herald Pub.
Assn., 1953), 1:585.

Paul always traveled with companions. He praised the Philippians for sending Epaphroditus who ministered to his needs (Phil 2:25). He valued Onesimus as a most useful helper (Phlm 13). He told the Corinthians that "God, who comforts the downcast, comforted us by the coming of Titus" (2 Cor 7:6 NIV); but then confronted the Corinthians with their lack of support for him especially in light of the severe trials he had suffered (2 Cor 6:3-13 NIV). The pastoral epistles were directed to the instruction and support of young ministers.

Jesus appears to have had special relationships among his disciples in his closeness with Peter, James, and John. And even something like a best friend may have been found in the "beloved disciple" (Matt 17:1; 26:37; John 13:23; 19:26; 20:2). He desired their support in his agony in Gethsemane. During his ministry he found periods of retirement necessary (e.g., Matt 14:23).

Even the strong need ministry, as Richard Baxter acknowledged.[1] Ellen White observed:

> We are too indifferent in regard to one another. Too often
> we forget that our fellow laborers are in need of strength
> and cheer. Take care to assure them of your interest and
> sympathy. Help them by your prayers, and let them know that
> you do it.[2]

In the last chapter of his book, Greeves admits the difficulty he had in discussing the cure of souls. Part of the time he found himself describing what pastors need to do and at other times what

---

[1]He said that the strong "also have need of our assistance, partly to prevent their temptations and declainings, partly to preserve the grace they have, and partly to help them to further progress and increase." Baxter, p. 17.

[2]White, _Ministry of Healing_, pp. 492-93.

they have need to be done for them. He concludes that the shepherds are also sheep.[1]

Perhaps the most helpful explanation is the one shared by Richard Frazier. He suggests that the model of shepherd and sheep may not fulfill all aspects of the pastoral situation. He likes the concept of "family" better. (Both Paul and John use this model.)[2] Frazier says that every man, every pastor, has need for three types of relationships, as in a family: father, brother, and son. With a father, a person "receives more than he gives, with a brother it is about equal, and with a son he usually gives more. And all are necessary and in some strange way very much interconnected."[3] So it is with a minister. There are many relationships where he does most of the giving, as with his people. These relationships are wanted and needed, contributing to his satisfaction. But he also needs the relationship in which he can be utterly weak and receive fully, as in a pastoral father. And he needs many pastoral brothers with whom he can share mutual concerns and who minister to each other. These types of relationships are part of the natural order. They are part of God's way of helping.

---

[1]Greeves, p. 174.

[2]For example, 1 Thess 2:11; 1 John is permeated with father, brother, children references.

[3]Richard Frazier, "The Role of 'Need' in Pastoral Care," The Journal of Pastoral Care 27 (March 1973):37.

CHAPTER III

THE CURRENT STATE OF SUPPORT SYSTEMS FOR

THE SEVENTH-DAY ADVENTIST MINISTRY

The Questionnaire

In chapter 1 the reasons why a minister might need a
support system were listed. In chapter 2 it was found that the
concept of support was theologically justifiable. Now we look
specifically at the SDA ministry to assess whether a support
system is functioning adequately or a need exists in this area.
We also wish to determine the attitude that ministers have toward
various support resources. To do this a questionnaire entitled
"The Support System of Local Church Pastors" was prepared and
sent to a random sample of SDA ministers in North America. As
noted previously, the ICM was doing a major church growth study and
a survey of pastoral morale. Arrangements were made to use the
sample of this concurrent study so as to build on the same data
bank. The original ICM study contained 281 pastors.[1] Eighty-
five percent (or 239) responded to the initial inquiries. This
became the base for obtaining information for this study. Six
of the 239 were eliminated due to death, leaving the country, and
other reasons, thus 233 questionnaires were mailed. Of those, 197

_____

[1]Appendix C contains the details regarding the methodology
of questionnaire construction, sample formulation, and data
retrieval.

were returned, which is 85 percent of the questionnaires sent and
70 percent of the original sample.

The questionnaire produced eighty-seven variables of information built around a number of objectives. The objectives included the measurement of fifteen subject areas: (1) general
attitude toward human support, (2) personal coping methods, (3) relatives other than spouse, (4) mentor, (5) peer pastors, (6) support
groups, (7) the sabbatical, (8) continuing education, (9) general
relationship with conference leadership, (10) conference president,
(11) conference ministerial secretary, (12) the conference advocate
concept, (13) church members, (14) professional counselors, (15) non-
SDAs. Some of these areas were touched rather briefly, the emphasis
being on resources that the denominational conferences could provide. The subject of "pastor's wife" was omitted because it was
measured in the ICM survey. However, it is included in this
report.

The questions that had to do with human relationships im-
plied (1) a general social relationship with a person, (2) a deep,
confiding relationship, or (3) an unspecified level of relationship
(since it was not critical to the question). The questions sought
the following types of information within the above categories:
(1) Is the support resource available to the pastor? (2) Has he
used it? (3) How effective is it, in his opinion? (4) What dynamics
influence the effectiveness and use of the support resource?
(5) How interested is the pastor in making use of the support resource? Not every combination of these categories was included.
Those judged to be most important, according to the preliminary

evidence (reading, conversations, experience), were measured. The way of responding to nearly all the questions was by choosing one number from a bipolar scale ranging from one to five. Occasionally a zero was used to indicate some exception.[1]

Findings from the Total Sample

The results of the questionnaire are reported as follows: In the written description only the percentages of those responding to the contrasting options will be noted. In other words, the percentages of numbers one and two in one direction and numbers four and five in the other direction are combined. The middle response is omitted unless it happens to be important. The zeros are also mentioned only when they are significant.[2]

We investigate first the results from the total 197 respondents. Each of the fifteen subject areas covered in the questionnaire will be reviewed. Later we study some of the sub-groups, such as age brackets and a few correlations among responses to some of the questions.

General Attitude toward Human Support

If there is a lack of support it is not because SDA ministers disdain general supportive human relationships. Eighty-two percent feel that human relationships are very helpful as

---

[1]The complete questionnaire, as well as table 9 showing which objectives were achieved in each question, is included in appendix C.

[2]Table 10 lists the percentages for all the response options and is found in appendix C. It also displays the mean or arithmetic average of the responses on the one to five scale. This indicates the balance point of the distribution of the responses and thus shows the general tendency of the overall sample.

opposed to only 3 percent who do not, according to question (Q) 3.
It must be remembered, however, that this sentiment applies only
to the general concept of social relationships. Feelings regarding
specific types of help and deeper confidences vary much more widely.
The pastors were asked to evaluate which of a list of factors might
keep them from seeking help for more sensitive problems. It was
not fear of wrong advice, concern for reputation, or job security;
it was not even distrust of others or the idea that man should
depend upon God that primarily keeps them from getting help in
times of need. All the factors but one had about twice as many
indicating that such things would not keep them from getting help
as opposed to those who felt they would be a definite hinderance.
But the one item that had a greater percentage in the other
direction was "no one to go to." Apparently many pastors feel
blocked from adequate resources to call upon in their times of
need. This confirms the assertions made in chapter 1 regarding
the ministers' isolation. Those hindered by the other factors,
although a smaller group, are still a significant number and
worthy of consideration. Specific percentages of the complete
list are shown in table 1.

The questionnaire provided an opportunity for additional
comments. It was in these personal expressions that the picture
was vividly colored with humanness and emotion. Quite a number
expressed a personal need and positive desire for some type of
help. A fifty-one-year-old man with over a quarter century as a
pastor wrote:

TABLE 1

FACTORS THAT KEEP ONE FROM SEEKING HELP FROM HUMAN
BEINGS REGARDING SENSITIVE PROBLEMS

Question 4	Item	Does Not Keep Me from Seeking Help	Definitely Keeps Me from Seeking Help
A.	Fear of wrong advice	71%	10%
B.	Can't trust others	46	22
C.	Might affect my reputation	54	23
D.	Should depend on God	52	26
E.	No one to go to	36	45
F.	Am a private individual	50	20
G.	Might affect my job security	61	19
H.	Believe we should solve our sensitive problems by ourselves	55	16
I.	It wouldn't really help	62	13

My wife is the only one I have felt free to share my frustrations
with and I can't share theological questionings with her because
I don't want to weaken her faith or to cause her concern about
mine. Right now I can't think of anyone with whom I can safely
discuss these issues for fear of . . . [appearing] weak in the
faith when I really am needing some help. So in the end I just
struggle on alone, trying to study as I can, holding questions
in my mind, and just trying to cope each day. The problems and
pressures get pretty heavy, but I don't know what else to do so
just "hang in there." I hope your study will prove helpful in
improving the situation.

In the group of only 197 responding ministers, five volunteered that

they had marital problems, four already being divorced. One said,

"Most of my recent interest in counseling is related to a marriage

problem I am now going through--and not related to church diffi-

culties. My church has not been the hard work." A wide variety

of concerns were expressed. A pastor with twenty-eight years in the

ministry said, "I feel like I am the weakest of the weak as far as

pastors are concerned. Pray for me." One wrote of his feelings of/
inadequacy when he first started in the ministry. Another appealed
in behalf of the special needs of Spanish-speaking ministers. Still
another mentioned the vast territory of his three-church district
and the isolation he feels. A pastor with a Ph.D. wrote: "I have
a great concern over all the 'administrivia!' . . . Another area
is the pastor's <u>health</u>. The pressures just about wipe you out!"
Pressures were referred to in another way in this note: "Obviously
you are getting into some touchy subjects (but needed). Somehow
the pressures from each other must be relieved so that we can
honestly look at our ministries." These pastors would welcome
some kind of support, some relief, someone to go to, or someone to
come to them.

Personal Coping Methods

There are many personal methods of coping with problems
that an individual might be able to utilize. Some of these are
suggested in chapter 5. This questionnaire measured only two.
One that is most important and could not be overlooked is spiritual
strength that comes from an active relationship with God. Q 2
asked how effective the person's personal Bible study, meditation,
and prayer were in coping with problems and frustrations in
ministry. It is reassuring to note that 90 percent find this
resource "very effective." To the degree that the finding of the
previous section is true, this may be the ministers' only resource.
On the other hand, we cannot know to what degree the always-
positive ministerial tendency is operating here. Ministers may

feel that a high mark on such a question is expected of them.

Others believe it with deep conviction. One minister wrote:

> I believe it is helpful to consult with fellow ministers on
> serious problems we have to face, and that we can profit much
> from such consultations; however, I think a minister can find
> solutions to most of the problems in his personal and pro-
> fessional life, by seeking the Lord in deep prayer--study
> sessions with our all wise Counselor and Saviour Jesus Christ.
> He invites us to come to him and He will help us.

While this, of course, is the ideal, there can be times when

spiritual things by themselves do not relieve the immediate human

problem.

Ministers often complain about their administrative duties

and general time pressures. Time management has been a popular tool

used to tune the organizational machine to function more smoothly.

Q 1 found that 31 percent of SDA ministers in this study have never

seriously tried time-management principles. However, 32 percent of

those who tried them found them to be "very helpful." Only 12

percent said they were "not helpful." In other words, if ministers

got involved at all, it usually was to their benefit. It may be

that many of those who have never tried time management have not

had opportunity to be exposed to it. And, of course, a large part

of its success depends upon personal motivation.

Relatives

In this questionnaire we asked only about supportive re-

lationships with relatives other than spouse. Surprisingly 30

percent had no other relative with whom they confide (Q 5). Whether

this is due to family tensions, differing ideologies, the minis-

terial pedestal operating even in the family, separation from extended family by distance, privacy and trust issues, or other things, we cannot know. Another 20 percent tried it, but without satisfaction. It seems that a total of 50 percent are without this resource. Only 30 percent found a confiding relationship with a relative "very helpful."

The frequency of contact with such relatives was measured in Q 28C. It asked how often within the last year had the ministers had a meaningful sharing time. Confirming Q 5, 33 percent had had no meaningful sharing time at all. In fact, 3 percent of those that had a relative to whom they could talk had not done so in the past year. In most other cases they had had a contact two or three times.

In regard to the minister's wife, the ICM survey, "The Pastor as Person and Husband," found that 91 percent of the ministers in this study had wives who encouraged and supported them in the ministry.[1] Similarly high percentages indicate that the ministers and their wives have a very open relationship wherein they can freely discuss their deepest feelings; they often counsel together on the work of ministry; and they always confer before making a major decision. The minister's wife is obviously one of the strongest support resources for the minister. Just as striking, however, is the effect of a stressful husband-wife relationship on pastoral morale. Those who gave negative responses to the above items (about 13.4 percent of the total) were singled out. Their responses to nine questions having to do with morale were compared

---

[1]Dudley, Cummings, and Clark, p. 5.

with the overall sample. The pastors experiencing marital stress also had lower morale in every one of the nine items. The differences from the total group were substantial. Table 2 shows these contrasts. Certainly the minister's family is a vital link in his support, and it is worth reciprocating care and concern to them to keep the relationship mutually healthy.

TABLE 2

MARITAL STRESS AND PASTORAL MORALE

Item	Pastors with Marital Stress	Total Sample
1. Satisfying personal devotional life	43%	74%
2. Professional-growth program effective	35	57
3. Regular family worship in home	52	70
4. Believe I am a successful pastor	74	87
5. Hope to be called to administrative, departmental, or teaching position	35	21
6. Sometimes want to leave the pastoral ministry	48	28
7. Wife and I have discussed transferring to another type of ministry	52	33
8. Counselor separate from administration needed for pastors and wives	91	70
9. Sometimes feel lonely and isolated	74	58

SOURCE: Material put together from Dudley, Cummings, and Clark.

Mentor

The word "mentor" was not used in the questionnaire lest misunderstandings should arise. Instead the concept of an older, experienced minister who would give nurture and guidance was presented. As is evident in table 3, less than half of the responding

TABLE 3

MENTOR RELATIONSHIP

Question	Item	None	Not Helpful	Very Helpful
6.	A nurturing relationship from an experienced minister in early ministry	17%	18%	45%
7.	Receive guidance from an older, experienced minister <u>now</u> (only up to age 39)	25	20	28

		Never	Regularly
8.	Nurture younger men in ministry , (only over age 40)	27%	50%

		Number of meaningful sharing times last year				
		0	1	2-3	4-6	6+
28A.	With an older, experienced minister	25%	16%	40%	8%	11%
28K.	With a college or seminary teacher	71	14	11	2	2

		No Interest	Much Interest
29A.	Interest in having an older, experienced minister to consult	15%	61%
	Same item--only those up to age 39	10	72

ministers had a "very helpful" relationship with such a person in their early ministry. Even fewer say they have a pastoral father now. This holds true even if the older pastors (who are the fathers) are eliminated, as in the table. More of the older pastors think they are nurturing younger men than there are younger men who feel nurtured. Either the mentoring is concentrated in a few, or what nurturing and guidance is to the older man is not what younger men think it should be. When contacts were made, they usually occurred only two or three times a year. Very few had any contact with college or seminary teachers. Many more desire to use this resource than presently have it available, especially younger pastors. A pastor with less than two years in the ministry and with the responsibility of three churches wrote:

> I would feel it very helpful to work under an experienced person for one year after coming out of college, providing it was someone willing to help and have you work right along side, at least for a few months. There's much in school that doesn't "sink in" until you experience it. Making sure an individual knows how to operate a church from the business side of things could be learned by working with someone, and ultra-helpful to someone younger and/or inexperienced.

Peer Pastors

Just over a third of the respondents say they have a fellow pastor with whom they can find effective help in sharing sensitive personal problems (Q 9). Competition among pastors apparently is not the only factor that keeps them apart, for 50 percent do not sense any competition to speak of. The rest recognized it to some varying degree (Q 10). Of all the possible support relationships, fellow pastors of neighboring districts were in second place in the frequency of meaningful contacts within the last year (Q 28B). This resource rates the highest of all in terms of the number who would like to use it more. A high 73 percent are "very interested" in more opportunities to work with and fellowship together with fellow pastors (Q 29B); 75 percent show that same enthusiasm for more opportunities for professional consultation among ministers on specialized ministry problems (Q 29C). Pastors generally seem to have a desire similar to this: "I have had the feeling that

pastors need to work together two by two for strength and effectiveness in their work." Another says, "I believe that the best support
system is that ordained by God--that of Team Ministry."

Support Groups

Not quite as much enthusiasm exists for a regular peer
support group. The group was described as an occasion when pastors
would get together, either among SDAs or interfaith, for the purpose of fellowship, learning, and support of one another. Only
55 percent are quite interested in belonging to such a group
(Q 29D). But then it must also be considered that only 22 percent
have had much involvement with groups (Q 11), and a number of
these thought in terms of the local ministerial associations.
Table 4 shows a list of possible problems with a group. This list
came from the free responses to Q 14, which were then categorized
into common classes. Some pastors wrote more than one response,
whereas the majority skipped the question. Most of those who had
some involvement said that their groups met monthly. The second
highest percentage met less than every other month--hardly often
enough to develop group cohesiveness (Q 12). And as one might
expect, the majority found only average fulfillment and satisfaction from it (Q 13). Still there are a significant number who
are favorable to this resource. A young pastor wrote: "Someway,
there desperately needs to be a support group for the pastor in the
field."

TABLE 4

PROBLEMS WITH A MINISTER'S SUPPORT GROUP

Rank	Item	Percentage of Times Mentioned
1	Different beliefs, values, needs among the group members, particularly with non-SDA participants	12
2	Lack of trust and confidentiality regarding discussions	11
3	Self-centeredness, competition, or exclusiveness among group members	9
4	Lack of honesty, openness, and self-disclosure	8
4	Lack of significant, meaningful accomplishment	8
5	Lack of regular commitment and motivation toward the group; irregular attendance	6
5	Lack of proper guidance in group communication and in situations of conflict	6
5	Tendency toward overdependence on human element; misdirection; neglect of divine element	6
6	Problem finding time to meet	5
7	Being expected to be more intimate, revealing things too personal or negative, than one wants to	3
7	Tendency for group to become a negative, gripe session or theological doubting experience	3
8	Distance and expense in meeting	2
9	Group has no authority or real answers to change problem situations	1
9	Conference leaders might disapprove of such a group	1

Sabbatical and Continuing Education

The sabbatical and continuing education are two separate areas since a sabbatical need not involve continuing education. But since their treatment in the questionnaire was so brief, both are discussed here. Almost no opportunities for sabbaticals presently

exist in the SDA Church.[1] Sometimes when a minister feels the
wear and tear of his situation, all he needs in order to rebound
is some extra time off to allow his own resources to function in
their natural course. When presented with the possibility of a
sabbatical,, 56 percent were eager for the opportunity (Q 29E).
Significantly more were anxious for continuing education--68 percent (Q 29F). Seventy percent evaluated continuing education as
highly effective in providing a strengthening, refreshing break
in their ministries (Q 15). Aside from the supportive role of this
resource, the ICM survey reported that 92 percent want a continuing-
education program to upgrade their skills.[2] One pastor wishes that
continuing education were a "must."

Conference Leadership

Every pastor has a conference president and most conferences
have ministerial secretaries as well as a number of other personnel.
To what degree is this component functioning as a support resource
for pastors? A great deal of space was used to elicit the dynamics
of these relationships, for the conference, as the employing
agency in the SDA church, has an undeniable imprint on the nature
of one's ministry. It is also, therefore, the most likely place
where supportive resources can be initiated.[3]

An overview of the questions on this subject reveal a great

---

[1]See chapter 4.   [2]Dudley, Cummings, and Clark, p. 5.

[3]Unless one opts for a management-labor division, where
labor organizes over against management and takes its own initiative
to find reprieves. Such a division does not seem healthy, or
necessary, for it does not utilize the Christian principles for
which the church stands.

variety of experiences. Some are enjoying a very positive relationship and others are enduring one that is very unsatisfactory. As
was mentioned in chapter 1 denominational organizations not only
tend to provide inadequate support but often are part of the
pressure causing the need for support. In this SDA sample,
57 percent feel that they are treated professionally; 22 percent
do not (Q 16A). About as many feel very great pressure to reach
conference goals as those who feel no pressure (Q 16B). There
are 18 percent who feel that their careers as ministers are very
seriously threatened if they do not reach conference goals or
other expectations (Q 16C). Another quarter feel moderately
threatened.

Table 5 shows the ministers' perception of their conference
presidents on a number of items. Quite consistently, about half
the individuals have positive perceptions of their presidents, a
quarter have quite negative views, and the rest are unsure. Only
in item E did this pattern change. In this a greater number perceived their presidents as more interested in the progress and
success of the organization than in the minister's personal welfare. The greatest percentage, however, marked the middle choice
indicating that they were either unsure of his emphasis or felt
that he judiciously had an equal interest in both.

In Table 6 the perceptions of the ministerial secretary
(or department director, as he is variously called) are revealed.
In comparison with the conference president, the ministerial
secretary does not have closer friendships with the ministers; he
is not more available to them time-wise. This is peculiar if he

TABLE 5

PERCEPTIONS OF THE CONFERENCE PRESIDENT

Item	Percentage Choosing Each		Item
Question 20			
A. A tense, obligatory relationship with him	29	48	A very close friendship with him
B. Will think less of me, going to him with a problem	24	50	Will not think less of me, going to him with a problem
C. Ignores what I say	25	54	Seriously considers what I say
D. Not accessible time-wise	26	52	Always accessible time-wise
E. More interested in the organization	38	19	More interested in my personal welfare
(42% marked the middle choice for item E)			

TABLE 6

PERCEPTIONS OF THE MINISTERIAL SECRETARY

Item	Percentage Choosing Each		Item
Question 21			
A. A tense, obligatory relationship with him	23	45	A very close friendship with him
B. Does mostly adminis-trative functions	48	26	Does mostly pastor's pastor functions
C. Not accessible time-wise	27	44	Always accessible time-wise
D. Not approachable or understanding	17	60	Very approachable and understanding
E. Not keep personal con-versations confidential	15	53	Will keep personal con-versations confidential
F. Would not stand by me in differences with the admin.	27	23	Definitely would stand by me in differences with admin.
(44% marked the middle choice for item F)			

is considered the pastor of pastors. Though he is considered very approachable and generally keeps confidences, his function to the pastors is perceived mostly as administrative and not as a pastor's pastor. His ties with the administration cause the ministers to suspect that his loyalties might edge in that direction should there be some difference between the pastor and his employer. Here too, the higher percentage marking the middle choice suggests that they are either unsure whether he would stand by them or feel he would try to be neutral.

In the year previous to the study, 39 percent had no meaningful sharing time with their ministerial secretary (Q 28E); 33 percent had none with their conference president (Q 28D). Approximately another quarter had only one meaningful contact with either of these officers in the year. Very few had four or more such occasions. Are the ministers reluctant to go to their conference administrators for support in sensitive personal problems knowing that they have influence over their placement and career reputation? Forty-six percent say that they are very reluctant, as opposed to 33 percent who are not (Q 17). How much of an advantage is it to go to the administrator in such times because he has official power? There is no advantage, say 52 percent, while 20 percent see a significant advantage (Q 18). Are conference administrators able to keep their roles of placement, supervision, and discipline distinct from a supportive role in order to be effective counselors? No, say 41 percent who believe they are not able to keep information obtained in one role from influencing decisions in the other role; 21 percent believe they can keep such

things in their proper place. Thirty-six percent marked the middle
choice suggesting that administrators may partially be able to do
it (Q 19). The tendency is definitely toward reluctance and
hesitation to turn to the conference leadership for help.

The questionnaire suggested the idea of an advocate or
pastor's pastor specifically designated by the conference to work
in behalf of the ministers' personal needs whether it be counseling,
facilitating colleague support and friendship, providing resource
help, or referring them to other resources. There were 57 percent
very interested in the idea (Q 29G). But who would be the best
person for the job? Table 7 shows the possibilities suggested and
how they rated. It is quite obvious that the ministers want someone
without ties to administration. The conference president was not
highly rated for the job, but neither was the ministerial secretary
as his position now stands. Ministers are interested either in a
change in the job description of the ministerial secretary or in
the creation of a new position. Some wrote that they were against
this latter option because it would add conference personnel of
which there are already too many.

The ICM survey found that 70 percent desired a counselor
separate from the administration. In the subgroup of those experiencing marital stress, 91 percent wished there were such. One
of the conclusions of the ICM study reads:

> There is a real need to appoint counselors who have no admin-
> istrative functions but who have a deep understanding of
> pastoral ministry to work with pastors and their wives in the
> solution of personal and professional problems.[1]

---

[1] Dudley, Cummings, and Clark, p. 23.

TABLE 7

PERSON TO BE THE PASTOR'S ADVOCATE

Person	Poorest Suited	Best Suited
Question 22		
A. The conference president	49%	27%
B. The ministerial secretary with a job description revised to omit administrative roles	14	56
C. The ministerial secretary as his position now stands	44	21
D. A totally new position in the conference office without administrative roles	25	56
E. An authorized church pastor	37	32
F. A professional counselor	29	41

Of course, the personality of the support person is a major factor in his ability to relate effectively. The evidence of need and interest in such a person is strengthened by the number and nature of additional comments that were written.[1]

> Having gone through a divorce last year opened my eyes to the crying need in our conferences for someone to help in sensitive times. Before my wife left (1 wk.) the ministerial secretary and wife visited us twice. . . . But after she left me the only time anyone came was the ministerial secretary and his replacement to discover if I would be willing to leave if the conference decided to let me go. For four lonely months I had to carry on by myself with no support . . . and then to have lost family, job, home, but knowing God was in control! . . . Yes we need a supportive advocate in the conferences who will really help when a pastor has problems.

> I left the ministry because as a minority I did not have any one to relate to. The president at that time would not listen to me; only took my senior pastor's evaluation. My experience as a ministerial intern was terrible. I came back because I love the ministry. God has been good to me. My ministry has been successful since returning. A conference evangelist and coordinator has been very supportive and helpful.

---

[1]Others, besides those presented here, are found in appendix C.

> I believe that a counselor completely divorced from the church would be the only effective way to go. There seems to be almost a total lack of mercy and compassion among the SDA clergy that I have known. May God help us all if we ever fall into their hands when in serious need of emotional support and indepth understanding. Would that the spirit of Jesus might reign in every heart.

> I would very much like to see the ministerial secretary really be one. Usually he has other roles. . . . My wife needs one also. May God hasten the time when all Christians can support each other. The ministry is basically a trial and error, swim or sink situation; a very lonely place.

> It is my dream to eventually see at least one professionally trained counselor in every conference, where services would be to lay person and ministers alike. This would be a full time ministry. The need is great and I pray that this dream will become a reality soon.

There are some who report effective experiences of support. One has a man retired from the General Conference of SDAs living in his area. Another reports that for the first time in his ministry a conference secretary is being for him a source of support and counsel. There are some bright spots. The challenge is to more widely and intentionally implement a program and practice of support.

Church Members

If the pastoral pedestal is not too high, lay members can often reciprocate the pastoral care they receive. They need not always be problems to the minister. According to this study, the SDA ministers had a higher number of meaningful sharing times with supportive church members in their congregations than with any other persons. Within the previous year 44 percent had four or more such occasions (Q 28F). The same percentage rated those relationships as very helpful (Q 23). Less than half had any such relationships with lay persons outside their congregations (Q 28G). It is

within one's own church family where this resource is operating
most effectively. And 57 percent of the pastors are very desirous
of even deeper, more open friendships with their church members
(Q 29H).

Professional Counselors

Nearly 90 percent of the respondents have made little or
no use of professional counselors for their needs (Q 24 and 28J).
This, according to over half of the ministers, is because they
have not had problems severe enough to demand professional attention.
Twenty-nine percent were kept from going to a professional counselor
because it was too expensive; 39 percent did not know of a good
counselor accessible to them; 24 percent feared they would be
found out by the wrong person; and 17 percent said they could not
take time from their work (Q 25A-E). Of these latter factors,
"not knowing of a good one accessible" was the greatest hinderance.
As noted above, there is an interest in having a professional
counselor serve as a conference-designated support person for
ministers (Q 22F). In general about 43 percent of the ministers
are quite interested in increased use of a professional counselor
for more serious problems (Q 29I). From the written comments, it
is evident that there is some ambivalence about submitting to the
psychological methods of professional counselors. This may explain the unenthusiastic interest.

Non-SDAs

Within one's own church family there is usually a greater
openness to sharing because of the mutual understanding that

pervades. However, a supportive relationship can develop with those outside one's own church--with a neighbor or a community pastor. Twenty-three percent of the SDA ministers in this study found a very helpful relationship with a non-SDA minister. A slightly smaller percentage had the same good experience with a non-SDA lay person (Q 26A-B). There were even 13 percent who definitely feel more free to confide with a non-SDA friend than with SDA associates (Q 27). Most of these relationships involved just one to three contacts within the last year (Q 28H-I).

Findings from Selected Subgroups

Two methods were used in comparing subgroups of the total sample. First, the percentages of positive responses to certain questions from each category were listed to pinpoint any differences. Second, a computer program applied Pearson's product-moment correlation formula (a two-tailed test) to each question in relationship to every other question. The result was a total inter-correlation matrix of all eighty-seven variables. Only correlation coefficients that were at least to the .01 level of significance are reported here.

Age

The age of ministers may be one of the most important determinants of the need for and interest in an improved support system. Three age categories were separated and compared: those under forty, those between forty and fifty-four; and those over fifty-four. Q 29 was chosen, first of all, to make an age comparison. It asked for the degree of interest that a person has in

each of nine support resources. The results seem to summarize
the questionnaire quite well. (A very active interest in the
resources seems also to imply a need for it.) Table 8 shows the
percentage of positive responses to each of the nine resources
by each of the three age categories. The percentage of positive
responses by the total sample is listed for comparison. The last
column gives the correlation coefficients for age and each of the
nine resources. The minus sign indicates a negative correlation.
It would seem that a person getting older becomes less interested
in support resources. The correlations are not high (which means
that there is not a large difference of interest between the extreme ages), but they are significant. Only in item H, "deeper,
more open friendships with church members," do we find older and
younger ministers with about the same degree of interest (hence
the low correlation and inadequate level of significance). It is
interesting that the middle-aged minister seems to have the least
interest in this resource.

To obtain an overall picture, the percentages for each age
category were averaged. The result was a summary of active interest
in all the resources by the ministers of each age. It is shown
in the bottom section of table 8. These average percentages
demonstrate that the younger minister shows a greater interest in
and possibly a greater need for support. Q 3 dealt with the general
attitude toward human support. As portrayed in table 8, evidence
again shows that younger ministers are more likely to feel that
supportive relationships with human beings would be very helpful.
Q 15 demonstrates that younger ministers are significantly more

TABLE 8

AGE CORRELATED WITH SELECTED VARIABLES

Item	Total Sample	Age Under 40	Age 40-54	Age Over 54	Correlation Coefficient
Question 29 -- Very interested in:					
A. An older, experienced minister to consult	61%	72%	52%	54%	*-.185
B. More opportunities to work with and fellowship together with fellow pastors	73	85	67	60	*-.245
C. More opport. for professional consultation	75	86	70	66	*-.200
D. A regular peer support group	55	67	49	46	*-.218
E. A sabbatical, to get self together	56	70	53	32	*-.313
F. A continuing-education experience	68	77	69	52	*-.313
G. A conference support person	57	64	60	43	*-.213
H. Deeper, more open friendships with church members	57	61	49	62	-.124
I. A professional counselor	43	53	45	26	*-.270
Average percentages for all resources	60.5	70.5	57.6	49	
3. Supportive relationships with human beings would be very helpful	82	87	79	76	*-.192
15. Time off for continuing education would be very strengthening and refreshing	70	85	69	51	*-.304
22B. Ministerial secretary without administrative roles, best suited for conf. advocate	56	65	56	43	*-.259

*Correlations at least to the .01 level of significance

likely to value time off for continuing education as a strengthening, refreshing break in their ministry. It is also younger ministers who want to have a ministerial secretary without ties to administration to help them in their needs (Q 22B). Older men apparently are not quite as concerned about mixing administration and support. This forcefully confirms the vulnerability of the initial entry into ministry as mentioned earlier.[1] Younger men may still be seeking a settled identity in ministry. However, they may feel that they might not get as sympathetic an ear from their administrators as the older men might get. They may be more overwhelmed by the idealistic goal of accomplishing great things. Whatever it is, this is not a group to be disregarded. Those under forty years of age comprise 42 percent of the local church pastors.

Miscellaneous Correlations

There are many interesting correlations, most of which simply demonstrate the logical and consistent outworking of a certain course. A few samples of correlations that are significant at the .001 level are given here. Among those who feel great pressure from the conference (Q 16B) are a number who also sense a great deal of competition in the ministry (.275). They are not as able to trust others (.240); and they do not feel as professionally treated (-.246). They tend to believe their careers are threatened (.618) and are very reluctant to confide in a conference administrator (.306). They feel a rather tense, obligatory relationship with the president (-.269) and believe he would think less of them

---

[1]See chapter 1.

for coming to him with a problem (.341). They perceive the ministerial secretary as not very accessible (-.256), not keeping confidences (-.243), and not standing by them (-.271).

Those who indicated that they had a problem requiring the
attention of a professional counselor (Q 25A) correlate with those
who found personal Bible study, meditation, and prayer not as
effective in coping with their problems (-.241). They also felt
they could not trust others (.240), they feared for their reputation (.255) and job security (.313), and had no one to whom to
go (.227).

Those who reported they now have a very helpful relationship with an older, experienced minister (Q 7) include those who
have a very close friendship with their ministerial secretary
(2.77), who find him very approachable (.237), and who see him as
one who would stand by them (.258). They see the president as a
person more interested in their personal welfare (.291) and find an
advantage in help from administrators (.307). Of course, the
opposite is true for those who do not have a very helpful relationship with an older, experienced minister.

Those who have a close friendship with the conference
president (Q 20A) can also say they have someone to whom to go
(-.322). They do not feel competition among ministers (-.264), nor
pressure (-.269), nor threat (-.421). They feel professionally
treated (.500) and are not reluctant to confide in an administrator
(-.450); in fact, it may be a real advantage (.282). They feel
that administrative and supportive roles can be kept separate
(.416). The president is accessible to them (.490), listens to

them seriously (.697), does not think less of them for coming with a problem (-.544), and is interested in their personal welfare (.513).

Summary

From this questionnaire we have found that many SDA ministers of the sample are doing well. About 50 percent have a very positive attitude and many meaningful, healthy relationships. Another 25 percent are ambivalent. They are not sure of their conference leaders. They find only partial fulfillment from the elements of their support system. Then there is the last quarter (or less) who seem to suffer from an inadequate support system. Either it simply is not there or they have had unfortunate encounters with those who could have been supportive. They report more pressure and have a variety of fears about receiving support.

In spite of that numerical pattern it is not just one-fourth or one-half that indicate great interest in improving their support system. Depending on the type of resource 50 to 75 percent indicate such eagerness, especially among the younger ministers. Each aspect of the support system is important, for each resource fulfills a need in a little different way. Some appeal more to one person than to another.

Pastors themselves can take the initiative in many areas. However, denominational leaders have a particular responsibility to be sensitive to the dynamics that may hinder the functioning of effective support, and most of all, to intentionally make available those resources that it is in their domain to provide. The evidence demonstrates both the need and the interest.

PART II

DESIGNS FOR A POTENTIAL PSYCHO-SOCIAL

SUPPORT SYSTEM

CHAPTER IV

A REVIEW OF EXISTING SUPPORT RESOURCES

Parallels from the Business World

The Failure of Success, the title of a book of business management,[1] captures the truth of a situation that too often exists in organizations and industries. Managers can succeed in achieving their work goals beyond their dreams, but that success is tainted with failure if the human beings involved are expended, discontented, and unhappy. Big industry does not have a long history. In its early period, soon after the industrial revolution, the emphasis was on authoritarian management, production output, and strict discipline. Henry Ford, it is reported, built his company on these principles. He allegedly made all the decisions and his workers only executed his orders. He told them how to live and how much to produce. It is said that his first line supervisors were regularly demoted every few years so they would not have too much influence. He had what amounted to a "secret police" watching for anyone who might be out of line. It is also observed that his company was riddled with conspiracy and insecurity and nearly collapsed. It recovered only when the management concepts were changed.[2]

---

[1]Alfred J. Marrow, ed., The Failure of Success (New York: AMACOM, 1972).

[2]Peter Ferdinand Drucker, The Practice of Management (New York: Harper and Row, 1954), pp. 111-117; Roger M. Bellows,

Drucker, an authority in the field of management, reports and promotes the philosophy of a more recent period that seeks to deal with the whole human being:

> In hiring a worker one always hires the whole man. It is evident in the IBM story that one cannot "hire a hand;" its owner always comes with it. Indeed, there are few relations which so completely embrace a man's entire person as his relation to his work.
>
> No matter what kind of work men do, whether they are skilled or unskilled, production workers or salaried clerks, professionals or rank-and-file, they are basically alike . . .[1] they are always human beings with human needs and motivations.[1]

The study of human needs and motivations has spirited new directions in the management policies of a number of organizations. IBM, mentioned above, decided that its operation should be guided by these principles. Instead of output norms imposed from above, each man works out his own norms with his supervisor. Instead of pay incentives, each worker is on a straight salary. A great deal of attention is given to placing a worker where his abilities enable him to do his best. There is increased emphasis on training. The worker is given knowledge about related departments so he has the big picture of how his job fits in. He is allowed to collaborate on product designs and work methods. Right after this plan was installed, worker output went up and continued to improve. Workers were more satisfied. They did not feel such strong competition. If one of their fellow-workers produced more, they did not resent it, for it neither resulted in a higher output norm for themselves nor endangered their job security. Drucker says that

---

Psychology of Personnel in Business and Industry (New York: Prentice-Hall, 1949), pp. 306-07.

[1]Drucker, pp. 262, 255.

fear is a poor motivator. "There is no worse sin than to turn man's capacity to grow into a threat to himself and his fellow men. It is also poor engineering."[1]

This sensitivity to human needs resulted also in the establishment of the personnel director whose responsibility is more than being "a procurer of warm bodies from the labor market and a keeper of books of account on human capital." The director is also looked to as "an advocate of a humanistic environment."[2] That includes occupational health, safety, employee development, compensation, managerial development, career counseling and career planning, equal employment opportunity, and even executive development. Albrecht refers to many companies that offer health screening and stress-reduction programs to their employees as part of their personnel policies.[3]

One benefit that is often part of this cluster is personal counseling for marital conflicts, financial problems, or other crises in the worker's life. A textbook on personnel policies says:

> An employee service which has traditionally been provided by staff of the personnel department is the counselling of employees who are experiencing personal problems. . . . Such problems often not only worry employees but may also affect the efficiency of the firm. If an employee has worries which derive from any one of the above sources, then his mind will not be fully on the job for which he is paid. His working efficiency, and the safety of both himself and his fellow employees, may be jeopardised. On humanitarian and economic grounds it is therefore desirable that a counselling service should be available to employees. . . .[4]

---

[1]Ibid., pp. 257-61, 266.   [2]Albrecht, pp. 300-01.

[3]Ibid., pp. 302-03.

[4]Robert Ashall, "Status and Security of Employees," in Administration of Personnel Policies, eds. Rachel Naylor and Derek Torrington (Epping, Essex, Great Britain: Gower Press, 1974), p. 238.

It is recommended in this setting also that counselors not have managerial responsibilities "for such assignments may adversely affect their confidential relationship with employees."[1]

Another method used to meet the human needs of individuals is the group experience. T-groups, encounter groups, and sensitivity training are used by workers from chief executives to production line employees. Leland Bradford, writing in 1972, suggests that more than a million people have been involved in such groups. Circumstances of a chief executive that he points out sound very reminiscent of what has been said here about ministers--loneliness, unable to share anxieties and uncertainties with others, the object of envy, the pressure to be a model above human weaknesses. A group, Bradford says, puts him in a society of peers where he can lower his defenses and learn about himself and grow in a safe environment.[2]

Drucker recommends the team approach to the chief executive's job. The demands and responsibilities of a company president are so multitudinous that he needs a partner for the sake of sanity. He is insulated from common contacts by the nature of his position-- contacts that would break his isolation. He needs a variety of viewpoints, opinions, and experiences that come from the openness of a colleague for sound decision making. It is imperative, therefore,

---

[1]Dale Yoder, Personnel Management and Industrial Relations (Englewood Cliffs, NJ: Prentice-Hall, 4th edition, 1956), pp. 646-47; Cary L. Cooper and Judi Marshall, Understanding Executive Stress (New York: PBI Books, 1977), pp. 178-79.

[2]Leland P. Bradford, "How Sensitivity Training Works," in The Failure of Success, ed. Alfred J. Marrow (New York: AMACOM, 1972), pp. 242, 252-53.

says Drucker, that several men work together. Standard Oil, General Motors, and General Electric all use the team approach in their chief executive position. In fact, Drucker says that a company "will not grow and survive unless the one-man top is converted into a team."[1]

An article in the Harvard Business Review points up another resource used in business not only to obtain success but also for satisfaction. The article, "Everyone Who Makes It Has a Mentor," describes the "first assistant philosophy" of the Jewel Tea Company, which is simply that executive responsibility involves assisting the people down the line to be successful. Each trainee is assigned a company officer as a sponsor. The sponsor knows more about the person than anyone else, but he is not the trainee's direct boss. This allows a sense of freedom in the relationship. In order to keep the sponsor from becoming an order-giving, domineering boss, the "first assistant" concept is used. The executive is the first assistant to the trainee. It is like turning the organizational charts upside-down mentally. The sponsor or executive leads by helping, teaching, listening, and assisting. Within this covering environment a great deal of latitude is allowed these trainees to take risks and use their own ideas to challenge the organization to grow. When the current president was asked if he noticed a qualitative difference between managers who were brought up with the sponsor and those who were not, he replied:

---

[1] Drucker, pp. 162-73.

> I don't know that anyone has ever succeeded in any business
> without having some unselfish sponsorship or mentorship, what-
> ever it might have been called. Everyone who succeeds has had
> a mentor or mentors. . . .[1]

Jewel Tea has a particularly strong reputation for developing

talented young executives.

This is just a sampling of resources used in the business

world that parallel in application to ministry situations. Others

could also be mentioned, such as workshops on burn-out for those in

helping professions[2] and other personnel benefits and organizational

adjustments.[3] The value of these resources in the eyes of business

is well summarized by an organizational development consultant who

writes:

> Throughout all the discussion in this book we have seen
> that there are really three bottom lines--the financial one,
> the social one, and the human one. We also know that they are
> inseparably linked. In the organization, what detracts from
> the economic bottom line eventually detracts from the human
> bottom line. Without an economically viable organization,
> there can be no jobs, no managers, and no social climate.
> And what detracts from the human bottom line eventually de-
> tracts from the economic bottom line. Without the human pay-
> off in money, job satisfaction, personal fulfillment, respect
> for human values and human rights, and opportunities for in-
> dividual growth, the economic bottom line becomes harder and
> harder to maintain. The price for inhuman use of human beings
> must be paid sooner or later, and I believe it is always paid
> in actual dollars and cents.[4]

---

[1] "Everyone Who Makes It Has a Mentor," Interviews with
F. J. Lunding, G. L. Clements, and D. S. Perkins, Harvard Business
Review 56 (July-August 1978):89-101; also Abraham Zaleznik,
"Managers and Leaders: Are They Different," Harvard Business
Review 55 (May-June 1977):77.

[2] Pines, Aronson, and Kafry, pp. 192ff.

[3] See Marrow; Naylor and Torrington.

[4] Albrecht, pp. 310-11.

Resources Independent from
Denominations

Support Groups and Consultation

In the early 1970s Duane Meyer, a conference minister of the Iowa Conference of the United Church of Christ, took some continuing education units in human-relations training, parent-effectiveness training, and principles of small groups. Being a leader of ministers and well aware of their needs, he began to encourage and facilitate support groups among them. The groups were not sponsored by the judicatory, but were conducted by the pastors themselves, often ecumenical. Meyer, as a consultant or facilitator, helped to get them started and occasionally sat in with them. As a result of the wide experience he gained, he wrote a thesis for his Doctor of Ministry degree which explained how ministers could set up their own local support group and gave the supporting rationale for this type of resource. This information has been marketed on cassette tapes by Minister's Life Resources and became a tool for ministers who wished to take their own initiative in this area.[1]

C. Umhau Wolf has done something similar. He is the pastor of the Hope Lutheran Church in Toledo, Ohio, but has also served as a professor of Old Testament at Chicago Lutheran Seminary

---

[1] Duane Meyer, Iowa Conference minister, United Church of Christ, personal letter, April 1, 1981; idem, "A Study of Professional Support Systems for Clergy" (D.Min. thesis, Eden Theological Seminary, 1975); idem, "How to Set Up Your Own Local Support Group" (Minneapolis: Minister's Life Resources, 1974, cassette recording); idem, "Group Support Tape" (Minneapolis: Minister's Life Resources, 1974, 4 cassette recordings). These cassettes are no longer available from Minister's Life but can be found in some seminary libraries.

and Director of the Lutheran Institute for Religious Studies at
Texas Lutheran College. Around 1975 he started eighty to ninety
clergy support groups in and around Texas. He has prepared a
cassette recording wherein he describes the value of and method
in forming such groups. He describes his own experience of how,
years before, this resource helped him survive the sudden death of
his wife and the normal challenges that come with teen-age
children and a step parent. He reports traveling sixty to
seventy miles just to meet with those who were a strength to him.
Their groups often had a study agenda or other specific plan, but
the highest priority was always the immediate personal needs of
a group member. Many times they simply postponed the scheduled
agenda in order to care for someone's distress.[1]

Cecil G. Osborne, a pastor for over forty years, founded
an organization called Yokefellows, Inc., in 1957.* Its purpose is
to "create in modern form the deep, satisfying fellowship of the
early Christians, and through this fellowship to stimulate greater
spiritual growth." Its primary tool is the small group, but
Yokefellows also offers counseling and other types of workshops for
more effective living. Although targeted to the general population, Osborne has applied the principles to minister's groups
as well. He writes that these minister's groups have "proven
highly effective." About twenty-three affiliated Yokefellow

---

[1]C. Umhau Wolf, "Clergy Support Groups," Thesis Theological
Cassettes series, May 1975.

*The asterisk throughout this chapter indicates that an
address is listed in appendix D for the indicated organization
where resources are available.

Centers are scattered throughout the United States. They report
establishing over seven thousand groups. A booklet, "How to Start
and Lead a Yokefellow Group," can be obtained from them. They also
publish a newsletter and have a catalog of resource materials
available.[1]

Family Clustering, Inc.,* begun in 1970 by Margaret M.
Sawin, is an organization that promotes small groups built
particularly around family units. This plan can help meet the
needs of the whole family of the minister together with other
minister's families. "A cluster," it is said, "provides mutual
support, training in skills to facilitate family living, and allows
for celebration of life and beliefs." The Family Clustering Organization makes available training events, books, a newsletter,
and various resources.[2]

A number of other reported ministerial support groups could
be described. For example, Oscar Eggers explains the twice-monthly
meeting of young clergymen in Kansas City, Missouri.[3] W. H. Lyon
and M. D. Riggs review their two-year experiment with a psychotherapy
group for ministers in connection with the Lyon Mental Hygiene
Clinic in California in which they explored the participants'

---

[1]Cecil G. Osborne, Executive Director, Yokefellows, Inc.,
personal letter, April 17, 1981. He mentions ministerial groups in
"Overcoming Guilt," Thesis Theological Cassettes series, December
1974, and also explains the role of small groups in The Art of
Understanding Yourself (Grand Rapids: Zondervan Publishing House,
1967), chapters 12-14.

[2]Margaret M. Sawin, "Congregations and Families: Building
Support Systems through Family Clusters," Action Information
(publication of the Alban Institute, Inc.), June 1980, pp. 5-6.

[3]Eggers, pp. 20-23.

personal and professional problems.[1] Lawrence H. Rockland, a psychiatrist, offered himself as a consultant to a group of clergymen.
In their weekly group meetings some teaching was done, some consultation was given on problem cases the ministers faced, and some
general support relating to personal issues in the ministers' lives
was shared.[2] Robert Worley has worked with groups of about fourteen
clergymen in the Chicago area in assessment of their ministry and
skill development.[3] These groups report high commitment and
enthusiasm.

Some seminaries are giving more attention to the personal
adjustment needs of their students and are utilizing small groups
in the process of education. One five-year experiment in the
Washington, D.C., area was called "Inter-Met" (for Interfaith
Associates in Metropolitan Theological Education). Each student
worked in some ministry project while belonging to a "core group"
of peers and supervisors. The groups developed supportive relationships for worship, feedback, reviewing cases, and relating theory
and practice. A college of preceptors taught courses under "field
conditions." This program took a large step in the attempt to meet
practical needs of seminary students.[4] Timothy J. Kidney designed a

---

[1]W. H. Lyon and M. D. Riggs, "Experience of Group Psychotherapy for the Parish Minister," Journal of Pastoral Care 18
(Autumn 1964):166-69.

[2]Lawrence H. Rockland, "Psychiatric Consultation to the
Clergy," Pastoral Psychology 21 (January 1970):51-53.

[3]Smith, Clergy in the Cross Fire, p. 130.

[4]John C. Fletcher and Tilden H. Edwards, Jr., "Inter-met:
On-the-Job Theological Education," Pastoral Psychology 22 (March
1971):21-30; Smith, Clergy in the Cross Fire, pp. 122-23. A

field education program utilizing small groups that deal with a
student's own self-actualization and adjustment to ministry as
well as professional skills.[1] Lancaster Theological Seminary requires a "collegium experience" of its students during the first
two years of the Master of Divinity program. Each group involves
six to ten seminarians, a pastor, and a faculty member. Professor Paul E. Irion says,

> It is our effort to begin to present to seminarians the value
> of and need for collegial support groups throughout their
> lifetime. . . . We have found it to be a very effective pro-
> gram in the six or seven years of its operation.[2]

Their Doctor of Ministry program also involves what is called
"Peer-Group Evaluation of Ministry" and is described thus:

> Under professional supervision, a small group of Fellows
> will carefully examine one another's ministry, exploring such
> things as theological and psychological self-understanding,
> perception of the social context, roles and role-conflicts,
> allocation of time, individual skills, etc. The process
> will include individual statements on theology of ministry,
> sharing of materials from the site of the ministry, peer
> visitation to the site of the ministry and lay evaluation.
> Since this process extends over approximately six months, there
> is ample opportunity to test new roles, styles and skills.
> Peer-Group evaluation concludes with written evaluations of
> each Fellow's practice of ministry.[3]

Many varied forms exist for ministers' groups, but they

---

final report on Inter-Met can be obtained from the Alban Institute:
"Inter-Met: Bold Experiment in Theological Education," ed. Celia
Hahn and Jack McKelvey.

[1]Timothy James Kidney, "A Supervision Program Including Both
the Individual Pastoral Care and the Social Ministry of Roman
Catholic Seminarians" (D.Min. dissertation, The Catholic University
of America, 1979).

[2]Paul E. Irion, Professor, Lancaster Theological Seminary,
personal letter (n.d.).

[3]"Handbook of the Doctor of Ministry Program at Lancaster
Theological Seminary," Lancaster, Pennsylvania, July 1, 1980,
pp. iv-4.

all provide an opportunity for the close interaction which has great potential for developing and maintaining a healthy ministry.

Career Development Centers and Other Counseling Services

In the five years prior to 1964 the United Presbyterian Church of the U.S.A. noticed that requests for professional counseling services for church workers had doubled. Its personnel office was overburdened with occupational counseling. Consequently, it established the Northeast Career Center in Princeton, New Jersey, as a three-year pilot project starting in 1965. In 1967, the American Baptist Church founded its Center for Ministry in Wellesley, Massachusetts. The success of these experiments opened the way for permanent status for career development centers. In 1969 the Church Career Development Council (CCDC)* was organized and a number of denominations joined in sponsoring this program. Since then a network of more than sixteen centers* across the country have been established and accredited by CCDC. They serve close to four thousand persons a year. Just the Northeast Career Center sees about two hundred persons a year in individual programs and has served more than 2800 since its doors opened in 1965.[1]

---

[1]Fred Petri, "Career Counseling for Professional Church Leaders," Pastoral Psychology 22 (February 1971):49-55; Thomas E. Brown, "Career Counseling for Ministers," Journal of Pastoral Care 25 (March 1971):33-40; Sybil B. Sim, Registrar and Administrative Assistant, Northeast Career Center, personal letter, April 2, 1981; Church Career Development Council, Church Career Development Council: Career Counseling Services for Professional Church Workers (New York: Church Career Development Council, n.d.), (brochure).

The Northeast Career Center describes its purpose as offering occupational and career counseling to persons who are

Seeking to assess their capabilities and potential within
their present situation
Dealing with adjustments related to early career, mid career
or preretirement
Considering change to a new position or specialization
Planning an individual continuing education program
Exploring questions of value or meaning for their life and
career
Considering the ordained ministry.[1]

These centers aim to work with normal individuals and are not equipped to deal with the deeply troubled person. The total program is centered on the personal initiative of the client. He/she must take responsibility for his/her own life. The basic staff for one of these centers includes a career counselor, a consulting clinical psychologist, a consulting physician, and an administrative assistant/secretary.

A typical program for an individual involves three major parts. Before a person actually comes to the center, he spends fifteen to thirty hours taking interest and personality tests, completing biographical questionnaires and capability analyses, and obtaining a complete physical examination. Then a two and one-half day period is spent at the center in direct counseling, analyzing achievements, strengths, abilities, values, interests, and skills. Time there is also spent in planning and setting goals under the guidance of the counselors. The spouse can participate as a full client or just take a portion of the testing and participate in some of the conferences. The involvement of the spouse is often

---

[1]Northeast Career Center, Exploring Dimensions in Personal Professional Development (Princeton, NJ: Northeast Career Center, n.d.), (brochure).

vital in the minister's experience, and the spouse may be helped just as much. The third phase of the program is the follow-up. As the client starts to implement his plan, he may be reviewing, re-thinking, and revising, or he may wish to explore new issues. Several hours of follow-up counseling provide for this.[1]

The cost of such a program seems to range from about $360.00 to $650.00, depending on the center and whether a person is coming from a denomination which helps to sponsor it. Some centers offer group programs such as workshops for career review and planning, team building for multiple staff churches or judicatories, consulting services for personnel programs, training in using the interview process for applicant assessment, dossier evaluation and selection criteria, etc. Centers may offer marriage counseling for clergy, retreats, special seminarian de-velopmental counseling, evaluation counseling, and just hourly counseling and consultation (at $55.00 per hour).

Thomas E. Brown, the first director of the Northeast Career Center, writes that many clients come saying, "If I could do some-thing else, I would quit tomorrow." But when they are helped to see that they can do something else, more often than not they decide to stay in church work. But the "deciding to" is important. Being free to leave frees them in their function as clergy. Not everyone is happy with his experience at the centers (some resent the honesty); but the files "document, in case after case, dramatic

---

[1]Thomas E. Brown, "Career Counseling as a Form of Pastoral Care," _Pastoral Psychology_ 22 (March 1971):15-20; Petri, pp. 53-55.

evidence of 'potential awakened and utilized, confidence restored, aimlessness turned to direction, hopelessness to faith, frustration to ambition.'"[1]

Specialized counseling for clergymen and their families can be found in other places also. For instance, Marble Retreat* in Marble, Colorado, was founded by Dr. Louis McBurney. It provides psychotherapy for pastors, other church workers, and their families.[2] There are private pastoral counseling centers such as the Pastoral Counseling and Educational Center of Dallas, Texas, and the Pastoral Care and Counseling Center of Abilene, Texas. Departments of pastoral care in some Christian hospitals provide counseling for clergy--especially those that also have Clinical Pastoral Education programs. A Directory of Counseling Services can be obtained from the International Association of Counseling Services, Inc.* It lists statistical data on all the accredited counseling centers in the country.[3]

Continuing Education and Personal Growth Resources

Far from being merely a means of increasing one's knowledge and skills, continuing education in the proper context has been found to be one of the best means of personal support. Dennis Doyle,

---

[1] Ibid.

[2] McBurney, Every Pastor Needs a Pastor, p. 24 (n. 3); McBurney, "A Psychiatrist Looks," p. 107; Russel Chandler, "Help for Christian Workers: Advance through Retreat: Pastoring the Pastor," Christianity Today, May 2, 1980, pp. 50-51.

[3] There are also halfway houses for clergy leaving church work, such as Bearings for Re-establishment and Next Step.

studying the effects of a Doctor of Ministry program in five
seminaries, found in about 80 percent of the cases that it helped
significantly to reduce stress, feelings of isolation, and loneliness; it helped establish personal priorities, redefine roles,
relieve frustration, and determine future goals. It not only
saved ministers from dropping out of the pastorate but also
greatly strengthened their commitment to it. Some of the comments
from those he interviewed include:

>It saved my career, if not my very life!
>It gave me new direction for my ministry.
>It's great. I just wish I had started sooner.
>It kept me in the pastorate.
>My self-confidence got a real boost. I began to feel more
>   satisfaction from the pastorate.
>After a month at the seminary, I always came home feeling like
>   I had dumped a load of garbage. I really miss those men.

Doyle concludes: "A pastor who is engaged in a program of continuing
education is not as likely to leave the parish ministry as one who is
not involved in such an endeavor." And of course in the parish he is
not as likely to become dysfunctional.[1]

Many things have been designed and are available for continuing education. Leaders in this field strongly recommend that a
person carefully assess his goals and establish a plan for a pur-
poseful, progressive program, rather than a here-and-there, hit-or-
miss smattering of unrelated experiences. Probably one of the best
books to help ministers plan and locate resources for continuing
education has been Mark Rouch's Competent Ministry. A few brief
examples of the many types of continuing education that have been
tried are mentioned here.

---

[1]Doyle, pp. 40-51.

One of the most immediate ways of growth is through the
reading of good books. Many new and excellent publications now on
the market cover very practical and timely aspects of ministry.
Tape clubs such as Thesis Theological Cassettes can bring exposure
to the personalities and ideas of others in condensed form, and in
a medium that can often conserve spare time. Ministerial colleague
groups, mentioned earlier, provide one of the most convenient
places and possibly one of the most useful means by which continuing education can happen. Besides sharing a book, studying
some subject together, or listening to a presentation, these
groups can make use of the ministry experiences of each of the group
members for learning. James Glasse feels that ministers should
take seriously the values in their own practices and proposes the
"case method" of learning. Writing, presenting, and discussing in
structured form specific cases that ministers actually face can be
a real help to all involved. It is a form of consultation and,
in some contexts, supervision.[1]

There are guided study programs such as one developed by
Richard Murray of Perkins School of Theology. Short study outlines
along with appropriate materials are sent in successive units.
Each is returned before the next arrives. At the end of a study,
a group of at least ten persons can have a one-day seminar under
the guidance of a specialist in the subject studied.[2] Many

---

[1]See Glasse, Putting It Together, chapters 6-8; Wesner
Fallaw, The Case Method in Pastoral and Lay Education (Philadelphia:
Westminster Press, 1963); Robert C. Leslie and Emily Hartshorne Mudd,
eds., Professional Growth for Clergymen (Nashville: Abingdon Press,
1970).

[2]Rouch, Competent Ministry, p. 76.

short workshops and seminars are offered by denominations and
seminaries.

A number of specialized centers maintain programs and resources for ministers. The Institute for Advanced Pastoral
Studies, Bloomfield Hills, Michigan, provides ten-day sessions for
experienced ministers where they can study and share, learn about
themselves and their work, support others and be supported.[1] Interpreter's House at Lake Junaluska, North Carolina, also inte-
grates continuing education, self-realization, and counseling for
ministers.[2] The Pastoral Institute of Washington in Seattle is
similar.

The Alban Institute* is not a place where one goes; it is
an agency that comes to pastors, churches, or denominations. It
comes by means of doing field research, providing consultations and
training workshops, and preparing publications. It has worked in
the areas of clergy-lay relationships, beginning and ending pastorates, new directions in ministry, dynamics of congregational life,
ministry of the laity, the parish during pastoral transitions,
theological education for parish leadership, and young adult
ministry.[3]

---

[1]Reuel L. Howe, "A Report on an Institute for Advanced
Pastoral Studies," in The Minister's Own Mental Health, ed. Wayne E.
Oates (Great Neck, NY: Channel Press, 1955; 1961), pp. 330-35.

[2]Carlyle Marney, "Interpreter's House: A Way Station for
Understanding," Thesis Theological Cassettes series, March 1972;
Rouch, Competent Ministry, p. 83; Robert T. Frerichs, "A History
of the Continuing Education Movement," The Drew Gateway 47/1,
1976-77, pp. 5-6.

[3]Loren Mead, "Mission Statement," Action Information,
May-June 1981, pp. 5-6.

Minister's Life is a mutual life insurance company, but it also has a division called Minister's Life Resources, Inc.* It markets a variety of professional aids for clergypersons: cassette tapes on such subjects as "How to Prepare Yourself for a Job Change," "Conflict Management," "How to Know Who You Are," etc.; financial counseling for ministers and two newsletters in financial areas; and a series of catchy posters on important issues in the life of the minister and his family, some directed to the minister himself and some to his congregation as a means of increasing understanding.[1]

Clergy associations have arisen with purposes similar to other professional organizations. The Academy of Parish Clergy* promotes continuing education and requires 150 clock hours of study in approved projects every three years.[2] The Clergy Development Network was an ecumenical effort in the Los Angeles area in the early 1970s to provide for the support needs of ministers. It was involved in continuing education, career planning and guidance, psychological counseling, and other things. It came to an end after a few years because the participating institutions seemed to prefer to work through their own structures.[3] Clinical Pastoral Education (CPE)* has been a successful type of training and personal growth. In a hospital or parish setting individuals are able to do counseling and practice ministry under supervision. Among peers and supervisors the person looks not just at his skills but

_____

[1]Arthur Bell, president of Minister's Life, personal letter and sample materials, April 9, 1981.

[2]Doyle, p. 32.   [3]Forney, pp. 182-205.

also at his own personal adjustment to life situations.[1] Action

Training Centers* have emphasized learning by involvement,

especially in urban settings where unique problems are confronted.[2]

There are the degree programs of seminaries, especially

the Doctor of Ministry which is usually designed for practicing

pastors and involves short intensive classes and guided field

work. So many alternatives exist for continuing education that The

Society for Advancement of Continuing Education for Ministry*

(SACEM) was formed. It maintains a comprehensive file of programs

and resources.

A Survey of Resources in
non-SDA Denominations

In contrast to the previous section, the resources mentioned

here are policies and provisions unique to specific denominations

and operate within their own structures. Generally they are avail-

able only to their own workers. Some information was gleaned from

available literature. In addition letters were written to twenty

selected major denominations inquiring about support programs for

ministers. Since it would be impossible to catalog all the re-

sources provided by each denomination here, only the most impor-

tant ones are highlighted.

The Southern Baptist Convention has created a number of

---

[1] Thomas W. Klink, "Clinical Pastoral Education," in The
Continuing Quest, ed. James B. Hofrenning (Minneapolis: Augsburg
Publishing House, 1970), pp. 93-103.

[2] Richard H. Luecke, "Urban Training Centers," in The
Continuing Quest, ed. James B. Hofrenning (Minneapolis: Augsburg
Publishing House, 1970), pp. 75-82; Rouch, Competent Ministry,
pp. 86-87.

support resources for its ministers. In 1971 an action was
passed by the Convention to establish a counseling ministry for
pastors and other church-related vocational workers and their
families.[1] The Church Administration Department of the Sunday
School Board established a career guidance section with a full
range of services: vocational guidance, including a "career
support timeline" that anticipates typical needs along the various
stages of one's career; a pastor-staff support service; career
assessment and development service; counseling and referral
service; and a ministry research service. Ministers' counseling
services have been established in many state conventions, such
as the Baptist General Convention of Texas. These provide crisis
intervention, preventive ministry in the form of retreats, conferences, and workshops, and general resources on crucial areas
of ministry. Many state conventions also have an office for
church-ministry relations that help with placement, counseling, and
referral.[2] The Director of Missions serves as a pastor's pastor,
visiting periodically, counseling, and assisting in placement and
adjustment to a new position. That the Baptists actively promote
forming support groups is evidenced by the articles in their publication for ministers, Church Administration.[3]

---

[1]Brooks R. Faulkner, "What's Going on in Pastoral Support?"
Church Administration, October 1976, pp. 8-9.

[2]Douglas Melton Dickens, "Pastoral Care of Ministers in the
Southern Baptist Convention" (Th.D. dissertation, Southwestern Baptist
Theological Seminary, 1978), p. 268; Albert McClellan, "Support System
for SBC Ministers," Church Administration, October 1976, pp. 2-7.

[3]Robert D. Dale, "Building Pastoral Support Systems in Your
Area," Church Administration, October 1976, pp. 14-15; Travis Hart,

The American Baptist Churches USA lists pastoral counselors, psychologists, and psychiatrists who have skills in
working with ministers. Its insurance plan covers psychological
treatment as well as medical problems. Visitation of local church
pastors is usually done by the Area Minister rather than the
Executive Minister of the region, state, or city offices. It also
has an organization called the Ministers' Council that is concerned
with pastoral care and support of all in the ministry. This denomination grants continuing education units and records them on
each person's personnel profile. In addition, it is an active sup-
porter of several career-development centers.[1]

The United Presbyterians launched the first career development center and now strongly advise their ministers to go through
this process three times in the course of their careers: (1) at the
beginning, when leaving seminary, (2) at mid-life during the time
of re-evaluating, and (3) at the time of retirement.[2] They also
operate what is called a Young Pastors Seminar in order to deal
with that critical entry time. The third year after graduation
from a seminary, every young Presbyterian pastor is invited to a

---

"We Pastor Each Other," Church Administration, June 1977, pp. 3-6;
Gary Holbrook, "Benefits of a Support Group," Church Administration,
October 1979, pp. 16-19; Robert Dale, "How to Find Where You Are,"
Church Administration, June 1977, pp. 13-16. A list of the activities
for the support of ministers in the Susquehanna Baptist Association
can be found in Jerry Graham, "The Development of a Support Ministry,"
pp. 81-94.

[1]Kathryn W. Baker, Projects Coordinator, Commission on the
Ministry, American Baptist Churches USA, personal letter, May 4,
1981.

[2]Frank A. Robinson, "Career Development," Thesis Theological
Cassettes series, July 1975.

retreat to spend several days with those who graduated with him. They live, study, and think together about their ministries and share disillusionments, successes, failures, uncertainties, hopes, and goals. Present also are several resource persons with expertise in ministry, group work, and counseling. For many this is a deeply meaningful experience. The opportunity is also repeated the next two years, the fourth and fifth year after leaving the seminary. Wives participate in the second and third times.[1]

For the same purpose, the United Methodist Church conducted a slightly different program in its Young Pastors Pilot Project. Cluster groups of five to eight young pastors, who were three to five years out of seminary and who lived close enough to get together, met once or twice a month for personal and professional development. An experienced fellow pastor, called a "pastoral associate" and chosen by the young pastors, met with the group. He served not so much as a teacher or supervisor, but as an enabler and working model of the professional practice of ministry. The pastoral associates met every six weeks for training sessions designed to help them in their role. Three- or four-day seminars were held at the beginning, in the middle, and at the end of the two-year program for those involved.[2]

A Methodist example of a general pastoral support system can be found in the work of Donald C. Houts in the Illinois area.

---

[1]Smith, Clergy in the Cross Fire, p. 128.

[2]Ibid., p. 129; Mark A. Rouch, "Young Pastors Pilot Project: An Experiment in Continuing Education for Ministry," The Journal of Pastoral Care 25 (March 1971):3-11.

He is Director of Pastoral Care and Counseling, lives ninety miles
from the area episcopal office, and is responsible to a committee
of eight persons--four clergy and four lay persons. Committee
members, in turn, are elected by two annual conferences that are
administered by the bishop of the Illinois area. Houts' job
description currently includes five main areas: crisis-intervention
services which include psychological testing, diagnostic evaluation,
counseling, and referral; consultation with pastors for problems of
their own ministry; coordinating continuing education programs;
training, pilot programs and research, which involve establishing
clergy support groups, program evaluation, marriage enrichment
opportunities, etc.; and career assessment, wherein he serves as
a contact agent to refer persons to one of the established career
development centers.[1]

The Reformed Church in America has passed a resolution requiring the classes (local judicatories) to make periodic inquiry
of each pastor to determine whether or not he has provided for the
pastoral needs of himself and his family. This approach gives the
local pastor autonomy to choose his own source of pastoral care,
but the denomination is responsible to make sure he has something.
A pastor may choose any available clergyperson to be his pastor.
The denomination subsidizes professional counseling when needed for
pastors, wives, and dependent children. Every church is required
to provide a minimum of one week's time and one hundred dollars per
year for continuing education. Many places double this and time and

---

[1]Donald C. Houts, "Pastoral Care for Pastors: Toward a
Church Strategy," Pastoral Psychology 25 (Spring 1977):194-96.

money is cumulative up to four years. Career-development counseling
is available to all clergy by virtue of the RCAs support of these
centers.[1]

In 1979-1980 the United Church of Christ conducted a major
project, "For the Renewal of Our Pastors." A great number of experiments were tried in conferences throughout the country to
learn more about the needs of pastors and how best to meet them.
The intention of the project was to determine what type of program
the Church should use in the care of pastors. Three of the eleven
recommendations are: a mentorship program should be developed
by conferences in order to assist in the ongoing development of a
pastor; mid-career counseling should be initiated; and beginning
pastors need a better integrated program between seminary and
parish.[2] Duane Meyer, mentioned above in connection with support
groups, is a pastor's pastor to ministers in his conference. He
says his organization recommends a three-month sabbatical for
clergy who have served a parish for five years.[3]

The Wisconsin Evangelical Lutheran Synod has a circuit
pastor who does the work of a pastor's pastor. He is a parish
minister elected by his peers. He is their chaplain when they are

---

[1] Alvin J. Poppen, Coordinator of Human Resources, Reformed
Church in America, personal letter, May 5, 1981; Dickson, p. 89;
McVay, pp. 64-65.

[2] United Church of Christ, Office for Church Life and Leadership, "For the Renewal of Our Pastors," 1979 Family Thank Offering
Project, A Final Report presented to the Special Appeals Committee
of the Executive Council, project manager, Ralph C. Quellhorst, New
York, New York, December 1980.

[3] Duane Meyer, personal letter, April 1, 1981; Meyer, "A
Study of Professional Support," p. 102.

ill; he visits them, and he helps new pastors adjust. The denomination has a "Handbook for Circuit Pastors" that outlines his duties.[1] In the Lutheran Church in America, the synods maintain a network of counselors for pastors. It is often done without the bishop's knowledge. One-half of the cost may be reimbursed. Pastors are usually visited every two or three years by bishops or their staff members. From 60 to 70 percent of the pastors are involved in an organized continuing education program. Their recommended plan is called PLACE, Professional Leaders Aid for Continuing Education. Two weeks each year is allowed, and two hundred dollars is contributed by the church and one hundred by the pastor. One of the strongest programs is the Growth in Ministry project, a series of seven workshops for pastors and spouses. One of these helps pastors build their own support system.[2]

The Christian Church (Disciples of Christ) publishes a booklet of "Study Opportunities for Ministers." The costs of continuing education are split four ways: the national Department of Ministry, the region, the congregation, and the individual clergy. The denomination maintains a training program in clergy-colleague formation and development believing that clergy can facilitate each other's personal and professional growth. A number of constituency groups are facilitated including the "Community of Clergy Couples"

---

[1]Carl H. Mischke, president of the Wisconsin Evangelical Lutheran Synod, personal letter, April 7, 1981.

[2]Joseph M. Wagner, assistant executive director of the Division for Professional Leadership, Lutheran Church in America, personal letter, April 10, 1981.

and the "Congress of Disciple Clergy." They also participate in the career-development centers.[1]

The Church of the Brethren has many features similar to the others. It has new pastors' orientation workshops for beginning pastors and experienced pastors who are in new situations. These are reported as very popular and increasing in number. The Church of Brethren seminary has several advanced pastoral seminars: a basic two-week period of reflection on one's ministry, a pastor-spouse seminar, and a seminar on management of time. A three-month sabbatical is recommended after five years in a particular parish. It has an annual or semi-annual retreat for ministers and spouses, promotes support and fellowship groups, provides at least an annual visitation of pastors by district executives, and covers half the cost of formal counseling. Continuing-education costs are split four ways: national office, district, congregation, and pastor. It, too, is involved with career-development centers.[2]

In response to an inquiry, Roscoe Snowden of the Church of God (Anderson, Indiana), wrote:

> This has been a prime interest to us for the past three years. We held some consultations nationwide to determine how much need really existed and if the pastors were concerned enough to share their needs. The response was overwhelming. We found people anxious to seek personal help and to find some support for their ministry.

He then outlined the church's plan to provide counseling and support

---

[1] L. Eugene Brown, director of Clergy Development in the Department of Ministry, Christian Church (Disciples of Christ), personal letter, June 4, 1981.

[2] Robert E. Faus, consultant for ministry, Church of the Brethren, personal letter, April 14, 1981.

resources. Much of it is similar to those already mentioned. However, there is also a plan to build a retreat center for ministers
and wives who can come for personal enrichment, family counseling,
marital enrichment, etc.[1]

Many other churches and programs could be mentioned--the
Roman Catholic House of Affirmation,[2] the Episcopal experiments
with consultation[3] and an intern group program,[4] the Washington
Episcopal Clergy Association,[5] and the several denominations which
have tried team ministries, clustering, or cooperative parishes,
wherein more than one church shares personnel and resources.[6] Not
all denominations are involved or interested in this pursuit. But
descriptions given have been sufficient to illustrate the interest
that many have and the methods already tried in creating a support
system for ministers.

---

[1]Roscoe Snowden, director of Church Service, Church of God
(Anderson, Indiana), personal letter, April 8, 1981.

[2]James P. Madden, ed., Loneliness: Issues of Emotional Living in an Age of Stress for Clergy and Religious (Whitinsville, MA:
Affirmation Books, 1977).

[3]Ruth B. Caplan, Helping the Helpers to Help (New York:
Seabury Press, 1972).

[4]Robert Mahon, "An Example of the Use of Professional Development Groups in Support of New Ministers," Pastoral Psychology
22 (March 1971):31-38.

[5]Edward R. Sims, "WECA--A Response to Passivity and Isolation Among Parish Ministers," Pastoral Psychology 22 (March 1971):
44-49.

[6]Smith, Clergy in the Cross Fire, p. 134; Judson Oscar Gears,
"Leadership Design and Positive Job Satisfaction in Staff Ministry
in United Methodist Town and Country Cooperative Parishes" (D.Min.
dissertation, Lancaster Theological Seminary, 1976). See also the
whole issue of Pastoral Psychology 14 (March 1963), for ten articles
on team ministries.

Resources in the SDA Denomination

In order to uncover resources that might not be generally
known, letters were written to each of the local conferences of the
North American Division of SDAs requesting descriptions of their
policies and practices in support of ministers. No attempt was made
to obtain more responses than what came as a result of the one
mailing. There was no intention to tabulate this information,
simply to report practices that are taking place and to show some
of the variety of possible ideas. Conferences vary widely in provisions made for support of ministers.

Looking first at the availability of professional counseling,
it was found that the British Columbia and Oklahoma Conferences have
on their staffs individuals with specialized training in counseling.[1]
Their services are available to workers at no charge. Potomac
Conference (Washington, D.C. area) has selected four professional
counselors who, though not employees of the church, provide services
to ministers and their immediate families. These approved counselors
bill the conference without revealing the identity of the counselees,
thus maintaining confidentiality and security of the workers.[2]
Oregon Conference recently took action to select several key psychologists or psychiatrists whom the pastors could use anonymously
for marriage counseling or other needs. A three-hundred-dollar
limit was placed on each particular case so that neither the

---

[1]G. E. Maxson, president, British Columbia Conference of
SDAs, personal letter, April 10, 1981; Robert Rider, president,
Oklahoma Conference of SDAs, personal letter, April 10, 1981.

[2]"Counseling Service for Employees" (Policy book of the
Potomac Conference of SDAs), p. C-11.

counselor nor the counselee would find it beneficial to unduly pro-
long the counseling process.[1] Ohio Conference is setting up a
program with Harding Hospital to provide psychiatric counseling
for pastors and families. For the first three visits the name is
not divulged to the Conference and the bill is paid as submitted by
the physician. After the third visit continuing care is handled
under the regular medical policy. The psychiatrists concerned felt
that many problems could be cared for in three visits. Beyond that
the situation is serious enough for the conference to know about
it and be involved.[2] Kansas-Nebraska Conference does not specify
the counselors that must be seen, and they pay on the basis of the
regular medical policy (three-fourths by the conference, one-fourth
by the pastor).[3] Texas Conference also pays for professional
counseling for pastors although the percentage was not indicated.[4]
The majority of conferences do not provide for any professional
counseling. A pastor would have to seek it and pay for it totally
on his own. Several conferences indicate that if the need would
arise, they would deal with each situation on an individual basis
and probably help with the expense.

Nearly all conferences have a ministerial secretary, but he

---

[1] Rankin H. Wentland, Jr., secretary, Oregon Conference of
SDAs, personal letter, April 7, 1981.

[2] John W. Fowler, president, Ohio Conference of SDAs, personal letter, April 27, 1981.

[3] L. S. Gifford, secretary, Kansas-Nebraska Conference of
SDAs, personal letter, May 1, 1981.

[4] Robert H. Wood, secretary, Texas Conference of SDAs, personal letter, April 7, 1981.

does not always fulfill a pastor's pastor function, at least from the perspective of the pastors.[1] Washington Conference is one that has taken seriously the need for a pastor of pastors. Lenard Jaecks writes:

> In my work I am really not the traditional coordinator of evangelism, but have been charged with the responsibility of being a pastor to the pastors. . . . I have a plan of being in the field with each pastor for a half day twice a year. Sometimes we visit in the field together, other times we spend time in their offices praying, planning and visiting together. I carry a lower profile for recruitment or transfer of personnel. This is by design so men will feel they can talk with me with less fear.[2]

Kansas-Nebraska Conference reports that their ministerial secretary visits the pastors in their districts on a quarterly basis.[3] Several other ministerial secretaries try to accomplish a visit at least once a year. Ohio Conference has even sought to reorganize its management structure so that it has several "assistants to the president" whose task is to spend time in the field helping pastors in the areas of their various specialities--pastoral nurture, local evangelism, church administration.[4] Other ministerial secretaries visit "as much as they can" or "when it is needed," without attempting any regular program. Although many report a visiting program the nature of the visit is the critical factor determining whether they are fulfilling a supportive role. A significant number revealed that their visits had to do with plans,

---

[1]This was noted in the results of the questionnaire reported in chapter 3.

[2]Lenard D. Jaecks, executive secretary and Ministerial Affairs, Washington Conference of SDAs, personal letter, April 9, 1981.

[3]Gifford.   [4]Robberson, see p. 42, n. 3 above.

evaluations, objectives, progress reports, and other promotional
items. Such visits may tend to increase stress rather than
communicate support.

All the conferences have one or two general workers' meetings each year where all pastors gather together. These can be
times of fellowship and group building if the official program
allows for it. Some conferences have smaller regional worker's
meetings as well. In the Montana Conference papers are assigned
to be presented at these smaller meetings. The presentations are
followed by discussion groups dealing with issues of the ministry.[1]
Washington Conference has four to six voluntary meetings where pastors
gather and discuss a topic of their choosing.[2] The Texas Conference
is divided into ten parishes and the pastors of each meet to discuss subjects and have social activities.[3] In the British Columbia
Conference each departmental director is a coordinator for an area
of ministers. Periodic meetings are held in each area.[4] Southeastern California Conference occasionally has support meetings
made up largely of interns.[5] Southern California Conference has
a pre-ordained worker fellowship meeting two or three times a year
for professional growth and a social outing.[6]

A few conferences have colleague groups organized among the

---

[1]Vernon L. Bretsch, secretary, Montana Conference of SDAs,
personal letter, April 7, 1981.

[2]Jaecks.   [3]Wood.   [4]Maxson.

[5]Elwood E. Staff, vice president for Administration, Southeastern California Conference of SDAs, personal letter, April 8, 1981.

[6]John Todorovich, ministerial director, Southern California
Conference of SDAs, personal letter, May 4, 1981.

ministers themselves. Alberta and Upper Columbia (eastern Washington, northern Idaho area) Conferences encourage their pastors to be involved in regional Adventist Ministerial Associations.[1] In the Oregon and Carolina Conferences the pastors in each of several regions meet once a month for a devotional, discussion/fellowship, and lunch.[2] Southern California reports ministerial fellowships in various parts of their conference. Participation is voluntary and some therefore are active and some are not.[3] Kansas-Nebraska Conference encourages fellowship groups:

> We have several groups meeting right now and these are totally planned and initiated by the local pastors with no conference involvement except for our active encouragement and support that they do this.[4]

Besides meeting together in groups, British Columbia Conference encourages ministers to work together in teams.[5]

Texas Conference is the only one that categorically stated, "Our man can have Sabbaticals." But no guidelines were described and it was not indicated if this option was written in a policy book. It was commented that there were few calls for these leaves.[6] Montana Conference noted that although sabbaticals are infrequent, one pastor who had taken a sabbatical leave had just written to the conference office informing them he was ready to be reassigned.[7] A

---

[1]Herb Larsen, president, Alberta Conference of SDAs, personal letter, May 20, 1981; David Parks, ministerial secretary, Upper Columbia Conference of SDAs, personal letter, April 13, 1981.

[2]Wentland; W. A. Geary, secretary, Carolina Conference of SDAs, personal letter, May 21, 1981.

[3]Todorovich.   [4]Gifford.   [5]Maxson.

[6]Wood.   [7]Bretsch.

few conferences might grant a short sabbatical based on an unusual need. But this resource is mostly absent in the SDA Church unless it is tied to a specific continuing-education program.

Many conference leaders seem to think of continuing education as a degree program such as the Master of Divinity, Master of Public Health, or Doctor of Ministry. The only other provision for continuing education is the speaker who comes to the workers' meeting. A few conferences use it as a reward or withhold it as punishment, depending on one's point of view. In one conference, a pastor must baptize a number equal to 10 percent of his membership, have a 10 percent increase in tithe, reach at least three-fourths of the local conference-offering objective for his churches, have at least two district active-youth weekends, and reach his Ingathering vanguard goal[1] in each church and company in his district before he can avail himself of continuing education. If he misses one of these objectives he can still receive funds for continuing education. The first year he meets these objectives he receives $350.00 for professional growth. This increases on succeeding successful years until a maximum of $600.00 is reached by the fifth year.[2] Another conference has other requirements:

> Each pastor who holds two evangelistic crusades per year, reads one of the following books, Evangelism, Welfare Ministry, or Christian Service, and holds spring and fall training classes in his church, is qualified to attend a seminar of his choice, with the larger portion (in some cases the full amount) of the expense paid.[3]

---

[1] Ingathering is a program of soliciting money and distributing literature in contact with the general public.

[2] D. K. Sullivan, president, Texico Conference of SDAs, personal letter, April 21, 1981.

[3] Robert Rider, president, Oklahoma Conference of SDAs, personal letter, April 10, 1981.

Some conferences have a policy that is more open. Southeastern California Conference encourages pastors to have at least twenty contact hours of seminar each year. For this a flat amount of two hundred dollars is granted. There is also provision for graduate-degree programs where 50 percent of the tuition is paid.[1] Iowa-Missouri Conference has voted to allow up to two hundred dollars and five days a year for each worker. This is cumulative up to three years for a total of six hundred dollars and fifteen days that can be taken at one time for approved programs. Degree programs are handled on an individual basis.[2] Central California Conference allows seven days and pays 75 percent of costs per year for seminars sponsored by the local conference. On alternate years pastors can attend a seminar of their choice within or outside the church. Two-thirds of tuition is generally paid when approval is granted for a pastor to take a degree program.[3] Ohio Conference is contemplating the requirement of a certain number of continuing education units for professional certification as in other professions. It has sent its men to a variety of continuing-education experiences such as management training at the American Management Association, seminars on church growth, institutes of evangelism, Clinical Pastoral Education, classes by guest professors from the S.D.A. Theological Seminary, Doctor of Ministry opportunities,

---

[1]Staff.

[2]Robert G. Peck, secretary, Iowa-Missouri Conference of SDAs, personal letter, June 29, 1981.

[3]George R. Elstrom, secretary, Central California Conference of SDAs, personal letter, April 16, 1981.

etc. The program is called the "Human Resource Development System." It actively seeks to assist a person to reach his own career objectives while also helping to achieve the corporate goals of the conference.[1]

Specifically for young pastors, many conferences have an internship program which means that they serve under the direction of an older, more experienced pastor. One conference that did not follow this practice but placed young men directly from college in a church of their own wrote, "We are finding that we need to reverse this and hope to work it out that each one will have some time with an older minister."[2] Another conference official wrote:

> We have a couple of young men in our field that I have just visited with recently. In the course of our conversation they mentioned the fact that they had not had this privilege and felt handicapped; in fact, they desired it even at this late date. So this is something we do intend to strengthen as our young men come into the field and to follow the practice of putting them, at least for a year and possibly two, with an older minister to give them experience.[3]

Three or four conferences have special retreats for interns. Central California Conference has an intern-supervisor workshop. The Kansas-Nebraska Conference does what is usually overlooked--trains the senior pastors to effectively work with interns.[4] New York Conference seems to be the only one that encourages a mentor relationship with a minister who is not the young minister's official supervisor.[5]

Other more general means of support include Ministry, the

---

[1] Fowler.

[2] Sullivan.

[3] Bretsch.

[4] Elstrom; Gifford.

[5] Nikolaus Satelmajer, secretary, New York Conference of SDAs, personal letter, April 13, 1981.

publication for Adventist ministers. In 1972 an Academy of Adventist Ministers was formed to encourage personal study and growth. But it had a faltering existence. In most cases the local conferences did not provide a local tie to the organization. Its desire for collegiality or spirit among ministers failed. To the local minister it looked like a lot of work that one could do on his own without the Academy. Where the local programming was strong, the spirit grew and the Academy was more successful. "Aspire," a tape-of-the-month club sponsored by the General Conference Ministerial Association, has been quite successful as a strengthening agent to ministers.

There is among top SDA administrators an apparent arousal of interest in improving the support of local church pastors. C. E. Bradford, vice president of the General Conference for the North American Division, invited representatives from various categories of pastors to meet during March 4-6, 1981. The purpose was to listen to the needs of pastors as they themselves expressed them. Concerns that are the focus of this project were among those raised by the pastors. A positive response and a hopeful sign came from Bradford in these words:

> Our emphasis on pastoral ministries is important and necessary. The church is in the hands of these servants who serve by speaking. When we rise up to strengthen them, to enhance and enrich ministry, we are but strengthening the ligaments and sinews that bind us all together and make the church a dynamic responsive organism fulfilling its purpose and mission in the world.[1]

---

[1] "Emphasis on Pastoral Ministries," reports from the March 4-6, 1981, meeting in Washington, D.C., with pastors, Office of the Vice President of the General Conference for the North American Division. (Mimeographed.)

A few things are being done. Some conferences are pioneering and experimenting, but much more can and should be done. The SDA Church needs a more complete and consistent support system for local church pastors throughout its conferences. An overview of such a support system is the purpose of the final chapter.

CHAPTER V

A DESIGN FOR A PSYCHO-SOCIAL SUPPORT SYSTEM FOR
PASTORS OF THE SDA CHURCH IN NORTH AMERICA

A psycho-social support system, it will be remembered, is
a network of various resources upon which a person might draw,
both from himself (psycho) and from people around him (social), to
help him relate positively to his life and career. Although all
human beings need some general social contacts for effective
living, many resources are not needed regularly by people. It is
in times of developmental transitions, stress and crisis, or
career frustrations that the need increases. Personal characteristics also help to determine the intensity of the need and the type
of resource that an individual would find most beneficial. The
facts are, however, that the times of need seem to occur quite
frequently in our world, especially if the goal is high quality
living as opposed to basic functioning. And in these times the
support that happens by chance may not be adequate. An intentionally designed support system can make a significant difference in
the quality of a person's life and work. Because of the many kinds
of needs and the differences among people, the best support system
has a great variety of resources available.[1]

---

[1]This is evidenced by a major research study reported by
Payne, "Organizational Stress and Social Support," p. 278.

With regard to the SDA pastor the responsibility for the
support system lies both with the individual and the corporate
church. Many pastors who spend so much time helping others seem
to wait for someone else to help them. They often deny their
needs until a crisis erupts. Mills and Koval found that clergypersons did not readily seek support, but they willingly received
it when it was offered.[1] Ministers need to seek help when they
need it. They need to create, encourage, and use resources of
support for themselves and each other. It is a sign of maturity
when a person recognizes his own limitations and does what he needs
to do to prevent dysfunction. He should not wait to be rescued
by someone else. Ministers can do many things on their own
initiative, some of which are suggested here.

Conferences also have a responsibility for the support
system of pastors. In the SDA Church conference officials are the
employers and they have a dominant role in the ministerial program
of each pastor. Their jurisdiction places them in a position where
they are best able to create such resources. It is questionable
if there is anything more important conferences could do than
support and encourage their pastors. Healthy pastors facilitate the
work of the church and make the work of the conferences easier.
Congregations can also take responsibility to provide support
resources to pastors. The ministry need not be all one way.
Seminaries should be involved, too. Here, then, are a number of
resources that pastors, conferences, and congregations should consider when designing an adequate support system.

---

[1]Mills and Koval, pp. 28, 55.

Personal Resources

Spiritual Strength

We want to clearly affirm that the power of God is the over-arching support resource, the real intervention. We previously established that God helps mankind directly, but he also helps through human agencies.[1] We must never be taken up with human potential in and of itself. We are what we are in Christ. Further-more, we must never look upon human agencies as the origin of our help and become fully dependent upon them. They are filled with faults and weaknesses. Nevertheless, God's help is mediated through them. We are dependent upon God, but his help often comes through human agencies. Whether direct or mediated we need to maintain that strengthening relationship with God. Bible study and prayer are the elements of a conversation with him. Meditation helps to free the mind from earthly cares, and contemplating the providence of God can be very reassuring. Faith can be cultivated in these ways. Many great preachers of the past kept spiritual journals that assisted them in their introspection and growth. Celia Hahn describes how some ministers seek "sabbath time" other than the regular day of worship (which is often a busy work day for them) for their own spiritual oasis.[2] Pastors must determine to reserve the highest priority for these things despite other pressing duties. Conferences and congregations can encourage pastors to take this

---

[1] See chapter 2.

[2] Celia Allison Hahn, "'Strung Out, Harried, Overextended'; How Can You Practice the Spiritual Life in a Busy Church," Action Information, March 1979, pp. 8-10.

time by verbally affirming it (thereby giving "permission"--not that
a pastor needs permission, but it helps to reduce the felt conflicts
in time demands) and by actually allowing time by limiting expectations.

Changes in Attitudes and Actions

What many support resources do is change a person's attitude
toward his situation and subsequently his way of acting or relating
to it. Many times a person can do this himself. The new way of
thinking is often discovered by good reading material--bibliotherapy,
as it is sometimes called. A multitude of books are available to
help pastors work through many of the issues that plague them. For
example, a little book entitled Help Yourself is a guide to self-
counseling.[1] Similar to Albert Ellis's "rational emotive therapy,"
this book helps a person examine his attitudes toward situations in
his life and deal with them himself. When the People Say No is a
book that helps ministers adjust their attitudes to the experiences
of rejection and frustration that they so often face.[2] Clergy in
the Cross Fire helps ministers understand and deal with role conflicts.[3]

There are books that deal with self-worth,[4] the stages of
a minister's career,[5] and the defenses that a minister often uses

---

[1]John Lembo, Help Yourself (Niles, IL: Argue Communications,
1974).

[2]Dittes, When the People Say No.

[3]Smith, Clergy in the Cross Fire.

[4]E.g., Maurice E. Wagner, The Sensation of Being Somebody
(Grand Rapids: Zondervan Publishing House, 1975); Idem, Putting It
All Together (Grand Rapids: Zondervan Publishing House, 1974).

[5]E.g., Paul, see p. 11 above.

in people relationships that hinder effectiveness and strike at
personal fulfillment.[1] There are books on assertiveness training,[2]
books on time management,[3] those which help ministers to create
for themselves an intentional ministry,[4] and many others. These
areas can be helpful to ministers. Sometimes a minister needs to
deal with his reasons for entering the ministry. There are those
who need to look behind a false front and find out who they really
are, in their humanity and variety of emotions. Sometimes a man
needs to feel free to leave the ministry in order to feel free to
stay. He can work more effectively when he freely chooses his
situation (knowing he has alternatives) than if he feels trapped.
Other ministers need to redefine success for themselves or reorder
priorities. Progress often can be made in these areas when a person draws on his own psychological resources. Some individuals are
able to create their own effective problem-solving methods. The
SDA minister may use his equipment allowance for self-development
books to help employ this resource.

---

[1] E.g., Zeluff, see p. 78 above.

[2] E.g., Paul Mickey and Gary Gamble, with Paula Gilbert,
Pastoral Assertiveness: A Model for Pastoral Care (Nashville:
Abingdon, 1978); David Augsburger and John Faul, Beyond Assertive-
ness (Waco, TX: Calibre Books, 1980).

[3] E.g., Leas, Time Management, see p. 29 above; Ted W.
Engstrom, and R. Alex Mackenzie, Managing Your Time (Grand Rapids:
Zondervan Publishing House, 1967).

[4] E.g., John Biersdorf, ed., Creating an Intentional Ministry
(Nashville: Abingdon, 1976).

Other Personal Resources

The eight natural remedies listed by Ellen White can also help a person cope with stress and various frustrations: the use of pure air and sunlight, abstemiousness, rest, exercise, proper diet, the use of water, and trust in divine power.[1] These remedies help a person to be physically healthy as well as to have a positive attitude. Some people practice relaxation exercises; others find that diversions or creative leisure, such as hobbies, travel, or other recreation, help significantly.[2] Ministers often need to work on establishing a balanced amount of free time.

Another method characteristic of ministers dealing with stressful situations is to move to a different church. But Edelwich points out that if a person is burned out, changing jobs does not prevent a new pattern of disillusionment unless other steps are taken also.[3]

We cannot deal with the many other specific kinds of personal resources that individuals have tried and found helpful. Instead, the importance of social resources draws our attention. Often persons need someone else to help them discover a new way of thinking, to pace them in a problem-solving technique or coping resource, to provide simple understanding, caring, or the transmission of strength, or to introduce any number of other interrelational supports. In the study reported by Mills and Koval, two-thirds of the ministers sought to relieve stress by self-helps. Yet,

---

[1] White, The Ministry of Healing, p. 127.

[2] Burke and Weir, pp. 301ff.   [3] Edelwich, pp. 194-204.

. . . consistently, those who report self-support--that is, no sources of support beyond themselves--reported fewer successful outcomes in the succeeding period. It seems that stress is hardest to resolve when external support is absent.[1]

Roy Payne concurs:

In stressful situations psychological mechanisms alone seem to have limited success; humans appear to need the constant physical and emotional contact with others to retain a sense of identity. Other people are the site for our identity.[2]

Consequently we turn to a wide variety of social supports.

Family Resources

Over and over again the research studies on the support of ministers indicate that the wife of the minister is his most important support person. Her attitude strongly influences the decision of those ministers who leave the ministry.[3] Chapter 3 indicated that the morale of SDA clergy is also tied closely to the support of the spouse. The family as a whole performs a number of important supporting functions. It is "a collector and disseminator of information about the world." It serves as a "feedback guidance system," whereby the family members help an individual to interpret the meaning of his life experiences in light of family values. It is also "a source of ideology" where belief systems, value systems, and codes of behavior help an individual understand the nature and

---

[1]Mills and Koval, pp. 32, 55.   [2]Payne, p. 269.

[3]E.g., Jud, Mills, and Burch, pp. 93-100; Dallas Anthony Blanchard, "Some Social and Orientative Correlates of Career Change and Continuity as Revealed among United Methodist Pastors of the Alabama-West Florida Conference, 1960-1970" (Ph.D. dissertation, Boston University, 1973), pp. 114, 266-70; Thomas Otis Fulcher, "Factors Related to Attrition of Parish Ministers in the North Carolina Conference of the United Methodist Church, 1966-1970" (Ed.D. dissertation, North Carolina State University at Raleigh, 1971), pp. 58, 70-71; Forney, pp. 128, 133; Cardwell and Hunt, pp. 128-30.

meaning of the universe. The family is a "guide and mediator in problem-solving." It is a "source of practical service and concrete aid," and a "haven for rest and recuperation." It is a "reference and control group" that applies sanctions for transgressing codes and values, but does it acknowledging that the individual will always be a member of the family. Security and identity thus result. Finally, the family contributes to a person's "emotional mastery" by strengthening his efforts in emotional struggles and keeping him from giving up too soon.[1]

Wife and family are a natural part of any man's support system, but ministers' families often bear too great a share of this function due to isolation and the lack of other resources. Even with other supports, the wife still plays a crucial role. Her effectiveness, in turn, may depend on her own sense of being supported. One SDA conference official wrote, "We are seeing a very great need for a support system for ministers' wives."[2] Efforts to improve family life are well worth the investment. As conferences take action in behalf of the minister's wife, they usually find that they have another support resource for the minister. Conferences can provide professional counseling, marriage retreats, family occasions, and a pastor for ministers' families. Minister/husbands should reciprocate support by taking time for wife and family; they should be encouraging, understanding, participating willingly in marriage-growth experiences (without feeling that it casts a negative reflection on them), and clarifying with their wives how they can be mutually supportive. Both

---

[1]Payne, pp. 279-81.   [2]Staff.

minister and conference should demonstrate sensitivity by not taking advantage of the spouse by making excessive demands. They should allow these women to develop their own identities rather than being swallowed up in the husband's role. Perhaps the pastor could stand before the congregation to negotiate role expectations in behalf of his wife. This is especially useful when a minister first moves to a church. A growing number of publications are available that deal with the situation of the minister's wife.[1] The suggestions above, as well as a number of others, can be found in these sources. Pastors, conferences, and congregations should pay attention to these things in an effort to establish interlocking support resources.

Training Resources

Seminary

The pattern of a young minister's vulnerabilities and his skillfullness in using various supports can be significantly determined by his initial training. Although the seminary cannot be blamed for not producing experienced ministers, it can intercept a number of personal and career issues by using certain tools of

---

[1]E.g., Mary LaGrand Bouma, "Ministers' Wives: The Walking Wounded," Leadership 1 (Winter 1980):63-75; Roy M. Oswald, Carolyn Taylor Gutierrez, and Liz Spellman Dean, Married to the Minister (Washington, D.C.: Alban Institute, 1980); Ruth Senter, So You're the Pastor's Wife (Grand Rapids: Zondervan Publishing House, 1979); Betty J. Cobble, The Private Life of the Minister's Wife (Nashville: Broadman Press, 1981); Charlotte Ross, Who Is the Minister's Wife? (Philadelphia: Westminster Press, 1980). A book that helps wives live with and help their husbands in their mid-life crisis is Sally Conway, You and Your Husband's Mid-Life Crisis (Elgin, IL: David C. Cook Publishing Co., 1980). Suggestions to denominational officials can be found in Mace, pp. 129-37.

support. Besides the testing and counseling which is being done,
it seems that the SDA Theological Seminary could make greater use
of small peer groups similar to those established at Lancaster
Theological Seminary and used in the Inter-met project.[1] Each
group should include a practicing pastor and a seminary faculty
member. These groups should be tied not merely to the field-
education program but in an on-going experience. They could be
the focal point for the development of a student's personal
spirituality and for general fellowship, which often seems to be
lacking. They could provide an opportunity for forming mentoring relationships with the pastor and faculty members.

McBurney and Hartung point out that many ministerial
problems stem from misunderstanding the "call" and entering the
ministry for the wrong reasons. A person may enter the ministry
to please his family, to atone for guilt, to find a place of
security and warmth, or to obtain power and prestige.[2] A support
group, as described above, may be able to deal with these issues
and save much later grief if a person learns to know himself
better and live accordingly. Sometimes those who are unsuited to
the ministry need "permission" to change into a line where they can
serve the Lord with effectiveness. It would be good if they could
do this before the costly investment of seminary education. Later
it is much harder to change. A support group could deal with

---

[1]See chapter 4.

[2]McBurney, Every Pastor, pp. 17-34; Bruce M. Hartung,
"Identity, the Pastor, and the Pastor's Spouse," Currents in
Theology and Mission 3 (October 1976):307-11.

issues of identity, self-worth, confidence, authority, and unresolved developmental tasks, all of which are so important to producing a well-adjusted minister.[1] Edelwich suggests that the intervention for burn-out should start in the first stage--enthusiasm:

> Intervention may be difficult at the stage of enthusiasm
> for the simple reason that it is hard to help people who do
> not realize they have a problem. On the other hand, it is
> most productive to reach people at a time when they have not
> gone very far down the road to disillusionment and when they
> still have a good deal of energy to put into their work.
> Interventions for enthusiasm are best made in training, so
> that trainees can learn to moderate their expectations before
> they go out into the field. Such interventions require an
> awareness of how and why unrealistic hopes arise and just
> what is unrealistic about them.[2]

This intervention falls into the lap of the seminary (as well as
the conferences) and possibly into the domain of support groups as
above. Such a group could establish a pattern of utilizing support which, hopefully, might be carried on throughout the student's
ministry--one of the goals for the program at Lancaster. Charles
Rassieur, of the North Central Career Development Center, writes:

> The seminarian who does not learn how to make a habit of
> cultivating a support system will end up trying to do ministry
> without a major resource necessary for survival. The "Lone
> Ranger" pastor is extremely vulnerable to stress and early
> burnout. . . . There can be no question about it. There is
> more stress in the ministry than can be handled by any one
> person alone.[3]

At the seminary, students should gain practice in self-disclosure
and friendship--things ministers generally tend to avoid.

------

[1] C. G. Fitzgerald, "Ordination Plus Six," Journal of
Pastoral Care 21 (March 1967):15-23.

[2] Edelwich, p. 46.

[3] Charles L. Rassieur, "How Will Stress Affect Your Ministry?"
Seminary Quarterly 22 (Fall 1980):2.

Mentor

The research studies of Cardwell and Hunt sought factors
that determined persistence in seminary and in ministry. They
found that individuals whose first ministry experience was as an
assistant to an older minister were the most likely to persist.
These young ministers had had a role model and a successful experience. The least likely to persist were those whose first
experience was full responsibility for a church.[1] We have else-
where in this study given evidence of the need (and desire) for
mentoring relationships.

Levinson describes the functions of a mentor like this:

> A good mentor is an admixture of good father and good friend.
> (A bad mentor, of which there are many, combines the worst
> features of father and friend.) A "good enough" mentor is a
> transitional figure who invites and welcomes a young man into
> the adult world. He serves as guide, teacher, and sponsor.
> He represents skill, knowledge, virtue, accomplishment--the
> superior qualities a young man hopes someday to acquire. He
> gives his blessing to the novice and his Dream. And yet, with
> all this superiority, he conveys the promise that in time they
> will be peers. The protégé has the hope that soon he will be
> able to join or even surpass his mentor in the work they both
> value.
> A mentor can be of great practical help to a young man as
> he seeks to find his way and gain new skills. But a good men-
> tor is helpful in a more basic, developmental sense. This
> relationship enables the recipient to identify with a person
> who exemplifies many of the qualities he seeks. It enables
> him to form an internal figure who offers love, admiration
> and encouragement in his struggles. He acquires a sense of
> belonging to the generation of promising young men. He reaps
> the varied benefits to be gained from a serious, mutual, non-
> sexual loving relationship with a somewhat older man or woman.[2]

Levinson says that a mentor is usually eight to fifteen years older
than the other person. If the age difference is too great, powerful

---

[1]Cardwell and Hunt, p. 128.

[2]Levinson, pp. 333-34; see also pp. 97-100.

feelings of paternalism may interfere with the mentoring function.
The two may never be able to move toward a peer relationship which
is the goal. If the difference in age is too small, the prospective
mentor cannot represent the advanced level toward which the younger
man is striving. Mentoring relationships last an average of two
or three years, eight to ten at the most.

As part of the support system, particularly of younger men,
conference leaders of the SDA Church need to encourage mentoring
relationships. They need to approve time for mentor and trainee
to spend together, plus special mileage and telephone reimburse-
ment as appropriate. Pastors should be allowed to choose their
own mentors, and it may not be their senior pastor/supervisor, if
they are interns or associates. Such a provision might help to
eliminate the hesitancy to be open and candid. Pastors should take
their own initiative to seek a mentor. One who wishes to find a
mentor must first admit his need of support. Prayerfully he should
make a list of ten individuals he admires. Next, he should plan
ways to meet these individuals, to get acquainted, and to ask
some questions that tap their resources. If a positive relationship seems to be developing, the pastor might ask the chosen person
if he could be his resource person. The pastor must be prepared to
risk sharing his dreams about the future and absorb his mentor's
positive insights. He must also recognize that this relationship
will change in time--either dissolving or becoming a peer friendship.[1]

---

[1]Adapted from Katie Funk Wiebe, "Passing Along the Faith,"
Today's Christian Woman, Winter 1980-81, p. 66.

Conferences should encourage older ministers to be available as mentors, something like the "first assistant" program of the Jewel Tea Company. Pastors who are willing to be mentors can fulfill that function best by studying other successful experiences, such as Paul's relationship to Timothy, Titus, and Onesimus. They need to feel comfortable with their own identity as a minister of the gospel and come to terms with their need for power and achievement so that they will not feel threatened by younger men whose talents and gifts are blooming and may become more effective than their own. They should look around for younger pastors who are struggling in an area in which they once struggled and make contact with a few in ways that are comfortable to both parties. They, too, need to pray about this ministry relationship and be prepared to share life stories, visions, hopes, and failures. Being realistic is more helpful than constant positive, but superficial, enthusiasm. The more experienced should be prepared to share "trade secrets" about their speciality and deliberately become teachers in an informal classroom. They must, of course, make room in their thinking and schedule for such friendships. Finally, they must at the proper time be prepared to let go of their superiority in the relationship and rejoice in the achievements of a new colleague.[1]

Continuing Education

Mark Rouch defines continuing education as

. . . an individual's personally designed learning program which begins when basic formal education ends and continues

---

[1] Ibid.

throughout a career and beyond. An unfolding process, it links together personal study and reflection and participation in organized group events.[1]

James Hofrenning makes the point that like people in other professions, ministers must also constantly renew, extend, and reorganize their knowledge or they will be beyond hope as an educator or practitioner in approximately eight years.[2] Furthermore, there are some things which simply cannot be learned or appreciated until a person has had some experience on the job. Sarata explains that new workers go through three phases in their initial adjustment. First, they are preoccupied with mastering the standard operating procedures. Next, they are concerned with the comparison of their work attitudes and philosophy with those of their co-workers and superiors. Finally, they begin to deal with their own adequacy for and commitment to the job. When an individual is preoccupied with standard operating procedures, he simply does not benefit much from a discussion of other matters.[3] When a young minister assumes full time responsibilities and is challenged and confronted by questions people ask, by ambiguities of human situations, by loneliness, feelings of inadequacy, and conflict over roles, then he has reached the primary learning moment. Discussion and training in these areas take on a whole new meaning.

---

[1] Rouch, Competent Ministry, pp. 16-17.

[2] James B. Hofrenning, "Preface," in The Continuing Quest, ed. James B. Hofrenning (Minneapolis: Augsburg Publishing House, 1970), p. 11.

[3] B. P. V. Sarata, "Now That We Have Identified Burnout, What Are We Going to Do about It?" in "Burnout in the Helping Professions," eds. Kenneth E. Reid and Rebecca A. Quinlan, papers presented at a symposium on burnout, Western Michigan University, Kalamazoo, Michigan, September 27-28, 1979, pp. 12-13.

Continuing education then doubles as a support resource for the individual.[1]

However, random continuing education for its own sake does not result in effective support. Thomas Brown who has had long experience with career-development centers has stated that many who come through the centers had engaged in continuing education, and many quite actively. Generally the education was unrelated to the central problems, hopes, and goals of their ministry. Continuing education, says Rouch, must be planned. It must be planned by each individual around those things he wishes to change in his life and ministry. It must affirm the person of the minister besides helping him develop skills for the practice of ministry. Continuing education experiences need to have both an immediate effect and a cumulative result.[2] Walter Wagoner gives this prescription for continuing education:

(1) it is long enough and recurring enough to make a lasting impact;
(2) it is largely designed for and shaped by the clergy themselves, not handed down from above, pro forma packaged, to carry out the educational or propagandistic goals of church officials;
(3) it is not to be equated with normal vacation periods and synodical cabals;
(4) it should be of the sort which can feed into the minister's or priest's own reading and work schedule;
(5) it has guaranteed financial support;
(6) it encourages a counseling process which enables the minister to ascertain his genuine needs.[3]

---

[1]See chapter 4; Rouch, Competent Ministry, pp. 115-16; Doyle, pp. 36-37.

[2]Mark Rouch, "Getting Smart about Continuing Education," in Growth in Ministry, ed. Thomas E. Kadel (Philadelphia: Fortress Press, 1979), pp. 124-31; Mills and Koval, pp. 52, 57; Sims, p. 40.

[3]Walter D. Wagoner, "A Prescription for the Health of the Church," in The Continuing Quest, ed. James B. Hofrenning (Minneapolis: Augsburg Publishing House, 1970), p. 24.

Continuing education needs to be a standard policy in the
conferences of the SDA Church, not merely "instances" where time
or financial help is granted "on an individual basis." Where there
is no policy, when a person must request each occasion, it implies
to the pastor that the conference is reluctant for him to have these
experiences. Opportunity for continued education should be willingly offered and encouraged. To hold it as a reward and/or
punishment related to conference goals completely misses the point
of its purpose. Only the successful and healthy can get help and
improve even more. The discouraged and unskilled are isolated to
perpetuate their failures even more.

The concept of continuing education needs to be much
broader than just degree programs (like the Doctor of Ministry).
These should be available but granted more selectively. The major
bulk of continuing education needs to be available to everyone and
to consist of short-term experiences, such as workshops and seminars designed for the practicing pastor. The responsibility of
each pastor is to choose the program that will further his own
plans and deal with his own needs. The responsibility of the
conference is to provide the opportunity for ministers to obtain
continuing education by establishing a clear policy, by cataloging
the various educational possibilities, and by actually offering
a variety of programs ministers could choose to attend.

An initial policy might offer each pastor one week per
year (the equivalent of one four-credit class) with 75 percent of
the costs reimbursed to an established upper limit. It could be
cumulative up to three years to allow for a more involved

experience within that period of time. This one week of continuing education would be the pastor's free choice (not an obligatory program prescribed for everyone), whereas the regular workers' meeting might involve continuing education that the conference wishes to provide to all. This establishes the possibility of two weeks per year in all. The conferences might even begin recording continuing education units as part of a minister's professional dossier.

Pastors in conferences which do not have these opportunities could do much on their own to fulfill their needs. They should unashamedly request such opportunities on an individual basis. They can purchase books, self-help courses, and other resources to use in personal study. One of the best methods would be to establish a learning program by means of a colleague group with other ministers. The books and resources could be studied together; guests could be invited to make presentations; or the case-study method could be used to learn from their own experiences. More is said about groups in a later section.

Sabbatical

The sabbatical is a biblical concept which in its essence implies rest. It is used in the academic community and for corporate executives. David McKenna believes it should be available to pastors also.[1] It is not just continuing education, nor is it

---

[1] David McKenna, "Recycling Pastors," Leadership 1 (Fall 1980):29. See also David C. Pohl, "Ministerial Sabbaticals," The Christian Ministry, January 1978, pp. 8-10; Connolly C. Gamble, "Continuing Education and Creative Leisure," The Christian Ministry, January 1978, pp. 4-7.

a vacation. It is an extended period of renewal, usually three to six months or even up to a year. The ministry is a demanding work in which much depends upon the continual output of fresh insights and clear vision. The unrelenting routine of preaching each week, counseling, evangelism, and administration can produce weariness of spirit and dulling of the capacity to be creative. A sabbatical can provide time for spiritual and intellectual rejuvenation. It may involve continuing education of a longer and more intense variety, such as a degree program. It may also be an opportunity for travel, for writing a book or articles that have been put off. It may involve associating with another minister of renown to observe and learn from his skills. It could be a time for introspective reflections, creative brooding, practicing the presence of God.

Sometimes persons who have suffered a severely stressful situation or an internal struggle need some time for their own personal resources to work their natural course to recovery. It is harder to recover when continually facing the grindstone. Some time to get themselves together, rather than counseling or other helps, may be all they need.

A goal to work toward as a general policy might be McKenna's suggestion of a three- to six-month period of a paid sabbatical after five to seven years of service. Special sabbaticals, such as for the Doctor of Ministry program, would be significantly longer. To make the general sabbatical useful, the pastor should present a proposal regarding his activities, followed by reports on the

results of his experiences.[1] Sabbaticals might be arranged between pastorates but are also possible during a longer pastorate.
The book Learning to Share the Ministry is the story of how one
church arranged the six-month sabbatical of its minister--of
organizing to cover his duties while he was gone, of preparing
the congregation mentally, of the letters and reports by the
minister during his sabbatical, and of the dynamics of the re-
entry period when he returned.[2]

It may be a long time before the SDA Church includes the
sabbatical as part of its policy for the minister other than the
special sabbatical for a degree program. In fact, a sabbatical
may not be as frequently needed as some of the other resources we
are discussing. But the leadership of the church, hopefully,
will recognize those times when a man simply needs some time off
to assist his recovery from extreme circumstances and will grant
a period for renewal on an individual basis.

Colleague Resources

Friendship

"Where there is competition, there can be no compassion,"
says Henri Nouwen. Competition often is a factor that keeps ministers from experiencing supportive relationships with one another.
A minister may feel insecure and defensive about his accomplishments in the presence of his peers. Time pressures, distance,

---

[1]McKenna, p. 29.

[2]James R. Adams and Celia A. Hahn, Learning to Share the
Ministry (Washington, D.C.: Alban Institute, 1975).

and other factors can also hinder the development of productive friendships. But as ministers resist professional rivalry, risk some self-disclosure, and emphasize some caring concern for one another, they find that others face much the same vulnerabilities they do; they find growing trust and a very helpful support resource.

Glasse believes that ministers can best help each other because no one else understands the ministry as well as the fellow pastor.[1] Some suggest that ministers pastor one another, either in a "buddy system" or a more formal arrangement.[2] Common friendship can be one of the best supports. Daniel Zeluff describes friendship:

> Everyone needs three or four people to whom he or she can be honest and open and candid about everything. . . . These are people you have met along the way with whom you confess and celebrate, weep and laugh, and no matter what you say or do, they will not cast you out. You share with each other anything you wish without fear of being rejected.
> These people are also your correctors, and you are theirs. They do not just hum the "Hallelujah Chorus" to everything you do or say, because there is no true affirmation without the occasional "You really were a jackass." When you say you acted stupidly they probably will agree, but they won't send you to your room without supper. They are friends, and in spite of anger, agreement, or disagreement they remain friends. You do not always praise them, nor they you, but when it's damning time you don't have to hit the road and find another set of people to whom to relate.[3]

Zeluff prefers this kind of support over the group. Groups, he feels, are often "too canned." Friends may never meet as a group. They may not all live in the same town or even be in a person's

---

[1] Glasse, Profession: Minister, p. 154.

[2] Hart, p. 6; Dale, p. 15; Dickson, p. 89.

[3] Zeluff, pp. 98-100.

same age group. Yet potential friends are all around, says Zeluff.
One must just look. "They are probably as frightened as you and
as hungry as you for someone to be real with."

SDA ministers need to invest in some friendships. They
may keep in touch with a schoolmate by letters, phone calls, or
maybe an occasional visit. They may develop a relationship with a
nearby pastor or a minister of another denomination in their own
community. It requires a venture in self-disclosure, honesty,
trust-building, giving, etc., but it is also a benefit in many
ways.[1]

Consultation

The variety and complexity of human problems and administrative situations that confront a minister could be so great that
he may find himself baffled. Another valuable support resource
could be a network of professional consultants. Physicians who
have difficult cases are responsible to obtain the consultation
they need to provide the best care for the patient. They often
talk over the situation with a specialist or a colleague. It gives
them more confidence in their decisions and actions. But ministers
often feel that they must carry on by themselves, that it is a
negative reflection upon them if they ask for help. It should
not be that way. Ministers also have specialties--some know how
to conduct building programs, some are specialists in marriage

---

[1]Principles for developing friendships can be found in Alan
Loy McGinnis, The Friendship Factor (Minneapolis: Augsburg Pub-
lishing House, 1979); Gerald L. Dahl, Everybody Needs Somebody
Sometime (Nashville: Thomas Nelson Publishers, 1980); Larry Graham,
"Ministers and Friendship."

counseling, a few have had experience with demon possession, others are successful in managing church conflict.

Conferences could open up this resource by cataloging the specialties of ministers and other professionals, then by encouraging the specialists to be available to consult with pastors, and finally by legitimatizing the use of these consultants. With a verbal encouragement and a well-established precedent, pastors might not be as hesitant to call a consultant. Conference departmental men perform some consulting roles. However, most conferences do not have departments that cover the most frustrating problems of a minister. For example, there is no department of conflict management nor is there any department of counseling. Furthermore, most conference personnel do not have specialized training and promotional duties often prevent them from having time or perspective to be effective consultants.

Ruth Caplan in Helping the Helpers to Help reports in detail the consultation program that the Episcopal Church established between psychiatrists and ministers to help in counseling problems. Sidney DeWaal outlines another approach to consultation.[1] He suggests that a pastor approach a colleague whom he respects as a person and professional for the purpose of consultation for one hour a week. The consulted pastor may in turn be a consulting pastor to someone else, or there may be reciprocal consultation. DeWaal wishes to explode the myth that the helper can never again be the helped. Consultation, he says, implies a basic equality between

---

[1] Sidney C. J. DeWaal, "The Minister as Colleague: A Pastoral Care Concern," Calvin Theological Journal 8 (November 1973):159.

the individuals. This is a model that SDA ministers could also implement.

Support Groups

Small numbers of pastors coming together in groups can yield a great variety of support benefits. Support groups can be the site for developing friendships, strengthening the bonds of brotherhood, and renewing one's spiritual life by communal study, prayer, and worship. They can provide the occasion for personal encouragement, practical help, and continuing education. They can help clarify an individual's personal identity, confront him with accountability, and affirm his commitment to his career. Duane Meyer says that a support group is a "community of understanding and acceptance, of sharing and caring for one another."[1]

However, there are some cautions. All these good things do not just happen by themselves. Edelwich says that without the proper structure, a burned-out person who ventilates his grievances may simply cause a contagion of burn-out rather than receive the constructive help he needs.[2] Also if no one in the group understands the principles of group building, the results may be unproductive and even negative. For instance, a group may deal with material that is too sensitive before a proper trust level is established. It may neglect some of the essential elements that produce group cohesiveness.

Generally a group should have no more than a dozen members

---

[1]Meyer, "A Study of Professional Support," p. 142.

[2]Edelwich, p. 37.

and, to obtain the benefits of group dynamics, no fewer than four.
Every group needs to go through the process of history giving,
affirmation, and goal setting. Without spending adequate time
getting to know each other during the history giving, there is no
basis for the trust, which in turn is necessary if the group is to
achieve honest and realistic self-disclosures. The material dealt
with in the group should not go beyond the level of relationship
established or resistance will occur. Affirmation is the verbal-
ization of a positive commitment to each other, and goal setting
is the clarification of what the group plans to accomplish. Every
group needs a contract which defines the guidelines governing it.
A contract for one group had these elements:

> A commitment to truly listen to one another and value each
> other's feelings and viewpoints.
> A commitment to encourage total participation and discourage
> domination of the group by any one person.
> A commitment to give the group priority and meet at ten o'clock
> for two hours on Sunday morning for eight weeks.
> A commitment to allow a person not to speak when it is his choice.
> A commitment to keep what each group member shares confidential.

To start with, it is good to contract for a specific number of
meetings. At the end of the contract time, members of the group
can drop out without embarrassment, agree to continue, or change
the group structure. Each person should be respected for what he
may or may not wish to share. And, of course, confidentiality is
supremely important for personal issues.[1]

---

[1]More details on the structuring of support groups can be
found in Luiz Melo, "A Rationale and Suggested Program for Ministers'
Support Groups for Seventh-day Adventist Pastors in Brazil" (D.Min
project report, Andrews University, 1981); William Clemmons and
Harvey Hester, Growth through Groups (Nashville: Broadman Press,
1974); Howard J. Clinebell, Jr., The People Dynamic (New York:
Harper and Row, 1972); Lyman Coleman, Encyclopedia of Serendipity

Groups can take a variety of directions in terms of their purpose. They may exist for discussion and sharing, recreation and social occasions, study and skill development, or consultation. Often groups schedule a specific agenda but are ready to table it whenever any group member has an immediate personal or professional concern. One of the most effective methodologies is the case-study method described by James Glasse and others.[1] In this method, a pastor writes out a ministry event, including background, description, analysis, and evaluation. The case is then presented to the group and discussed for the benefit of all.

The support group is one resource that lies in the domain of pastors to organize and carry on. They do not need the conference to make it possible. One or two pastors can solicit interest from other pastors and get something started. It needs to be well-planned or pastors will lose interest and it will simply be another unprofitable meeting. Conferences can encourage such groups by verbal approval and by providing leadership skilled in group building to help facilitate them. Conferences might even provide some mileage for the get-togethers. However, such groups should never be required for that would completely offset their effectiveness.

Support groups are not intended to be official organizations

(Littleton, CO: Serendipity House, 1976); Kenneth Johnson, "Personal Religious Growth;" Rouch, Competent Ministry, pp. 141ff.; Wolff, "Clergy Support Groups;" Meyer, "How to Set Up Your Own Local Support Group;" idem, "Group Support Tape;" Holbrook; Hart; Dale.

[1]Glasse, Putting It Together, pp. 72-105; see also Fallow; Leslie and Mudd.

or associations. There may be a place for something like an Academy of Adventist Ministers, if it could provide some beneficial services and have a corresponding function on the local level, but certainly there is no intention to have any union-like organization that would represent pastors and their interests before conference officials, as some have suggested. Support groups are simply one means that can enable the personnel of the church to work together with greater effectiveness. Groups that include conference officials certainly should not be excluded. There are appropriate times for each kind of group.

Team Ministries

Another support resource can be found in colleague relationships through team ministries. We find this in the multiple staff of a larger church. Although mutual support is not automatic, a good staff can bring significant satisfaction to each of its members.[1] In order to apply this resource to smaller churches, some denominations have tried "cooperative parishes." In this arrangement, several churches are all served by two or more pastors who form a staff rather than one pastor working alone in a church or two. This gives opportunity for specialization (no one pastor must be an expert in everything nor do everything) and gives opportunity for mutual support of the pastors in their work. In order to make this plan, or even the large church staff, successful, there must be some

---

[1]Randy Karschner suggests that one staff member perform the function of minister of relationships and that he also be a minister to the senior pastor. "How to Be a Minister's Minister," Church Administration, April 1981, pp. 29-30.

investment in team building--trust, openness, and a good executive head.[1] Others have suggested that smaller churches be linked to larger churches in nearby towns so young ministers can have some contact with other ministers and the life of larger churches.[2] This could be tied to the internship program, as it is already done in some conferences. It could be applied by means of the district system, as in the Michigan Conference, where smaller churches are linked to a larger one whose pastor is the district leader. This plan of organization needs to have more than administrative purposes, however. It is the responsibility of the conference to review the various options and to evaluate their merits in each situation.

Pastors might also be able to initiate the option of team ministry. It is possible for neighboring pastors to arrange to work together occasionally for a day or two. It might be visiting, giving Bible studies, or doing business Ingathering. It is especially helpful in major projects like evangelistic campaigns or even building programs.

Ellen White has certainly given strong counsel in this area of team ministry which should raise the interest of SDAs in this particular resource. After referring to the example of Jesus who sent out his disciples two by two, she says,

God never designed that, as a rule, His servants should go out singly to labor. . . . Unless a speaker has one by his side

---

[1]See chapter 4, and Gears; R. A. Rhem, "Staff Ministries: Advantages, Challenges, and Problems," Reformed Review 31 (Winter 1978):78-81.

[2]Burnett, p. 159; Jud, Mills, and Burch, pp. 122-23.

with whom he can share the labor, he will many times be placed in circumstances where he will be obliged to do violence to the laws of life and health. Then, again, important things sometimes transpire to call him away right in the crisis of an interest. If two are connected in labor, the work at such times need not be left alone.

There is need of two working together; for one can encourage the other, and they can counsel, pray, and search the Bible together. In this they may get a broader light upon the truth; for one will see one phase, and the other another phase of the truth. If they are erring, they can correct one another in speech and attitude, so that the truth may not be lightly esteemed because of the defects of its advocates. . . .

Why is it that we have departed from the method of labor which was instituted by the Great Teacher? Why is it that the laborers in His cause today are not sent forth two and two? "Oh," you say, "we have not laborers enough to occupy the field." Then occupy less territory. Send forth the laborers into the places where the way seems to be opened, and teach the precious truth for this time. Can we not see the wisdom of having two go together to preach the gospel?[1]

Professional Resources

Pastor's Pastor

One long-standing suggestion for the support of ministers is the pastor pastorum. Although this function can be performed by colleagues (usually in a more limited way), it is one area that conferences are in a position to do effectively. There are, however, some factors that determine the success of this service. One seems to be the threat that results from overlapping administrative and support roles. The local conference president functions in both of these roles. He is the chief executive officer who oversees the hiring, transferring, and ongoing work of each pastor in his jurisdiction, as well as the promotion of conference programs. But as a pastor himself, he also frequently functions as a spiritual counselor to pastors. There are some ministers who do not find

---

[1]White, Evangelism, pp. 72-74.

this situation a threat. However, as pointed out before a significant number do fear that the revealing of personal problems
adversely affects their standing and future opportunities in the
work of the church.[1] They do not believe that conference presidents
can keep these roles distinct, nor do they perceive that concern
for the pastor's personal welfare is always well-balanced with
interest in the progress and success of the organization.

Other studies yield the same result. For example, the
Lutheran Institute of Religious Studies found that Lutheran pastors
have a high degree of distrust in their synod presidents and others
in authority. It comments, "Perhaps the suggestion of the pastoral
counselor's office separate from that of president would give the
'loneliest man in town' a place to go."[2] Of course, the spirit
of pastoral care and nurture should never be absent from administration. The effectiveness that conference presidents can have in
the counseling and support of pastors is largely dependent upon
their personalities and attitudes, the degree to which they cultivate trust relationships and then consistently maintain that reputation in their actions, and the amount of time they make available for unhurried sharing. The Lutheran study mentioned above
found that clergy who had training and experience in interpersonal
and group skills, with emphasis on trust and openness, had a much
higher degree of trust in the president than the others. They
recommended:

---

[1]See chapter 3.

[2]C. Umhau Wolf, "Do Pastors Trust Their Synod Presidents?"
Dialog 11 (Winter 1972):58-60; see also Wagner, p. 167.

> There would be great value in the president's participation in small groups on interpersonal and group skills with his clergy until all in his synod have been able to interact and to trust the president. Such programming is not a one shot deal, but a continuing one because of change in personnel and change in the situation of clergy and presidents.[1]

The president needs to be an open, self-disclosing human being for that trust to grow. It does not happen merely out of awe and respect for the office.

Because some apprehension seems unavoidable and because the president is usually overwhelmed with administrative demands, there also needs to be a separate pastor's pastor who can work to fulfill the many needs that have not been touched. The ministerial secretary should be such a person, but as noted earlier, pastors perceive his functions so closely tied with the administration that he has no advantage in overcoming this major barrier to effective support.[2] He seems to be an extension of the president, a person to whom pastors are responsible for achieving goals and complying with conference programs. Conferences report ministerial secretaries often visiting pastors, but their visits frequently deal with objectives, promotion, or evaluation.[3] In other cases, the ministerial secretary is an evangelist who does not always understand the perspective of the local pastor. Evangelists are also primarily promotors; and one who has a theory to prove or a program to push does not make a good counselor. Donald Houts, himself a pastor's pastor whose program was described before, writes this appropriate description:

> In working with the United Methodist structure, it seems clear to me that my power must be informal and indirect, based

---

[1]Ibid.   [2]See chapter 3.   [3]See chapter 4.

upon the trust of both hierarchy and fledgling pastor. I
cannot enter into decisions that have to do with termination,
admission, or discipline--except where confidentiality, client
initiative, and administrative authority are treated with
respect.

By no means can the minister to ministers skirt responsible
relationship between self, the judicatory authorities, boards
that admit candidates into membership, committees that relate
to continuing education programs, and other ecclesiastical
committees and agency staff persons. At the same time, it
seems imperative that this person not be appointed as a
regular member of any ongoing administrative or program
committees; rather, he/she should be free to attend them when
requested or even occasionally to request an opportunity to
appear before them in the service of common goals.[1]

The options seem to be: change the job description of the
ministerial secretary, create a new position, or use a local church
pastor. A church pastor would need to have very limited duties
associated with a church in order to accomplish much with other
ministers. A program that ministers need in a pastor pastorum
would require a full-time position. A new position would add another salary, which conferences do not need. But this option
would have the benefit of a position with a clean record and have
the impact of a new program. The most pragmatic idea would be to
change the job description of the ministerial secretary to eliminate promotional or administrative duties. However, it would be an
uphill struggle for a ministerial secretary to change his image because of the traditional image associated with him. In spite of
this, according to the results of our questionnaire, ministers
express a high interest in this option. Perhaps the personal
characteristics of the man chosen would mean the most in making
the new role function successfully.

---

[1]Houts, p. 193.

Another factor that determines the effectiveness of a conference support person is confidentiality. Often there is too much
talk in the conference office. If the conference president and
ministerial secretary collaborate on administrative matters, they
will certainly, in the pastor's mind, share nearly everything
they know with each other. Certainly there are appropriate times
for sharing information. But a pastoral counselor must always
remember that the secret belongs to the counselee, not to the
counselor. There are several levels of confidentiality, and the
pastoral counselor should contract with the counselee regarding the
way the information will be used. The counselor must not assume
consent. This is not only a moral obligation, but is vital to
establishing the person as a human being. Without confidential
relationships a person is isolated. When confidences are broken,
people are isolated because such a betrayal works against trust
and relationship building.[1]

Studies reveal that people who counsel and help others
effectively have certain personal characteristics. One list of
these essential traits reads thus:

> empathy--"the ability to perceive accurately what another per-
>   son is experiencing and to communicate that perception"
> respect--appreciation of "the dignity and worth of another
>   human being," and of that person's right to make his or her
>   own choices in his or her own time
> genuineness--"the ability of an individual to be freely and
>   deeply himself"

---

[1]Several very helpful articles on confidentiality are
DeLoss D. Friesen, "Confidentiality and the Pastoral Counselor,"
Pastoral Psychology 22 (January 1971):48-53; A. A. Cramer, "Go
Tell the People? The Ethics of Pastoral Confidentiality,"
Pastoral Psychology 17 (March 1966):31-41; Robert M. Cooper,
"Confidentiality," Anglican Theological Review 59 (January 1977):
20-32.

concreteness--"specificity of expression concerning the client's
    feelings and experiences"
confrontation--the capacity to challenge the client on dis-
    crepancies in his or her statements, feelings, and actions
self-disclosure--"the revealing of personal feelings, attitudes,
    opinions, and experiences on the part of the therapist for
    the benefit of the client"
immediacy--the ability to deal with "the feeling between the
    client and the counselor in the here and now"
warmth--the expression of verbal and nonverbal concern and
    affection
potency--"the dynamic force and magnetic quality of the therapist"
self-actualization--the capacity to "live and meet life directly,"
    to be "effective at living"[1]

Such a person in the position of a pastor's pastor would
accomplish a great deal in the support of ministers and their
families. What would he do? What does a pastor do in his parish?
The function would not be identical but similar. A pastor regularly
visits his people in their homes. He teaches, counsels, and enables
them to function more efficiently. He is a spiritual leader. He
represents and mediates the help of God in times of crisis and
tragedy. The list could go on and on. The description that Donald
Houts gives of his role seems viable for a pastor's pastor in the
SDA conferences. He does crisis intervention, counseling, referral,
consultation, continuing education, training, pilot programs, research, and career assessment.[2] The pastor's pastor could be en-
visioned as facilitating a number of other support resources
described above. For instance, he could be trained in group
dynamics and facilitate the starting of support groups. He could
be an advocate for the pastor to the pastor's congregation, helping

---

[1]Edelwich, pp. 41-42, partially quoting Sidney Wolf,
"Counseling--for better or worse," Alcohol Health and Research World,
Winter 1974-75, pp. 27-29.

[2]Houts, pp. 194-95.

them to better understand his work, or to the conference leaders. He could be a consultant, as described previously,[1] plus many other things. Overall, he could be a coordinator of resources for the local church pastor. Most SDA conferences desperately need this kind of support resource for their ministers. They need to give it high priority for action. Pastors need to have courage to express how such a support system can best help them and then use it when it is made available.

Professional Counseling

Professional counseling is sometimes greatly needed and can be very helpful among workers. Marriage and family problems, personal upsets and crises often need some special skill in treatment. Although some ministers have a negative attitude toward psychology and psychiatry because of possible conflicts with religion, many realize that a significant number of Christian professionals can encourage rather than attack one's faith. SDA conferences should all have a policy that informs workers of the provisions for this resource. Unless the information is volunteered, a minister might never know that the conference provides help "as the need arises" or "on an individual basis." When there is no policy providing professional help, the worker's family could seek help on its own. However, family members might not be able to afford professional help or know of a reliable counselor. The problem

---

[1] James D. Anderson describes the role of a consultant, such as could be filled by a conference pastor's pastor. "Pastoral Support of Clergy: Role Development within Local Congregations," Pastoral Psychology 22 (March 1971):9-14.

could then become very serious before conference help is offered. When there is no policy there is no prevention.

Professional counseling could be made available in several ways. The conferences could compile a list of reputable Christian counselors in their area and allow workers to go to any one of them with the costs reimbursed according to the regular medical policy. This list would also be useful to the pastors for their own work of counseling and referring church members. A second method, typified by that used in the Potomac Conference, selects certain counselors who can treat workers and send the bill to the conference without identifying counselees. Third, a conference could maintain a resident counselor. The British Columbia Conference has established a department of health and family services directed by a person who is trained both in counseling and health education. This person provides counseling both for workers and church members in the conference. Some have suggested that a resident professional counselor should be in the union conference office. This would alleviate the greater expense for smaller conferences, and workers would find greater anonymity when going to see him. Mileage expense could also be provided for the trips.

Another idea would be to provide a minister's hotline by means of an 800 telephone number. Ministers could call for crisis intervention or consultation in both personal and professional issues.[1] Conferences need to evaluate which provision might fit their situation best.

---

[1]This idea is suggested by Delmar W. Holbrook, Director of Home and Family Service, General Conference of Seventh-day Adventists, personal letter, April 10, 1981.

Career-Development Centers

Career-development centers are an excellent support resource for clarifying and/or strengthening one's relationship to his career and for dealing with many personal issues.[1] Several now also provide general counseling. This would be a valuable resource to have available to the SDA ministry. An SDA center could be established as an adjunct organization of the North American Division, or possibly the Theological Seminary. Sponsorship from the various levels of the church organization would have to augment the fees clients would pay. A career center located near the seminary could benefit students--those just beginning as well as older persons returning to school--besides the many people who pass through the area. This resource could also be made available to SDA ministers if the church were to participate in one or more of the already established centers. Even if the SDA church does not participate, a pastor could go on his own to one of the established centers. However, coming from a non-participating denomination, he would find the costs significantly higher.

Congregational Resources

Lay leaders and other lay persons have been rated quite highly as a support resource by the ministers in many of the other studies as well as our own.[2] The pastoral pedestal can be reduced as we recognize common humanity and the priesthood of all believers.[3]

---

[1] They are described more fully in chapter 4.

[2] See Jud, Mills, and Burch, pp. 94, 182; Blanchard, p. 114; Fulcher, pp. 70-73; Forney, p. 133. See also chapter 3 for the results of our questionnaire.

[3] See chapter 2.

There are inappropriate as well as appropriate ways, however, of
doing it. Lovett says that pastors sometimes leap from the pedestal
when the threat of being discovered as human creates too many
emotional tensions. The goal is to escape pain, but instead "he
or she lands in a pool of crocodiles." Furthermore, she says,
there is no benefit in deliberately flaunting one's weaknesses.
"Nothing is less acceptable to a congregation than seeing before
them a vivid portrayal of their own potential for unacceptable behavior." But she adds:

> A multitude of pastors have demonstrated that through
> growth in personal identity and careful nurturing of the
> potential of the congregation to grow in understanding, it is
> possible to step down from the pedestal with dignity and lead
> the congregation in a realistic Christian ministry. . . . By
> avoiding some of the defenses which impair relationships and
> by being honest about limitations and abilities, the pastor
> will go a long way to diminish the pedestal effect.[1]

Reducing the pedestal does involve self-disclosure. Like
other people, pastors are often hesitant to reveal themselves to
their people for fear that they may not be liked, accepted, or
respected.[2] Also the ministerial image that church people place
upon their pastor is intertwined with their own anxieties, needs,
and hopes.[3] Pastors need to address those underlying factors,
both in themselves and in their congregations, that contribute to
the unrealistic features of their relationship.

Emory Griffin, a professor at Wheaton College, writes that

---

[1] Lovett, pp. 90-91.

[2] John Powell discusses this with clarity and insight in
Why Am I Afraid to Tell You Who I Am? (Niles, IL: Argus Communications, 1969).

[3] Holifield, pp. 377-78.

he has a picture on his office wall of a turtle with an elongated

neck. The caption reads: "Behold the turtle who makes progress

only when he sticks his neck out." Although many would say that

the turtle is an example of what not to be--retreating into his

shell because he is fearful of exposing himself to others--Griffin

feels that this funny-looking creature is a model of appropriate

disclosure.

> Picture two turtles--face to face--with their heads almost
> completely hidden. One turtle extends his neck just a bit.
> If the other turtle responds in kind, then the first one
> ventures out some more. In a series of minute movements the
> first turtle ends up with his head in the sunshine, but only
> if his counterpart follows his lead. At any time he's pre-
> pared to slow the progression, come to a complete stop, or even
> back off.[1]

This illustrates the principle of reciprocity. Self-disclosure is

not best as a solo act. The leader takes the initial risk and is

slightly ahead of the norm--testing, probing, hoping. But another

principle is evident in that the process is gradual. It takes

time. In order for a minister to have friendships among his members,

he must hold in balance such polarities as his special relationships

and his universal commitments, his personal involvement and ethical

standards, his personal needs and his sacrificial service.[2]

But when a minister discloses himself and develops closer

relationships, Ron Flowers testifies, it can open up one's ministry

to greater effectiveness. Deeper feelings of compassion emerge.

The church program operates more smoothly. Sinners are drawn

---

[1] Emory A. Griffin, "Self-disclosure: How Far Should a Leader Go?" _Leadership_ 1 (Spring 1980):130.

[2] Larry Graham, p. 487.

magnetically to the church as a theater of grace. Church members become more honest, open, and comfortable with the pastor and themselves. The pastor feels better about himself. Flowers says, "I was trusting them with the real me, and they were accepting me, showing me love!"[1]

Here SDA pastors can take the initiative in cultivating the congregation as a support resource. Based on the theological presupposition that the elders of the church are in essence fellow ministers, the pastor might well develop a support group among them.[2] Friendship, working relationships, and other kinds of groups can be very supportive particularly for certain kinds of problems. Speed Leas offers a detailed plan to pastors for negotiating their roles and time commitments with the congregation.[3] Other studies indicate that discussion between laity and clergy over matters of role expectations and methods used actually increases consensus between them. The report says, "A significant correlation exists between the amount of discussion and the increase in laymen-minister agreement."[4] It could be quite helpful for a conference

---

[1]Flowers, pp. 12-13. Other writings on reducing the pedestal and its benefits are Paul G. Johnson, Buried Alive (Richmond, VA: John Knox Press, 1968); Carlyle Marney, Priests to Each Other (Valley Forge, PA: Judson Press, 1974).

[2]For another plan, see Henry B. Adams, "Effectiveness in Ministry--A Proposal for Lay-Clergy Collegiality," Christian Ministry, January 1971, pp. 32-35.

[3]Leas, Time Management, pp. 56-89.

[4]Paul S. Higgins and James E. Dittes, "Change in Laymen's Expectations of the Minister's Roles," Ministry Studies 2 (February 1968):4-23. There are several books written for lay people to help them understand the work of the pastor and learn how to be supportive: G. Curtis Jones, The Naked Shepherd (Waco, TX: Word, 1979); William E. Hulme, Your Pastor's Problems (Garden City, NY: Doubleday

pastor's pastor to assist in this negotiation. Others speak of training the congregation to carry on a more effective caring ministry for one another, including the pastor.[1] Certainly in a number of judicious ways, a pastor can find support right in his own congregation. And it is probably a resource more available than any other except wife and family.

Conference Administrative Resources

Methods of management and administration form another whole field of study. But it is important to at least mention that the way conferences conduct their business with pastors and churches is a significant factor in the pastor's morale, stress, and the degree of support he feels. One major area that needs to be re-considered by many conferences is the whole process of goal-setting, promotion, defining success, and evaluation of pastors. One author says:

> The judicatories closer to the local church give off mixed signals. They are more conscious of the need of institutional success, and keep the pastor's eyes focused on more money and more members but at the same time constantly feed him signals and models which suggest that institutional success is not what it is all about after all. This double kind of incongruent signal therefore contributes to the pastor's role confusion.[2]

The expectations of administrators need to be clarified. Further-more, writers on the subject of burn-out repeatedly point out that

---

and Company, 1966; Minneapolis: Augsburg Publishing House, 1967); Lucille Lavender, They Cry Too! (Wheaton, IL: Tyndale House Publishers, 1979).

[1]Paul, pp. 112-20; Jay Lane Beavers, "Building a Support Community for People in Crisis" (D.Min. dissertation, Southern Methodist University, 1975).

[2]Jud, Mills, and Burch, p. 120.

externally imposed goals are a definite contributing factor to burn-out.[1] Workers need to be the authentic source of their own choices. When success is defined in terms of an industrial model of statistics, it tends to encourage competition rather than cooperation. The evaluation of pastors needs to be done on a much more comprehensive basis. It needs to include important things a minister does that are not statistical. There are a number of models being suggested that would help to improve this procedure.[2]

The ministers who met with Bradford in Washington, D.C., mentioned that the position of the pastor needed to be enhanced.[3] Since he plays a key role in the work of the church, he should not be looked upon as the most insignificant of all positions in con-trast to all conference positions. Pastors need to be treated as professionals. One pastor wrote: "How can a pastor become im-portant enough in the church structure so he will not seem un-successful if he remains a pastor for life?" In the ICM study of pastoral morale the question was asked, "What changes would you like to see in the profession of pastoral ministry?" Some of the responses that ranked the highest included:

---

[1]E.g., Freudenberger, p. 19. Some good books that outline the principles of goal-setting, etc., that take into consideration theology and the uniqueness of the church include Richard G. Hutcheson, Jr., Wheel Within the Wheel: Confronting the Management Crisis of the Pluralistic Church (Atlanta: John Knox Press, 1979); Robert C. Worley, Dry Bones Breathe! (Chicago: The Center for the Study of Church Organizational Behavior, 1978). This latter source is addressed to the local church, but principles also apply to conferences.

[2]Judy, pp. 40-61; Hutcheson, chapter 11; Loren B. Mead, Evaluation: Of, by, for, and to the Clergy (Washington, D.C.: Alban Institute, 1977).

[3]"Emphasis on Pastoral Ministries" report.

Raise professional level with more continuing education and
    in-service education
Less promotion of conference programs
More emphasis on soul-winning
Decrease pastor's multiple roles, less administrative work, and
    increase lay responsibility
More understanding and sensitivity from the conference
Increase spiritual emphasis
Reduce multi-church districts
Less administrative direction
More opportunities for inter-relationships with other Adventist
    pastors
More input from pastors in setting conference goals[1]

Most of all, conference leaders should encourage free and
open communication so pastors can discuss the issues and make suggestions without fear of sanctions. They could also provide and
encourage the use of the above resources, neither apathetically nor
as a handed-down requirement. Working together as colleagues and
treating each other with respect is an effective support in itself.

Conclusion

In this project we have expressed the vulnerabilities of
ministers and their need for support. We have reflected upon the
theological implications of the situation and the proposal for
relief. The ministers of the SDA Church in North America were
allowed to express their perceptions and opinions regarding the
effectiveness of the support system they presently have. Some of
the efforts to provide support that already have been tried were
investigated. Finally, a design for a support system for the SDA
Church in North America was outlined.

Though it may seem that the proposed support system is almost overdone, it must be remembered that not all methods are used

---

[1]Dudley, Cummings, and Clark, p. 16.

by any one minister. Each resource can best serve specific kinds
of needs. Conferences need to evaluate their own situations and
implement those supports that fit. For instance, some conferences
may have a number of professional counselors available; others may
have to deal with great distances that would prevent ready access
to counselors. In such conferences there is the need to put together a support system for their isolated pastors that might draw
more heavily on congregational or local resources, the pastor's
pastor, the telephone, and maybe extra sabbatical time when needed
contacts could be made. The use of the various support resources
is also partly determined by individual and personal preferences.
The best support systems are those that have as many different resources available as possible. Conferences have a responsibility
to provide as many as they can. George Anderson was director of
the Academy of Religion and Health when he wrote this moving
appeal:

> We need to restore the concept of the church denomination as a
> community of individuals who have joined together for a common
> task. In a Christian community there is no place for a self-
> righteous hierarchy, or for disregard or ignorance of another's
> problems, or for hate or condemnation of a brother who has be-
> come spiritually sick. A Christian community should be a heal-
> ing community where the weaknesses of all may be known but un-
> uttered, where the strength that comes from genuine love brings
> relief and healing. The manner by which a church denomination
> serves the deep-seated needs of its clergy is a fair indication
> of its worth as a community of Christ. At the risk of sounding
> trite I suggest that we should remember that a church is as
> strong as its weakest link. When the weak link is one of its
> own clergy, the need for support becomes obvious. From the
> viewpoint of sound organizational practice, one might expect
> a church to take steps to remedy the matter. But in minister-
> ing to ministers we must be stirred by something much higher
> than a desire to preserve the church's reputation. The supreme
> motivation must be love.[1]

---

[1]George C. Anderson, "Who is Ministering to Ministers?"
Christianity Today, January 18, 1963, p. 7.

Pastors also have a responsibility to care for their own needs. Many may look upon these resources and think of the risks they entail. Some fear they may be betrayed or their reputation or job may be threatened. But there is risk entering into any relationship. Some support methods could have negative results. But a person never achieves his growth or fulfillment potential if he constantly isolates himself for fear of the risk. Edgar Mills says:

> One reason intentional ministries are lost is that they are done in isolation: each minister striving more or less alone to do an endless job against powerful resistance (usually inside as well as outside the minister). Firm resolve and heroic dedication are eventually undermined by solitary struggle.
> In contrast to this experience is that of people who begin to work together, to share their ministries (and often their lives), and who thereby gain both insight and support for intentionality.[1]

Furthermore, in the absence of support resources, we more frequently face that periodic regret of a minister who drops out. He is lost to the service of God, either because he could not take the stress anymore or because he has broken health, is bitter, or has used some unacceptable coping method.

Ministry will never be easy. There will always be sacrifices to make.

> The more dedicated, intelligent and sensitive a minister is, the more he will be wearied by the tedium of the daily rounds, frustrated by his frequent inability to get things done, harassed by the petulant, grumbling, meddlesome members of which every parish has its share. Every day he will die a little under the weight of his cross. He will be many times tempted to flee from such ordeals. But he remains on the job because he knows that the parish--not the bishopric, the professorship, the executive office or any other laudable

---

[1]Edgar W. Mills, "Intentionality and the Ministry," The Journal of Pastoral Care 28 (June 1974):79.

ministerial post--is the arena where Christ's battle for the world must be fought.[1]

Of course, all these other positions have their place in the work of God, but the local church and, consequently, the local pastor is central in the task of reaching the world for Christ. Let us "bear one another's burdens, and so fulfill the law of Christ"!

Personal Postscript

As I was writing this last chapter, in startling coincidence, I was visited by the person referred to in the first words of the introduction to this paper. The visit was totally unexpected for he lives across the country and we had not contacted one another for some time. In the course of our conversation he remarked that he found it very strange when he reflected on how he had started out so committed to one direction of life, but ended in a completely different place. He still wonders how he got where he is. Perhaps this man would not be so far from his original call to ministry if there had been some effective means of support during the time of his crisis.

---

[1]"Ministers Are Not Quitters" (editorial), The Christian Century, December 5, 1962, p. 1471.

APPENDICES

and

BIBLIOGRAPHY

APPENDIX A

STRESS AND BURN-OUT INVENTORIES

1. Clergy Life Changes Rating Scale

2. Stressful Work Conditions

3. Stress in Everyday Living

4. Typical Strain Responses

5. Decile Groups for the Diagnostic Questionnaires

STRESS AND BURN-OUT INVENTORIES

Complete each of the following inventories. Then add your score for each one and refer to the chart of "Decile Groups for the Diagnostic Questionnaires" on page 207. On this chart you will find an indication of the level of stress you may be experiencing.

Clergy Life Changes Rating Scale

Source: Roy M. Oswald, Director of Training and Field Studies, The Alban Institute, Inc., 1981.

For each of the events below which you consider yourself to have experienced directly during the past twelve months, transfer its "Average Value" to the line in the "Your Score" column. Then add these for your total Life Change Score. The following Life Change Rating Scale was adapted from the Holmes/Rahe Scale and field tested with clergy groups from various denominations.

Event	Average Value	Your Score
Death of spouse	100	_____
Divorce	73	_____
Marital separation	65	_____
Death of close family member	63	_____
Personal injury or illness	53	_____
Marriage	50	_____
Serious decline in church attendance	49	_____
Geographical relocation	49	_____
Segment of congregation meeting privately to discuss your resignation	47	_____
Immediate family member starts drinking heavily	46	_____
Marital reconciliation	45	_____
Retirement	45	_____
Change in health of family member	44	_____
Problem with children	42	_____
Pregnancy	40	_____
Sex difficulties	39	_____
Alienation from one's Board/Council/Session/ Vestry	39	_____
Gain of new family member	39	_____
New job in new line of work	38	_____
Change in financial state	38	_____
Death of close friend	37	_____
Increased arguing with spouse	35	_____
Merger of two or more congregations	35	_____

Event	Average Value	Your Score
Parish in serious financial difficulty	32	_____
Mortgage over $50,000 (home)	31	_____
Difficulty with member of church staff (Associates, Organist, Choir Director, Secretary, Janitor, etc.)	31	_____
Foreclosure of mortgage or loan	30	_____
Church burns down	30	_____
New job in same line of work	30	_____
Son or daughter leaving home	29	_____
Trouble with in-laws	29	_____
An influential church member irate over something you did	29	_____
Slow, steady decline in church attendance . . .	29	_____
Outstanding personal achievement	28	_____
Introduction of new humnal to worship service	28	_____
Failure of church to make payroll	27	_____
Remodeling or building program	27	_____
Spouse begins or stops work	26	_____
Going away for a holiday	27	_____
Begin or end school	26	_____
Death of peer	26	_____
Receiving a call to another parish	26	_____
Change in living conditions	25	_____
Revision of personal habits	24	_____
Former pastor active in parish in negative way	24	_____
Difficulty with confirmation class	22	_____
Change in residence	20	_____
Change in schools	20	_____
Change in recreation	19	_____
Change in social activities	18	_____
Death/Moving away of good church leader	18	_____
Mortgage or loan less than $50,000 (home) . . .	17	_____
Change in sleeping habits	16	_____
Developing a new friendship	16	_____
Change in eating habits	15	_____
Stressful continuing education experience . . .	15	_____
Major program change	15	_____
Vacation at home	13	_____
Christmas	12	_____
Lent	12	_____
Easter	12	_____
Minor violations of the law	11	_____

Your Total: _____

Stressful Work Conditions

Source: Roy M. Oswald, Director of Training and Field Studies,
         The Alban Institute, Inc., 1981.

There frequently are day to day conditions at work which we find
stressful. On the items below, indicate how often each source of
stress is true for you by placing the appropriate number on the
blank beside the item.

| 1 - Never | | 4 - Often |
| 2 - Infrequently | 3 - So-so | 5 - Always |

_____ 1. The congregation and I disagree as to my role as pastor.

_____ 2. The governing board is unclear about what my job prior-
           ities ought to be.

_____ 3. I do not have a cadre of people in the congregation who
           support me.

_____ 4. A group of people in the congregation wish I would move
           elsewhere.

_____ 5. There are several members of my governing board who con-
           sistently oppose my perspectives on parish life.

_____ 6. Our church plant is in such bad shape that we consistently
           need to deal with maintenance problems.

_____ 7. The parish consistently has trouble meeting its financial
           obligations.

_____ 8. I lack confidence in our parish decision-making process.

_____ 9. There is conflict between my parish and the judicatory.

_____ 10. My governing board expects me to interrupt my work for new
           priorities.

_____ 11. I only get feedback when my performance is unsatisfactory.

_____ 12. Decisions or changes that affect me are made without my
           knowledge or involvement.

_____ 13. There are opposing factions in the congregation each of
           which expects my loyalty and support.

_____ 14. I am expected to accept the decisions of my judicatory
           without being told the rationale.

_____ 15. I must attend meetings to get my job done.

_____ 16. I have too much to do and too little time to do it.

_____ 17. I do not have enough work to do.

_____ 18. I feel over-qualified for the work I actually do.

_____ 19. I feel under-qualified for the work I actually do.

_____ 20. The people I work with (parishioners) do not understand the demands of my job.

_____ 21. I have unsettled conflicts with the people I work with (staff).

_____ 22. I spend my time "fighting fires" rather than working to a plan.

_____ 23. I don't receive the right amount of supervision (too much or too little) at work.

_____ 24. I don't have opportunity to use my knowledge and skills on my job.

25. The morale of the congregation is low.

_____ 26. There is a socio-economic/cultural gap between my congregation and its immediate neighborhood.

_____ 27. I appear unable to receive a call to another parish.

_____ 28. My job requires me to hire/fire/supervise personnel.

_____ Total Score

29. Are there ongoing sources of stress for you at work which are not included above? If so, please list them here.

Stress in Everyday Living

Source: Roy M. Oswald, Director of Training and Field Studies,
          The Alban Institute, Inc., 1981.

There are many on-going conditions of life at home and in our society
generally which we find stressful. Several potentially stress pro-
voking conditions are listed below. Please indicate how stressful
each of these is for you, personally, by placing appropriate number
on the blank beside the item.

1 - Not Stressful   3 - Moderately   4 - Very Stressful
2 - Somewhat Stressful   Stressful   5 - Extremely Stress-
                                                   ful

_____ 1. Noise (traffic, airplanes, neighbors, etc.)

_____ 2. Pollution.

_____ 3. Own standard of living and ability to make ends meet
           financially.

_____ 4. Crime and vandalism in my immediate neighborhood.

_____ 5. Law and order in society.

_____ 6. Personal long term ill health.

_____ 7. Long term ill health of family member or close friend.

_____ 8. Racial tensions.

_____ 9. Regular drug or alcohol abuse of family member or close
           friend.

_____ 10. Concern over future of own career.

_____ 11. Concern over values/behaviors of family members.

_____ 12. Political situation in this country.

_____ 13. Possibility of war.

_____ 14. Financing own retirement, children's education, etc.

_____ 15. Economic situation in this country.

_____ 16. Changing morals in our society (about family life,
            sexuality, etc.).

_____ TOTAL

       17. Are there on-going sources of stress for you at present
            (other than at work) which are not included above? If
            so, please list them here.

Typical Strain Responses

Source: Roy M. Oswald, Director of Training and Field Studies,
         The Alban Institute, Inc., 1981.

Our natural physical and psychological response to stress is referred
to as strain. The 24 items below are examples of strain responses.
That is, when we are experiencing stress, it is likely that we will
respond as described by one or more of these items. This instrument
is designed to help you become more aware of your strain response
patterns. It is not a complete list, by any means, but should provide
a point of departure for further investigations. Please assign a
value to each item according to how often it is true of your behavior
or feelings as follows:

                0 - Never   2 - Frequently
                1 - Infrequently   3 - Regularly

_____ 1. Eat too much.

_____ 2. Drink too much alcohol.

_____ 3. Smoke more than usual.

_____ 4. Feel tense, uptight, fidgety.

_____ 5. Feel depressed or remorseful.

_____ 6. Like myself less.

_____ 7. Have difficulty going to sleep or staying asleep.

_____ 8. Feel restless and unable to concentrate.

_____ 9. Have decreased interest in sex.

_____ 10. Have increased interest in sex.

_____ 11. Loss of appetite.

_____ 12. Feel tired/low energy.

_____ 13. Feel irritable.

_____ 14. Think about suicide.

_____ 15. Become less communicative.

_____ 16. Feel disoriented or overwhelmed.

_____ 17. Difficulty getting up in the morning.

_____ 18. Headaches.

_____ 19. Upset stomach.

_____ 20. Sweaty and/or trembling hands.

_____ 21. Shortness of breath and sighing.

_____ 22. Let things slide.

_____ 23. Misdirected anger.

_____ 24. Feel "unhealthy."

_____ TOTAL SCORE

Decile Groups for the Diagnostic Questionnaires

Source: Roy M. Oswald, Director of Training and Field Studies,
         The Alban Institute, Inc., 1981.

Place your scores from the previous inventories on this chart in order
to rate your level of stress.

Percentile	Life Changes Rating Scale	Stressful Work Conditions	Stresses of Everyday Living	Strain
Low Stress				
10	65	42	20	13
20	85	46	27	17
30	110	53	31	20
40	136	58	34	22
50	160	62	37	24
60	176	64	41	26
70	203	69	46	29
80	230	72	50	31
90	283	78	56	35
High Stress				

Scores in the 70 or 80 percentile range or higher can cause
some individuals to exceed their stress tolerance with resulting
physical and/or psychological reactions. Remember, however, that
this is only a general guideline. Each person has a different
threshold of stress. What is important is that you begin to recognize when your threshold level for stress is being reached or sur-
passed, and what things are causing you the most stress.

APPENDIX B

SELECTED COUNSELS OF ELLEN G. WHITE THAT RELATE

TO SUPPORT AND MINISTERS

Counsels of Ellen G. White

The duty to preserve health

"I am pained at heart as I see so many feeble ministers, so many on beds of sickness, and so many closing the scenes of their earthly history--men who have carried the burden of responsibility in the work of God, whose whole heart was in their work. The conviction that they must cease their labor in the cause they loved was far more painful to them than their sufferings from disease, or even death itself.

"Is it not time for us to understand that nature will not long suffer abuse without protesting? Our heavenly Father does not willingly afflict or grieve the children of men. He is not the author of sickness and death. He is the source of life; He would have men live, and He desires them to be obedient to the laws of life and health, that they may live." (Counsels on Health, p. 563.)

"As the true watchman goes forth, bearing precious seed, sowing beside all waters, weeping and praying, the burden of labor is very taxing to mind and heart. He cannot keep up the strain continuously, his soul stirred to the very depths, without wearing out prematurely. Strength and efficiency are needed in every discourse. And from time to time fresh supplies of things new and old need to be brought forth from the storehouse of God's word. This will import life and power to the hearers. God does not want you to become so exhausted that your efforts have no freshness or life.

"Those who are engaged in constant mental labor, whether in study or preaching, need rest and change. The earnest student is constantly taxing the brain, too often while neglecting physical exercise, and as the result the bodily powers are enfeebled and mental effort is restricted. Thus the student fails of accomplishing the very work that he might have done had he labored wisely." (Ibid., pp. 563-64.)

"If they worked intelligently, giving both mind and body a due share of exercise, ministers would not so readily succumb to disease. If all our workers were so situated that they could spend a few hours each day in outdoor labor, and felt free to do this, it would be a blessing to them; they would be able to discharge more successfully the duties of their calling. . . .

"Some of our ministers feel that they must every day perform some labor that they can report to the conference, and as the result of trying to do this, their efforts are too often weak and inefficient. They should have periods of rest, of entire freedom from taxing labor. But these cannot take the place of daily physical exercise.

"Brethren, when you take time to cultivate your garden, thus gaining the exercise you need to keep the system in good working order, you are just as much doing the work of God as in holding meetings. God is our Father, He loves us, and He does not require any of His servants to abuse their bodies." (Ibid., p. 564.)

"Our workers should use their knowledge of the laws of life and health. They should study from cause to effect. Read the best authors on these subjects, and obey religiously that which your reason tells you is truth." (Ibid., p. 566; see also <u>Gospel Workers</u>, pp. 239-240, 242.)

Danger from overwork

"When the apostles returned from their first missionary journey, the Saviour's command to them was, 'Come ye yourselves apart into a desert place, and rest awhile.' They had been putting their whole souls into labor for the people, and this was exhausting their physical and mental strength. It was their duty to rest.

"Christ's words of compassion are spoken to His workers to-day just as surely as to His disciples. 'Come ye yourselves apart, . . . and rest awhile,' He says to those who are worn and weary. It is not wise to be always under the strain of work and excitement, even in ministering to men's spiritual needs; for in this way personal piety is neglected, and the powers of mind and soul and body are overtaxed. Self-denial is required of the servants of Christ, and sacrifices must be made; but God would have all study the laws of health, and use reason when working for Him, that the life which He has given may be preserved.

"Though Jesus could work miracles, and had empowered His disciples to work miracles, He directed His worn servants to go apart into the country and rest. . . ." (<u>Gospel Workers</u>, p. 243.)

"The servants of Christ are not to treat their health indifferently. Let no one labor to the point of exhaustion, thereby disqualifying himself for future effort. Do not try to crowd into one day the work of two. At the end, those who work carefully and wisely will be found to have accomplished as much as those who so expend their physical and mental strength that they have no deposit from which to draw in time of need.

"God's work is world-wide; it calls for every jot and tittle of the ability and power that we have. There is danger that His workers will abuse their powers as they see that the field is ripe for the harvest; but the Lord does not require this. After His servants have done their best, they may say, The harvest truly is great, and the laborers are few; but God 'knoweth our frame; He remembereth that we are dust.'" (Ibid., p. 244.)

"God is merciful, full of compassion, reasonable in His requirements. He does not ask us to pursue a course of action that will result in the loss of physical health or the enfeebling of the mental powers. He would not have us work under a pressure and strain until exhaustion follows, with prostration of the nerves.

". . . There are those who might be with us to-day, to help forward the cause both at home and in foreign lands, had they but realized before it was too late that they were in need of rest. These workers saw that the field is large and the need for workers great, and they felt that at any cost they must press on. When nature uttered a protest, they paid no heed, but did double the work they should have done; and God laid them in the grave to rest until the last trump shall sound to call the righteous forth to immortality." (Ibid., p. 245.)

"Let not God be dishonored by breaking down the man in the process of educating him; for a broken-down, discouraged man is a burden to himself. To think that in any work that he may plan to do God will sustain him, while he piles upon himself studies and subjects himself to exposures that imperil health and life and violate the laws of nature, is contrary to the light that God has given. Nature will not be imposed upon. She will not forgive the injuries done to the wonderful, delicate machinery." (Medical Ministry, Mountain View, CA: Pacific Press Publishing Association, 1932; 1963, p. 79.)

Sharing the work

"Sometimes ministers do too much; they seek to embrace the whole work in their arms. It absorbs and dwarfs them; yet they continue to grasp it all. They seem to think that they alone are to work in the cause of God, while the members of the church stand idle. This is not God's order at all." (Evangelism, p. 113.)

"One man usually performs the labor which should be shared by two; for the work of the evangelist is necessarily combined with that of the pastor, bringing a double burden upon the worker in the field." (Testimonies for the Church, 4:260.)

"There are a few who are working day and night, depriving themselves of rest and social enjoyments, taxing the brain to the utmost, each performing the labor of three men, wearing away their valuable lives to do the work that others might do, but neglect. Some are too lazy to perform their part; many ministers are carefully preserving them- selves by shunning burdens, remaining in a state of inefficiency, and accomplishing next to nothing. Therefore those who realize the worth of souls, who appreciate the sacredness of the work and feel that it must go forward, are doing extra labor, making superhuman efforts, and using up their brain power to keep the work moving. Were the interest in the work and the devotion to it equally divided, were all who profess to be ministers diligently devoting their interest wholly to the cause, not saving themselves, the few earnest, God- fearing workmen who are fast wearing away their lives would be relieved of this high pressure upon them, and their strength might be preserved so that, when actually required, it would tell with double power, and produce far greater results than can now be seen while under the pressure of overwhelming care and anxiety. The Lord is not pleased with this inequality." (Ibid., 2:502-503.)

"The idea that the minister must carry all the burdens and do all the work, is a great mistake. Overworked and broken down, he may go into the grave, when, had the burden been shared as the Lord designed, he might have lived. That the burden may be distributed, an education must be given to the church by those who can teach the workers to follow Christ and to work as He worked." (Christian Service, pp. 68-69.)

Interdependence of human beings

"We are all woven together in the great web of humanity, and whatever we can do to benefit and uplift others will reflect in blessing upon ourselves. The law of mutual dependence runs through all classes of society." (Mind, Character, and Personality, 2 vols., Nashville: Southern Publishing Association, 1977, 2:431.)

"In the Lord's plan human beings have been made necessary to one another. If all would do their utmost to help those who need their help, their unselfish sympathy and love, what a blessed work might be done. To everyone God has entrusted talents. These talents we are to use to help one another to walk in the narrow path. In this work each one is connected with the other, and all are united with Christ. It is by unselfish service that we improve and increase our talent." (Ibid., 2:431.)

"In our intercourse as Christians, we lose much by lack of sympathy one with another, by a want of sociability. He who talks of independence, and shuts himself up to himself, is not filling the position that God designed he should. We are all children of God, mutually dependent upon one another for happiness. The claims of God and of humanity are upon us. It is the proper cultivation of the social elements of our nature that brings us in sympathy with our brethren, and affords us happiness in our efforts to bless others." ("Christian Work," Review and Herald, October 10, 1882, p. 625.)

God works through the human agent

"The Lord has need of you. He does not do His work without the co-operation of the human agent." (Testimonies for the Church, 6:40.)

"Angelic agencies, though invisible, are co-operating with visible human agencies, forming a relief-association with men. . . .
    "Human agencies are the hands of heavenly instrumentalities; for heavenly angels employ human hands in practical ministry. Human agencies as hand-helpers are to work out the knowledge and use the facilities of heavenly beings. By uniting with these powers that are omnipotent, we are benefited by their higher education and experience. Thus, as we become partakers of the divine nature, and separate selfishness from our lives, special talents for helping one another are granted us. This is Heaven's way of administering saving power." ("Help for Our Scandinavian Institutions," Review and Herald, March 19, 1901, p. 177.)

"The Holy Spirit is to work through human agencies. A partnership between God and the workers must be maintained. Man works because God works in him; all the efficiency and power is of God. Yet God has so arranged that all the responsibility rests with the human instrument. These are the appointed conditions of partnership. Men are required to move among men, doing a divine work." ("'If Ye Know These Things, Happy Are Ye If Ye Do Them,'" Review and Herald, November 4, 1902, p. 9.

Support for ministers

"We are too indifferent in regard to one another. Too often we forget
that our fellow laborers are in need of strength and cheer. Take care
to assure them of your interest and sympathy. Help them by your
prayers, and let them know that you do it. . . .
         "Regard yourselves as missionaries, first of all, among your
fellow workers. . . ." (Ministry of Healing, pp. 492-93.)

"Help those who have erred, by telling them of your experiences. Show
how, when you made grave mistakes, patience, kindness, and helpfulness
on the part of your fellow workers gave you courage and hope."
(Ibid., p. 494.)

"We are dependent upon one another, closely bound together by the ties
of human brotherhood.

> Heaven forming each on other to depend,
> A master or a servant or a friend,
> Bids each on other for assistance call,
> Till one man's weakness grows the strength of all."
> (Ibid., p. 496.)

Divine counselor most important

         "When in trouble, many think they must appeal to some earthly
friend, telling him their perplexities, and begging for help. Under
trying circumstances unbelief fills their hearts, and the way seems
dark. And all the time there stands beside them the mighty Counselor
of the ages, inviting them to place their confidence in Him. Jesus,
the great Burden-bearer, is saying, 'Come unto Me, and I will give
you rest.' Shall we turn from Him to uncertain human beings, who
are as dependent upon God as we ourselves are?" (Ibid., p. 512.)

"The solemn work in which we are engaged demands of us a strong,
united effort under divine leadership.
         "The Lord desires His workers to counsel together, not to
move independently. Those who are set as ministers and guides to
the people should pray much when they meet together. This will give
wonderful help and courage, binding heart to heart and soul to soul,
leading every man to unity and peace and strength in his endeavors.
         "Our strength lies in taking our burdens to the great Burden
Bearer. God confers honor on those who come to Him and ask Him for
help, in faith believing that they will receive.
         "Human help is feeble. But we may unite in seeking help
and favor from Him who has said, 'Ask, and it shall be given you; seek,
and ye shall find; knock, and it shall be opened unto you.' Divine
power is infallible. Then let us come to God, pleading for the
guidance of His Holy Spirit. Let our united prayers ascend to the
throne of grace. Let our requests be mingled with praise and thanks-
giving." (Testimonies to Ministers and Gospel Workers, Mountain View,
CA: Pacific Press Publishing Association, 1923; 1962), p. 485.)

APPENDIX C

INFORMATION ON "THE SUPPORT SYSTEM OF LOCAL

CHURCH PASTORS" QUESTIONNAIRE

1. Methodology of sample formulation, questionnaire
   construction, and data retrieval.

2. Sample questionnaire.

3. Table of objectives.

4. Sample letters.

5. Percentages and means for each question.

6. Additional comments written by the respondents.

Methodology

Sample formulation

The ICM's original church growth study was based on a population of all White, Black and Hispanic churches in the North American Division which were in existence at the close of 1978. The method for drawing the sample is indicated in the following excerpt from the written research proposal:

> The sample size for this study has been determined by the standard power formula (Welkowitz, Ewen & Cohen, 1976, chap. 13) as calculated on the APL program at the Andrews University computing center, Berrien Springs, Michigan. The significance criteria was set at the .05 level of rejection which means that there is only a 5 percent probability that any significant correlations could have occurred by chance. The population effect size was set at $\pm$ .30 which means that the researchers are only interested in multiple correlations larger than $\pm$ .30, or accounting for more than 9 percent of the variance in the church-growth rate.
> The power for this study was set at .95 which will provide a 95 percent probability of finding statistical significance if a multiple correlation greater than $\pm$ .30 exists in the population. Entering these three values for each of the three populations into the power equation yields the following sample sizes: . . . 155 white English-speaking churches, 97 Black churches, and 66 Hispanic churches. To draw this sample the churches of each of the three populations were numbered separately, and the desired number were selected by computer using the APL random number general program of the Andrews University computing center. Inspection of the randomly-drawn sample churches reveals that they are distributed in such a way as to represent all areas of the division, urban and rural churches, large and small churches, and fast-growing and declining churches. (Roger L. Dudley, "A Study of Factors Relating to Church Growth in the North American Division of Seventh-day Adventists," A Research Proposal commissioned by the General Conference of Seventh-day Adventists, July 1979, pp. 13-14.)

Actually ninety-nine Black churches were used, making a total of 320 churches in the original sample. Twenty-five of these churches were disbanded or otherwise unavailable. This left 295 for the working sample. The number of individual pastors was smaller yet since in fourteen cases the same person pastored two churches within the sample.

Thus there were 281 pastors in the original working sample. Eighty-five
percent (or 239) responded to the initial surveys. This became the new
working sample for the collection of additional data which could be
integrated with that already in hand, and thus the base for this
questionnaire. Before mailing the questionnaire, six more pastors
were eliminated--one due to death, four because they had moved to
another part of the world, and one because the individual was not
a minister. Finally, 233 questionnaires were mailed.

Questionnaire construction

Before starting to write the questionnaire considerable time
was spent getting acquainted with the issues. A thorough bibliographical
search of books, periodicals, dissertations, and tapes was completed.
Conversations and informal interviews were conducted with ministers,
teachers, colleagues, and friends. My own personal experience was
analyzed. Previous questionnaires of the ICM were studied for design
and content. All or part of the following books were read: Earl R.
Babbie, The Practice of Social Research, 2nd edition (Belmont, CA:
Wadsworth Publishing Co., 1979); James Engel, How Can I Get Them to
Listen? (Grand Rapids: Zondervan, 1977); A. N. Oppenheim, Question-
naire Design and Attitude Measurement (New York: Basic Books, 1966);
Mildred Parten, Surveys, Polls, and Samples: Practical Procedures
(New York: Cooper Square Publishers, 1950; 1966); John L. Phillips,
Jr., Statistical Thinking (San Francisco: W. H. Freeman and Co.,
1971; 1973).

The basic hypothesis as stated in the project proposal is
that an evaluation of the current situation of the local pastor in
the SDA Church in North America will indicate a need for an improved

psycho-social support system in the Church. Specific objectives for the questionnaire have been discussed in chapter 3. A table showing which objectives are achieved in each question follows in this appendix. The initial brainstorming resulted in a list of about one hundred questions. They were reduced and revised about seven times with the help of various faculty members and the use of a pretest given to about twenty ministers in the Andrews University area.

Data retrieval

The address list of the sample of 233 ministers was updated according to the latest information. The envelopes were stamped with "Address Correction Requested" in order to obtain the proper addresses for subsequent mailings. Two cover letters were prepared for the first mailing--one by Roger Dudley, director of the ICM survey, and my own. My letter was personalized with the name of the minister in the salutation and was personally signed. The return envelope was addressed and had a commemorative stamp on it. (Those who live in Canada received two dimes for Canadian stamps for the return envelope.) The material was sent in #10 business envelopes and return envelopes were #9 business envelopes. Each questionnaire was coded with the church code used by the Institute for this sample.

Three mailings were sent, each one eliminating the names of those who had responded to the previous one. They were spaced two to three weeks apart. Samples of each of the letters sent with the mailings appear in this appendix. Returns were received from 85 percent of the questionnaires mailed and 70 percent of the original sample.

THE SUPPORT SYSTEM OF LOCAL CHURCH PASTORS

Please indicate your answers to the following questions.
Circle the <u>number</u> that represents your <u>current</u> opinion or situation.
In most questions you can choose from a scale between 1 and 5. Mark
only <u>one</u> answer.

1. To what degree has a time   0   1 2 3 4 5
    management program ever   Never   Not   Very
    been helpful to you in   seriously helpful   helpful
    reducing the frustrations   tried one
    of ministry?

2. How effective do you find personal   1 2 3 4 5
    Bible study, meditation, and prayer   Not   Very
    in coping with personal problems   effective   effective
    and frustrations in your ministry?

3. How helpful would it be to have   1 2 3 4 5
    supportive relationships with   Not   Very
    human beings?   helpful   helpful

4. To what degree do the following
    factors keep you from seeking   Does <u>not</u>   Definitely
    help from human beings regarding   keep me from   keeps me from
    sensitive problems?   seeking help   seeking help
    A. fear of wrong advice   1 2 3 4 5

    B. can't trust others   1 2 3 4 5

    C. might affect my reputation   1 2 3 4 5

    D. should depend on God   1 2 3 4 5

    E. no one to go to   1 2 3 4 5

    F. am a private individual   1 2 3 4 5

    G. might affect my job security   1 2 3 4 5

    H. believe we should solve our   1 2 3 4 5
        sensitive problems by ourselves

    I. it wouldn't really help   1 2 3 4 5

    J. other_____   1 2 3 4 5

5. To what degree do you have   0   1 2 3 4 5
    some relative, other than   Have Relation-   Relationship
    your spouse, in whom you   no   ship <u>not</u>   very
    confide?   one   helpful   helpful

continue on reverse side

6. To what extent did a more experienced minister have a nurturing relationship with you in your early ministry?

0	1	2	3	4	5
Had no one	Relation-ship not helpful				Relation-ship very helpful

7. To what degree do you <u>now</u> have an older, experienced minister to whom you look for guidance?

0	1	2	3	4	5
Have no one	Relation-ship not helpful				Relation-ship very helpful

8. How much do you nurture younger men in the ministry?

1	2	3	4	5
Never				Regularly

9. To what degree do you have a fellow pastor with whom you feel free to share sensitive personal problems?

0	1	2	3	4	5
Have no one	Relation-ship not helpful				Relation-ship very helpful

10. How much do you feel a sense of competition among the pastors in your conference?

1	2	3	4	5
No competition				Much competition

Sometimes pastors will get together in "support groups" or "growth groups" (either among SDAs or interfaith) for fellowship, learning, and support of one another:

11. How much involvement have you had with a regular support group among ministers?

1	2	3	4	5
None				A lot

If you had some involvement:
12. How often did the group meet? (Choose one answer)

1. every week
2. every other week
3. every month
4. every other month
5. less than every other month

13. How fulfilling and satisfying was the group to you?

1	2	3	4	5
Not fulfilling				Very fulfilling

14. What problems might there be with such a group? (Write your own answer.)

_____

_____

_____

15. To what degree would you consider time off for continuing education to be a strengthening, refreshing break in your ministry?

1	2	3	4	5
Not strengthening refreshing				Very strengthening refreshing

continue on next page

16. To what degree do you feel the conference leadership:

A. seems to treat the local pastor with the level of professionalism that his place deserves?

1 2 3 4 5
Not treated professionally — Treated professionally

B. seems to pressure you to reach conference goals?

1 2 3 4 5
No pressure — Very great pressure

C. seems to threaten your career as a minister when you are not able to reach goals or other expectations?

1 2 3 4 5
Not feel threatened at all — Feel very seriously threatened

17. How reluctant are you to go to one of your conference administrators for support in sensitive personal problems knowing that he has influence over your placement and career reputation?

1 2 3 4 5
Not reluctant at all — Very reluctant

18. How much of an advantage is it to seek support in sensitive personal problems from him because he has official power that could help you?

1 2 3 4 5
No advantage — Very great advantage

19. To what degree do you believe conference administrators are able to keep their roles of placement, supervision, and discipline distinct from a supportive role in order to be effective counselors?

1 2 3 4 5
Not able at all — Definitely able

20. To what degree do you perceive your conference president as:

A. a very close friend rather than one with whom you have a rather tense, obligatory relationship?

1 2 3 4 5
Obligatory relationship — Very close friendship

B. likely to think less of you if you go to him with a problem since you did not handle it yourself?

1 2 3 4 5
Will not think less of me — Will think less of me

C. likely to really listen to you and seriously consider what you say in his decision-making?

1 2 3 4 5
Ignores what I say — Seriously considers what I say

D. accessible to you time-wise to discuss your personal concerns?

1 2 3 4 5
Not accessible — Always accessible

E. seemingly more interested in your personal welfare than in the progress and success of the organization?

1 2 3 4 5
More in the organization — More in my personal welfare

continue on reverse side

21. To what degree do you perceive
     your ministerial secretary as:

     A. a very close friend rather   1 2 3 4 5
         than one with whom you have   Obligatory   Very close
         a rather tense, obligatory   relationship   friendship
         relationship?

     B. performing more administrative   1 2 3 4 5
         functions (assisting the president) Mostly   Mostly
         than "pastor's pastor" functions?   pastor's   administration
                                              pastor

     C. accessible to you time-wise to   1 2 3 4 5
         discuss your personal concerns?   Not   Always
                                              accessible   accessible

     D. an approachable, sympathetic,   1 2 3 4 5
         understanding person?   Not   Very
                                              approachable   approachable

     E. likely to keep confidential   1 2 3 4 5
         your conversations of a   Not keep it   Will keep it
         personal nature?   confidential   confidential

     F. likely to stand by you in   1 2 3 4 5
         case of differences with   Would not   Definitely would
         the administration?   stand by me   stand by me

     An advocate for the pastor would be someone
     who ministers in behalf of his personal needs
     whether it be counseling, facilitating colleague
     support and friendship, providing resource help,
     or referring to other resources.

22. If such an advocate was designated by
     the conference, how would you rate   Poorest   Best
     the following persons for the job?   suited   suited

     A. the conference president   1 2 3 4 5

     B. the ministerial secretary with a   1 2 3 4 5
         job description revised to omit
         administrative roles

     C. the ministerial secretary as   1 2 3 4 5
         his position now stands

     D. a totally new position in the   1 2 3 4 5
         conference office without
         administrative roles

     E. an authorized church pastor   1 2 3 4 5

     F. a professional counselor   1 2 3 4 5

     G. other _____   1 2 3 4 5

23. To what degree do you have close   0   1 2 3 4 5
     relationships with church members   Have Relation-   Relation-
     from whom you receive support, in   no   ship not   ship very
     a ministry to you?   one   helpful   helpful

continue on next page

24. How much have you used a professional   1 2 3 4 5
    counselor for your own needs?   Never   Very often

25. To what degree have the following   Definitely   Did not
    reasons kept you from going to a   kept me   keep me
    professional counselor?   from going   from going
    A. never had a problem needing   1 2 3 4 5
        such attention

    B. it was too expensive   1 2 3 4 5

    C. didn't know of a good one   1 2 3 4 5
        accessible to you

    D. feared someone you didn't want   1 2 3 4 5
        to know would find out

    E. you couldn't take time off   1 2 3 4 5

    F. other _____   1 2 3 4 5

26. To what degree have you had a   Have Relation-   Relation-
    friendly, mutually supportive   had ship not   ship very
    relationship with: no one helpful   helpful
    A. a non-SDA minister   0   1 2 3 4 5

    B. a non-SDA lay person   0   1 2 3 4 5

27. How often do you feel more free to   1 2 3 4 5
    confide with a non-SDA friend than   Never more   Always more
    with your own SDA associates?   free with   free with
                                          non-SDAs   non-SDAs

28. How often within the last year have
    you had a meaningful sharing time with: Times last year
    A. an older, experienced minister   0   1   2-3   4-6   6+

    B. a fellow pastor of a neighboring   0   1   2-3   4-6   6+
        district

    C. a relative other than your spouse   0   1   2-3   4-6   6+

    D. your conference president   0   1   2-3   4-6   6+

    E. your ministerial secretary   0   1   2-3   4-6   6+

    F. a supportive church member in   0   1   2-3   4-6   6+
        your congregation

    G. a lay person outside your congregation 0   1   2-3   4-6   6+

    H. a non-SDA minister   0   1   2-3   4-6   6+

    I. a non-SDA lay person   0   1   2-3   4-6   6+

    J. a professional counselor   0   1   2-3   4-6   6+

    K. a college or seminary teacher   0   1   2-3   4-6   6+

    L. other_____   0   1   2-3   4-6   6+

continue on reverse side

29. To what degree are you interested   Not   Very
    in using the following resources: interested   interested
    A. an older, experienced minister to   1 2 3 4 5
        consult

    B. more opportunities to work with and   1 2 3 4 5
        fellowship together with fellow pastors

    C. more opportunities for professional   1 2 3 4 5
        consultation among ministers on
        specialized ministry problems (as
        physicians do in the medical profession)

    D. a regular peer support group   1 2 3 4 5

    E. extra time off--like a sabbatical--   1 2 3 4 5
        to get yourself together

    F. a continuing education experience   1 2 3 4 5

    G. a person designated by the conference   1 2 3 4 5
        to be an advocate for pastor's needs

    H. deeper, more open friendships with   1 2 3 4 5
        your church members

    I. a professional counselor for more   1 2 3 4 5
        serious problems

30. How many churches do you have in your care? _____

31. What is(are) the current membership(s)? 1. _____ 2. _____ 3. _____

32. Which category are you in: 1. The only pastor of your church(es)
                                   2. Senior pastor on a multistaff
                                   3. Staff pastor on a multistaff

33. How many years have you been a local church pastor? _____

34. What is your current age? _____

35. Additional comments are welcome below:

Thank you very much for your time!

TABLE 9

OBJECTIVES FOR EACH QUESTION

Subject Area	Question Number	Relationship			Information Objectives				
		General Social	Deep Confiding	Unspecified	Available	Used	Effectiveness	Dynamics	Interest in Using
1. Personal	1					X	X		
coping meth.	2						X		
2. General	3			X			X		X
attitude	4A		X					X	
toward human	4B		X					X	
support	4C		X					X	
	4D		X					X	
	4E		X		X				
	4F		X					X	
	4G		X					X	
	4H		X					X	
	4I		X					X	
3. Relatives	5		X		X	(X)	X		
	28C			X		X			
4. Mentor	6			X	X	(X)		X	
	7			X	X	(X)		X	
	8			X	X				
	28A			X		X			
	29A			X					X
	28K			X		X			
5. Peer Pastor	9		X		X	(X)	X		
	10	X						X	
	28B			X		X			
	29B	X							X
	29C	X							X
6. Support	11			X		X			
groups	12			X		X			
	13			X			X		
	14			X				X	
	29D			X					X
7. Sabbatical	29E								X
8. Continuing	15						X		X
education	29F								X
9. General	16A	X						X	
relationship	16B	X						X	
with Conf.	16C	X						X	
leadership	17		X					X	
	18		X					X	
	19		X					X	

Subject Area	Question Number	Relationship			Information Objectives				
		General Social	Deep Confiding	Unspecified	Available	Used	Effectiveness	Dynamics	Interest in Using
10. Conference President	20A	X						X	
	20B		X					X	
	20C	X					X	X	
	20D			X	X			X	
	20E			X				X	
	22A			X			X		
	28D			X		X			
11. Conference Ministerial Secretary	21A	X						X	
	21B			X				X	
	21C			X	X			X	
	21D			X			(X)	X	
	21E		X					X	
	21F			X				X	
	22B			X			X		
	22C			X			X		
	28E			X		X			
12. Conference advocate concept	22D			X			X		
	22E			X			X		
	29G			X					X
13. Church members	23	X			X	(X)	X		
	28F			X		X			
	28G			X		X			
	29H			X					X
14. Professional counselors	22F			X			X		
	24		X			X			
	25A		X					X	
	25B		X					X	
	25C		X		X				
	25D		X					X	
	25E		X					X	
	28J			X		X			
	29I		X						X
15. Non-SDAs	26A	X			X	(X)	X		
	26B	X			X	(X)	X		
	27		X					X	
	28H			X		X			
	28I			X		X			

TABLE 10

PERCENTAGES AND MEANS FOR THE RESPONSES TO THE QUESTIONNAIRE
"THE SUPPORT SYSTEM OF LOCAL CHURCH PASTORS"

Item	Meaning	0	Meaning	Percentages for Each Response					Meaning	Mean (Zeros Excluded)
				1	2	3	4	5		
1. The helpfulness of a time management program	Never seriously tried one	31%	Not helpful	3%	9%	25%	19%	13%	Very helpful	3.45
2. Effectiveness of Bible study, meditation, and prayer	No response	0	Not effective	0	3	7	24	66	Very effective	4.54
3. Helpfulness of supportive relationships	"	1	Not helpful	1	2	14	29	53	Very helpful	4.32
4A. Fear of wrong advice	"	2	Not keep from seeking help	44	27	17	8	2	Keeps from seeking help	1.94
4B. Can't trust others	"	0	"	25	21	32	13	9	"	2.60
4C. Might affect my reputation	"	3	"	33	21	20	17	6	"	2.42
4D. Should depend on God	"	3	"	34	18	19	15	11	"	2.49
4E. No one to go to	"	4	"	20	16	15	23	22	"	3.12
4F. Am a private individual	"	3	"	30	20	27	13	7	"	2.45
4G. Might affect my job security	"	3	"	40	21	17	12	7	"	2.24
4H. Believe we should solve our sensitive problems ourselves	"	3	"	35	20	26	12	4	"	2.28
4I. It wouldn't really help	"	3	"	39	23	22	9	4	"	2.12

TABLE 10--Continued

Item	Meaning	0	Meaning	1	2	3	4	5	Meaning	Mean (Zeros Excluded)
					Percentages for Each Response					
5. Confide in relative other than spouse	Have no one	30%	Relationship not helpful	9%	11%	20%	18%	12%	Relationship very helpful	3.18
6. Nurturing relationship with experienced minister in early ministry	Had no one	17	"	7	11	20	22	23	"	3.54
7. Guidance by an experienced minister now	Have no one	32	"	11	14	20	13	10	"	2.96
8. Nurture younger ministers	No response	3	Never	5	24	25	28	15	Regularly	3.26
9. Fellow pastor to share with	Have no one	25	Relationship not helpful	7	15	18	20	15	Relationship very helpful	3.26
10. Feel competition among pastor	No Response	1	None	25	25	25	16	8	Much	2.55
11. Involvement with support group	"	1	"	37	23	17	17	5	"	2.30
12. How often the group met	"	37	Every week	5	2	32	7	17	Less than every other month	3.49
13. Fulfillment from the group	"	37	Not Fulfilling	3	14	20	19	7	Very fulfilling	3.20
14. (See Table 4)										
15. Continuing education as strengthening, refreshing	"	1	Not strengthening	3	7	19	23	47	Very strengthening	4.06
16A. Conference leadership-- treats pastor professionally	"	1	No	5	17	20	33	24	Yes	3.56

TABLE 10--Continued

Item	Meaning	0	Meaning	1	2	3	4	5	Meaning	Mean (Zeros Excluded)
				Percentages for Each Response						
16B. Pressures for goals	No response	0%	No	9%	26%	31%	25%	9%	Very much	2.98
16C. Threatens career over goals	"	1	No threat	35	23	23	13	5	Great threat	2.30
17. Reluctant to go to administrator for support	"	1	Not reluctant	21	12	20	21	25	Very reluctant	3.17
18. Advantage to seek support from administrator	"	1	No advantage	29	23	27	14	6	Very great advantage	2.46
19. Administrators ability to keep roles distinct	"	2	Not able at all	10	31	36	15	6	Definitely able	2.74
20A. Perceive conference president as close friend or obligatory relationship	"	0	Obligatory relationship	13	16	23	32	16	Very close friendship	3.23
20B. Think less of you if you go to him with a problem	"	0	Will not think less	21	29	26	17	7	Will think less	2.58
20C. Really listen to you	"	1	Ignores you	8	17	20	30	24	Listens	3.44
20D. Accessible time-wise	"	1	Not accessible	6	20	21	32	20	Always accessible	3.40
20E. More interested in you or organization	"	1	More in organization	17	21	42	14	5	More in me	2.68
21A. Perceive ministerial secretary as close friend or obligatory relationship	"	4	Obligatory relationship	8	15	28	30	15	Very close friendship	3.30
21B. More admin. or pastor's pastor functions	"	4	Pastor's pastor	7	19	22	32	16	Mostly admin.	3.32
21C. Accessible time-wise	"	4	Not access.	6	21	25	28	16	Always acces	3.27

TABLE 10--Continued

Item	Meaning	0	Meaning	1	2	3	4	5	Meaning	Mean (Zeros Excluded)
				Percentages for Each Response						
21D. Approachable	No response	4%	Not so	4%	13%	19%	34%	26%	Very much	3.67
21E. Keeps confidences	"	6	Does not	5	10	26	27	26	Does	3.63
21F. Would stand by you	"	6	Would not	9	18	44	16	7	Would	2.93
22A. Persons for conf. advocate the conference president	"	4	Poorest suited	29	20	20	16	11	Best suited	2.58
22B. Ministerial sec. with revised job description	"	7	"	6	8	23	30	26	"	3.68
22C. Ministerial sec. as pres.	"	6	"	15	28	29	16	5	"	2.65
22D. New position	"	6	"	14	11	13	12	44	"	3.64
22E. Authorized church pastor	"	6	"	20	17	25	20	12	"	2.85
22F. Professional counselor	"	6	"	17	12	24	19	22	"	3.18
23. Support from church members	Have no one	7	Not helpful	6	15	28	26	18	Very helpful	3.40
24. Used a prof. counselor	No response	1	Never	77	12	5	5	0	Very often	1.38
25A. Not use prof. counselor: had no problem needing one	"	3	Kept me from going	42	12	15	11	17	Did not keep me from going	2.45
25B. It was too expensive	"	13	"	21	8	11	11	36	"	3.36
25C. Didn't know of one	"	14	"	29	10	13	8	26	"	2.89
25D. Feared someone would find out	"	14	"	15	9	13	11	38	"	3.58
25E. Couldn't take time off	"	15	"	11	6	13	8	47	"	3.87

TABLE 10--Continued

Item	Percentages for Each Response								Mean (Zeros Excluded)
	Meaning	0	Meaning	1	2	3	4	5	Meaning	
26A. Support from non-SDA minister	Had no one	37%	Not helpful	10%	14%	16%	15%	8%	Very helpful	2.98
26B. Support from non-SDA lay person	"	42	"	9	13	16	10	10	"	2.98
27. More free with non-SDAs	No response 3		Never more	55	12	17	7	6	Always more	1.92

Percentages for Each Response

Item	Times last year				
Meaningful sharing time with:	0	1	2-3	4-6	6+
28A. An older, experienced minister	25%	16%	40%	3%	11%
28B. A fellow pastor of a neighboring district	23	16	33	15	13
28C. A relative other than your spouse	33	12	31	12	12
28D. Your conference president	33	26	30	5	5
28E. Your ministerial secretary	39	27	24	5	4
28F. A supportive church member in your congregation	16	16	24	22	22
28G. A lay person outside your congregation	56	12	21	5	5
28H. A non-SDA minister	65	17	14	3	2
28I. A non-SDA lay person	65	13	15	3	4
28J. A professional counselor	87	5	6	0	2
28K. A college or seminary teacher	71	14	11	2	2

TABLE 10--Continued

Item	Meaning	0	Meaning	\multicolumn{5}{c}{Percentages for Each Response}					Meaning	Mean (Zeros Excluded)
				1	2	3	4	5		
29A. Resources interested in using: experienced min.	No response	2%	Not interested	8%	7%	22%	25%	36%	Very interested	3.76
29B. Work and fellowship with fellow pastors	"	1	"	3	8	15	30	43	"	4.05
29C. Consultation among ministers	"	3	"	6	4	12	24	51	"	4.15
29D. Peer support group	"	2	"	12	9	22	26	29	"	3.53
29E. Sabbatical	"	2	"	13	14	15	13	43	"	3.62
29F. Continuing education	"	2	"	4	7	19	18	50	"	4.06
29G. Conference advocate	"	3	"	11	9	20	20	37	"	3.67
29H. Support from church members	"	3	"	4	13	23	27	30	"	3.70
29I. Professional counselor	"	3	"	21	12	21	20	23	"	3.14
30. Number of churches in your care	"	4		32	39	19	5	1		2.01

TABLE 10--Continued

	Size of Church Memberships									
	No Response	to 50	51-100	101-150	151-200	201-350	351-500	501-750	751-1000	1000+
31. First church	4%	16%	22%	13%	14%	17%	6%	6%	1%	1%
Second church	36	37	19	6	0	2	0	0	0	0
Third church	74	19	3	1	1	1	1	0	0	0
Fourth church	94	5	1	0	0	0	0	0	0	0
Total district memberships	4	2	14	16	16	32	8	6	1	1

32. The only pastor of your church(es) 82%
Senior pastor on a multistaff 11
Staff pastor on a multistaff 2
No response to the question 5

	Years as a Pastor									
	No Response	1-5	6-10	11-15	16-20	21-25	26-30	31-35	36-40	Over 40
33.	1%	27%	25%	14%	9%	7%	6%	5%	5%	1%

	Age of Ministers									
	No Response	to 28	28-33	34-39	40-44	45-49	50-54	55-59	60-65	Over 65
34.	0%	3%	20%	19%	12%	10%	10%	10%	10%	6%

APPENDIX D

ADDRESSES FOR RESOURCES OF SUPPORT

Organizations and Addresses:

Resources Available:

Yokefellows, Inc.
19 Park Road
Burlingame, Calif. 94010

Booklet on how to lead groups
Spiritual Growth Tests
Catalogue of materials

Family Clustering, Inc.
P.O. Box 18074
Rochester, NY 14618

Books and other resources
Workshops, training, retreats
Write for descriptive info.

Church Career Development Council
Room 770
475 Riverside Drive
New York, NY 10115
(212) 870-2144

Helps to establish and accredit
regional centers, that provide
career counseling for ministers,
and other services.

Accredited centers include:

_____

Career Development Center
St. Andrews Presbyterian College
Laurinburg, NC 28352
(919) 276-3162

Career Development Center
Eckerd College
St. Petersburg, FL 33733
(813) 867-1166

Career Development Center of the
531 Kirk Road   Southeast
Decatur, GA 30030
(404) 288-0022

Lancaster Career Development Center
561 College Avenue
Lancaster, PA 17603
(717) 397-7451

Center for the Ministry
7804 Capwell Drive
Oakland, CA 94621
(415) 635-4246

Midwest Career Development Serv.
2501 North Star Road, Suite 200
Columbus, OH 43221
(614) 486-0469

Center for the Ministry
40 Washington Street
Wellesley Hills, MA 02181
(617) 237-2228

Midwest Career Development Center
P.O. Box 249
1840 Westchester Blvd.
Westchester, IL 60153

Judicatory Career Support System
3501 Campbell
Kansas City, MO 64109
(816) 931-2516

New England Career Development Center
40 Washington Street
Wellesley Hills, MA 02181
(617) 237-2228

Northeast Career Develop. Cent.
291 Witherspoon Street
Princeton, NJ 08540
(609) 924-4814

North Central Career Development Center
3000 Fifth Street, N.W.
New Brighton, MN 55112
(612) 636-5120

Southwest Career Develop. Cent.
P.O. Box 5923
Arlington, TX 76011
(817) 265-5541

Accreditation Pending:
Career and Personal Counseling Center
1904 Mt. Vernon Street
Waynesboro, VA 22980
(703) 943-9997

Accreditation Pending:
Mid-South Career Development Cent.
P.O. Box 120815, Acklen Station
Nashville, TN   37212
(615) 327-9572

Programs in Canada, contact:
Resources for Ministry
600 Jarvis Street
Toronto, Ontario M4Y2J6
(416) 924-9192

Addresses:

Resources:

International Association of
Counseling Services, Inc.
Two Skyline Pl. Suite 400
5203 Leesburg Pike
Falls Church, VA   22041
(703) 820-4710

A Directory of Counseling
Services, including accredited
pastoral counseling centers.

Dr. Louis McBurney
Marble Retreat
Marble, Colorado   81623

Psychotherapy and other help
pastors, other church workers,
their families.

The Alban Institute, Inc.
Mount St. Alban
Washington, D.C.   20016

Helpful publications on issues
in ministry; workshops;
periodical, Action Information

Ministers Life Resources, Inc.
3100 West Lake Street
Minneapolis, MN   55416

Cassettes, posters, brochures,
newsletters.

Association for Clinical Pastoral
Education, Inc.
475 Riverside Drive
New York, NY   10115

Directory of accredited CPE
centers and member seminaries

Society for the Advancement of
Continuing Education for Ministry
3401 Brook Road
Richmond, Virginia   23227

Information on continuing
education programs available.

Action-Training Coalition
c/o M.E.T.C.
1419 V Street, NW
Washington, D.C.   20009

Information on Action
Training centers

Academy of Parish Clergy
3100 West Lake Street
Minneapolis, MN   55416

BIBLIOGRAPHY

1. Books

Adams, James R., and Hahn, Celia A. Learning to Share the Ministry.
    Washington, D.C.: Alban Institute, 1975.

Albrecht, Karl. Stress and the Manager. Englewood Cliffs, NJ:
    Prentice-Hall, 1979.

Antonovsky, Aaron. Health, Stress, and Coping. San Francisco:
    Jossey-Bass, 1979.

Augsburger, David, and Faul, John. Beyond Assertiveness. Waco,
    TX: Calibre Books, 1980.

Babbie, Earl R. The Practice of Social Research. Belmont, CA:
    Wadsworth Publishing Company, 1979.

Bartlett, Laile E. The Vanishing Parson. Boston: Beacon Press,
    1971.

Baxter, Richard. The Reformed Pastor. Edited by Jay Green.
    Marshallton, DE: National Foundation for Christian
    Education, n.d.

Bellows, Roger M. Psychology of Personnel in Business and In-
    dustry. New York: Prentice-Hall, 1949.

Biersdorf, John, ed. Creating an Intentional Ministry. Nashville:
    Abingdon, 1976.

Blazer, Dan G. II. Healing the Emotions. Nashville: Broadman
    Press, 1979.

Bouma, Mary LaGrand. Divorce in the Parsonage. Minneapolis:
    Bethany Fellowship, 1979.

Bowers, Margaretta K. Conflicts of the Clergy. New York: Thomas
    Nelson and Sons, 1963.

Brister, C. W.; Cooper, James L.; and Fite, J. David. Beginning
    Your Ministry. Nashville: Abingdon, 1981.

Caplan, Gerald. Support Systems and Community Mental Health. New
    York: Behavioral Publications, 1974.

241

Caplan, Ruth B. Helping the Helpers to Help. New York: Seabury Press, 1972.

Cattell, Raymond B.; Eber, Herbert W.; and Tatsuoka, Maurice M. Handbook for the Sixteen Personality Factor Questionnaire. Champaign, IL: Institute for Personality and Ability Testing, 1970.

Church Career Development Council. Church Career Development Councils: Career Counseling Services for Professional Church Workers. New York: Church Career Development Council, n.d. (brochure).

Clemmons, William, and Hester, Harvey. Growth Through Groups. Nashville: Broadman Press, 1974.

Clinebell, Howard J., Jr. The People Dynamic. New York: Harper and Row, 1972.

Coble, Betty J. The Private Life of the Minister's Wife. Nashville: Broadman Press, 1981.

Coleman, Lyman. Encyclopedia of Serendipity. Littleton, CO: Serendipity House, 1976.

Collins, Gary. How to Be a People Helper. Santa Ana, CA: Vision House, 1976.

Conway, Jim. Men in Mid-Life Crisis. Elgin, IL: David C. Cook Publishing Co., 1978.

Conway, Sally. You and Your Husband's Mid-Life Crisis. Elgin, IL: David C. Cook Publishing Co., 1980.

Cooper, Cary L., and Marshall, Judi. Understanding Executive Stress. New York: PBI Books, 1977.

Cooper, Cary L., and Payne, Roy, eds. Current Concerns in Occupational Stress. New York: John Wiley & Sons, 1980.

Cox, Harvey. The Secular City. New York: Macmillan Company, 1965.

Dahl, Gerald L. Everybody Needs Somebody Sometime. Nashville: Thomas Nelson Publishers, 1980.

Dittes, James E. When the People Say No. San Francisco: Harper & Row, Publishers, 1979.

Donne, John. "Devotions Upon Emergent Occasions" (1624), no. 17 in John Bartlett. Familiar Quotations. 15th ed. Edited by Emily Morison Beck. Boston: Little, Brown, 1980.

Drucker, Peter Ferdinand. The Effective Executive. New York: Harper & Row, 1967.

_____. The Practice of Management. New York: Harper & Row, 1954.

Edelwich, Jerry, with Brodsky, Archie. Burn-out--Stages of Dis-illusionment in the Helping Professions. New York: Human Sciences Press, 1980.

Engel, James. How Can I Get Them to Listen? Grand Rapids: Zondervan Publishing House, 1977.

Engstrom, Ted W., and Mackenzie, R. Alec. Managing Your Time. Grand Rapids: Zondervan Publishing House, 1967.

Fallaw, Wesner. The Case Method in Pastoral and Lay Education. Philadelphia: Westminster Press, 1963.

Freudenberger, Herbert, with Richelson, Geraldine. Burn-out: The High Cost of High Achievement. Garden City, NY: Doubleday & Company, Anchor Press edition, 1980.

Friedman, Meyer, and Rosenman, Ray H. Type A Behavior and Your Heart. New York: Alfred A. Knopf, 1974.

Glasse, James D. Profession: Minister. Nashville: Abingdon Press, 1968.

_____. Putting It Together in the Parish. Nashville: Abingdon Press, 1972.

Gould, Roger L. Transformations. New York: Simon and Schuster, 1978.

Greeves, Frederic. Theology and the Cure of Souls. Manhasset, NY: Channel Press, 1962.

Grider, Edgar M. Can I Make It One More Year? Atlanta: John Knox Press, 1980.

Hadden, Jeffrey K. The Gathering Storm in the Churches. Garden City, NY: Doubleday, 1969.

Handbook of the Doctor of Ministry Program at Lancaster Theological Seminary. Lancaster, Pennsylvania: Lancaster Theological Seminary, 1980.

Harris, John C. Stress, Power and Ministry. Washington, D.C.: Alban Institute, 1977.

Hartley, Loyde H. A Study of Clergy Morale. Lancaster, PA: Research Center in Religion and Society, Lancaster Theological Seminary, 1980.

244

Hofrenning, James B., ed. The Continuing Quest. Minneapolis: Augsburg Publishing House, 1970.

Hulme, William E. Mid-Life Crises. Christian Care Books, No. 7. Philadelphia: Westminster Press, 1980.

_____. Your Pastor's Problems. Garden City, NY: Doubleday and Company, Inc., 1966; Minneapolis: Augsburg Publishing House, 1967.

Hutcheson, Richard G., Jr. Wheel Within the Wheel: Confronting the Management Crisis of the Pluralistic Church. Atlanta: John Knox Press, 1979.

Johnson, Paul G. Buried Alive. Richmond, VA: John Knox Press, 1968.

Jones, G. Curtis. The Naked Shepherd. Waco, TX: Word, 1979.

Jud, Gerald; Mills, Edgar W., Jr.; and Burch, Genevieve Walters. Ex-Pastors; Why Men Leave the Parish Ministry. Philadelphia: Pilgrim Press, 1970.

Kadel, Thomas E., ed. Growth in Ministry. Philadelphia: Fortress Press, 1979.

Kahn, R. L.; Wolfe, D. M.; Quinn, R. P.; Snoek, J. D.; and Rosenthal, R. A. Organizational Stress: Studies in Role Conflict and Ambiguity. New York: John Wiley & Sons, 1964.

Katz, Daniel, and Kahn, Robert L. The Social Psychology of Organizations. New York: John Wiley & Sons, 1966.

Kemper, Robert G. The New Shape of Ministry. Nashville: Abingdon, 1979.

Kraemer, Hendrik. A Theology of the Laity. Philadelphia: Westminster Press, 1958.

Lavender, Lucille. They Cry, Too! Wheaton, IL: Tyndale House Publishers, Inc., 1979.

Leas, Speed B. Should the Pastor Be Fired? Washington, D.C.: Alban Institute, 1980.

_____. Time Management. Nashville: Abingdon, 1978.

Lembo, John. Help Yourself. Niles, IL: Argus Communications, 1974.

Leslie, Robert C., and Mudd, Emily Hartshorne, eds. Professional Growth for Clergymen. Nashville: Abingdon Press, 1970.

Levinson, Daniel J. The Seasons of a Man's Life. New York: Ballantine Books, 1978.

Liepsner, B. F., ed. The Young Pastor and His People: Bits of Practical Advice for Young Clergymen. New York: N. Tibbols & Sons, 1878.

Lowder, Paul D. Feed Whose Sheep? Waco, TX: Word Books, 1973.

Luther, Martin. "An Appeal to the Ruling Class of German Nobility as to the Amelioration of the State of Christendom." In Martin Luther: Selections from His Writings. Edited by John Dillenberger. New York: Doubleday, 1961.

McBurney, Louis. Every Pastor Needs a Pastor. Waco, TX: Word Books, 1977.

McClelland, David C. "Sources of Stress in the Drive for Power." In Psychopathology of Human Adaptation. Edited by George Serban. New York: Plenum Press, 1976.

McGinnis, Alan Loy. The Friendship Factor. Minneapolis: Augsburg Publishing House, 1979.

McNeill, John T. A History of the Cure of Souls. New York: Harper & Row, Publishers, 1951; paperback edition, 1977.

Mace, David, and Mace, Vera. What's Happening to Clergy Marriages? Nashville: Abingdon, 1980.

Madden, James P., ed. Loneliness: Issues of Emotional Living in an Age of Stress for Clergy and Religious. Whitinsville, MA: Affirmation Books, 1977.

Marney, Carlyle. Priests to Each Other. Valley Forge, PA: Judson Press, 1974.

Marrow, Alfred J., ed. The Failure of Success. New York: AMACOM, 1972.

Mayer, Nancy. Male Mid-Life Crisis. Garden City, NY: Doubleday, 1978.

Mead, Loren B. Evaluation: Of, by, for, and to the Clergy. Washington, D.C.: Alban Institute, 1977.

Mickey, Paul, and Gamble, Gary, with Gilbert, Paula. Pastoral Assertiveness: A New Model for Pastoral Care. Nashville: Abingdon, 1978.

Miller, William A. Why Do Christians Break Down? Minneapolis: Augsburg Publishing House, 1973.

Mills, Edgar W., and Koval, John P. Stress in the Ministry. Washington, D.C.: Ministries Studies Board, 1971.

Morse, Donald Ray, and Furst, M. Lawrence. Stress For Success. New York: Van Nostrand Reinhold Co., 1979.

Naylor, Rachel, and Torrington, Derek, eds. Administration of Personnel Policies. Epping, Essex, Great Britain: Gower Press, 1974.

Neufeld, Don F., ed. Seventh-day Adventist Encyclopedia. Washington, D.C.: Review and Herald Pub. Assn., 1966.

Niebuhr, H. Richard, and Williams, Daniel D., eds. The Ministry in Historical Perspectives. New York: Harper and Bros., 1956.

Northeast Career Center. Exploring Dimensions in Personal and Professional Development. Princeton, NJ: Northeast Career Center, n.d. (brochure).

Nouwen, Henri J. M. The Wounded Healer. Garden City, NY: Doubleday, 1972.

Oates, Wayne E., ed. The Minister's Own Mental Health. Great Neck, NY: Channel Press, 1955; 1961.

Oglesby, William B., Jr., ed. The New Shape of Pastoral Theology. Nashville: Abingdon Press, 1969.

Osborn, Ronald E. In Christ's Place: Christian Ministry in Today's World. St. Louis: Bethany Press, 1967.

Osborne, Cecil G. The Art of Understanding Yourself. Grand Rapids: Zondervan Publishing House, 1967.

Osgood, Don. Pressure Points; The Christian's Response to Stress. Chappaqua, NY: Christian Herald Books, 1978.

Oswald, Roy M. Crossing the Boundary. Washington, D.C.: Alban Institute, 1980.

_____. New Beginnings: Pastorate Start Up Workbook. Washington, D.C.: Alban Institute, 1977; reprint, 1980.

_____. The Pastor as Newcomer. Washington, D.C.: Alban Institute, 1977.

_____. Running Through the Thistles. Washington, D.C.: Alban Institute, 1978.

Oswald, Roy M.; Gutierrez, Carolyn Taylor; and Dean, Liz Spellman. Married to the Minister. Washington, D.C.: Alban Institute, 1980.

Page, Robert Collier. How to Lick Executive Stress. Englewood Cliffs, NJ: Prentice-Hall, 1961; reprint edition, New York: Cornerstone Library, 1977.

Paul, Cecil R. Passages of a Pastor. Grand Rapids: Zondervan Publishing House, 1981.

Phillips, John L., Jr. Statistical Thinking: A Structural Approach. San Francisco: W. H. Freeman and Co., 1973.

Pines, Ayala M., and Aronson, Elliot, with Kafry, Ditsa. Burnout: From Tedium to Personal Growth. New York: Free Press, 1981.

Powell, John, S.J. Why Am I Afraid to Tell You Who I Am? Niles, IL: Argus Communications, 1969.

Ragsdale, Ray W. The Mid-Life Crises of a Minister. Waco, TX: Word, 1978.

Rassieur, Charles. The Problem Clergymen Don't Talk About. Philadelphia: Westminster Press, 1976.

Reid, Kenneth E., and Quinlan, Rebecca A., eds. "Burnout in the Helping Professions." Papers presented at a Symposium on Burnout, Kalamazoo, MI, Sept. 27-28, 1979.

Richards, Lawrence O., and Hoeldtke, Clyde. A Theology of Church Leadership. Grand Rapids: Zondervan Publishing House, 1980.

Rogers, Carl R. On Becoming a Person. Boston: Houghton Mifflin, 1961.

Ross, Charlotte. Who is the Minister's Wife? Philadelphia: Westminster Press, 1980.

Rouch, Mark A. Competent Ministry. Nashville: Abingdon Press, 1974.

St. Clair, Robert James. Neurotics in the Church. Westwood, NJ: Fleming H. Revell Company, 1963.

Scott, William, and Mitchell, Terence R. Organization Theory. Homewood, IL: Dorsey Press, 1972.

Selye, Hans. Stress Without Distress. Philadelphia: J. B. Lippincott, 1974.

Senter, Ruth. So You're the Pastor's Wife. Grand Rapids: Zondervan Publishing House, 1979.

Sheehy, Gail. Passages: Predictable Crises of Adult Life. New
    York: E. P. Dutton, 1974; Bantam Books, 1976.

Smith, Donald P. Clergy in the Cross Fire. Philadelphia:
    Westminster Press, 1973.

Stewart, Charles William. Person and Profession: Career Develop-
    ment in the Ministry. Nashville: Abingdon Press, 1974.

Toffler, Alvin. Future Shock. New York: Random House, 1970;
    Bantam edition, 1971.

Vaillant, George E. Adaptation to Life. Boston: Little, Brown,
    1977.

Wagner, C. Peter. Your Church Can Grow. Glendale, CA: Regal
    Books Division, G/L Publications, 1976.

Wagner, Maurice E. Putting It All Together. Grand Rapids:
    Zondervan Publishing House, 1975.

_____. The Sensation of Being Somebody. Grand Rapids:
    Zondervan Publishing House, 1975.

Walker, Daniel D. The Human Problems of the Minister. New York:
    Harper & Brothers, 1960.

White, Ellen G. Christian Service. Washington, D.C.: Home
    Missionary Department of the General Conference of Seventh-
    day Adventists, 1947.

_____. Counsels on Health. Mountain View, CA: Pacific Press
    Pub. Assn., 1951.

_____. Evangelism. Washington, D.C.: Review and Herald Pub.
    Assn., 1946.

_____. Gospel Workers. Washington, D.C.: Review and Herald
    Pub. Assn., 1948.

_____. Mind, Character, and Personality. 2 vols. Nashville:
    Southern Pub. Assn., 1977.

_____. Ministry of Healing. Mountain View, CA: Pacific
    Press Pub. Assn., 1905; 1942.

_____. Testimonies for the Church. 9 vols. Mountain View,
    CA: Pacific Press Pub. Assn., 1948.

Wise, Carroll A. The Meaning of Pastoral Care. New York: Harper &
    Row, Publishers, 1966.

Worley, Robert C. _Dry Bones Breathe!_ Chicago: The Center For the Study of Church Organizational Behavior, 1978.

Yoder, Dale. _Personnel Management and Industrial Relations._ Englewood Cliffs, NJ: Prentice-Hall, 1956.

Zeluff, Daniel. _There's Algae in the Baptismal 'Fount'._ Nashville: Abingdon, 1978.

2. Periodicals

Adams, Henry B. "Effectiveness in Ministry--A Proposal for Lay-Clergy Collegiality." _Christian Ministry_, January 1971, pp. 32-35.

Aden, Leroy. "Minister's Struggle with Professional Adequacy." _Pastoral Psychology_ 20 (March 1969):10-16.

Anderson, George C. "Who is Ministering to Ministers?" _Christianity Today_, January 18, 1963, pp. 6-7.

Anderson, James D. "Pastoral Support of Clergy: Role Development Within Local Congregations." _Pastoral Psychology_ 22 (March 1971):9-14.

Blizzard, Samuel W. "The Minister's Dilemma." _The Christian Century_, April 25, 1956, pp. 508-10.

Bouma, Mary LaGrand. "Ministers' Wives: The Walking Wounded." _Leadership_ 1 (Winter 1980):63-75.

Bowers, M. K. "Psychotherapy of Religious Personnel; Some Observations and Recommendations." _Journal of Pastoral Care_ 17 (Spring 1963):11-16.

Bradshaw, Samuel L. "Ministers in Trouble: A Study of 140 Cases Evaluated at the Menninger Foundation." _Journal of Pastoral Care_ 31 (December 1977):230-42.

Brennan, Eileen, and Weick, Ann. "Theories of Adult Development: Creating a Context for Practice." _Social Casework: The Journal of Contemporary Social Work_ 62 (January 1981):13-19.

Broadus, Loren A. "Constructive Approach to Frustration in the Practice of Ministry." _Pastoral Psychology_ 22 (April 1971):39-44.

Brown, Thomas E. "Career Counseling as a Form of Pastoral Care." _Pastoral Psychology_ 22 (March 1971):15-20.

_____. "Career Counseling for Ministers." _Journal of Pastoral Care_ 25 (March 1971):33-40.

_____. "Vocational Crises and Occupational Satisfaction among Ministers." Princeton Seminary Bulletin 63 (December 1970): 52-62.

Bustanoby, Andre. "How to Cope with Discouragement." Christianity Today, January 7, 1977.

_____. "The Pastor and the Other Woman." Christianity Today, August 30, 1974, pp. 7-10.

_____. "Why Pastors Drop Out." Christianity Today, January 7, 1977, pp. 14-16.

Cardwell, Sue Webb, and Hunt, Richard A. "Persistence in Seminary and in Ministry." Pastoral Psychology 28 (Winter 1979): 119-31.

Cedarleaf, J. Lennart. "Pastoral Care of Pastors." Journal of Pastoral Care 27 (March 1973):30-34.

Chandler, Russell. "Help for Christian Workers: Advance through Retreat: Pastoring the Pastor." Christianity Today, May 2, 1980, pp. 50-51.

Cohen, Jeffrey L. "Male Metapause." Ministry, January 1978, pp. 18-20.

Collins, Gary R. "Burn-out: The Hazard of Professional People-Helpers." Christianity Today, April 1, 1977, pp. 12-14.

Collie, Robert M. "Counseling the Middle-yeared Pastor." Pastoral Psychology 22 (March 1971):50-53.

Cooper, Robert M. "Confidentiality." Anglican Theological Review 59 (January 1977):20-32.

Cramer, A. A. "Go Tell the People: The Ethics of Pastoral Confidentiality." Pastoral Psychology 17 (March 1966):31-41.

Dale, Robert D. "Building Pastoral Support Systems in Your Area." Church Administration, October 1976, pp. 14-15.

_____. "How to Find Where You Are." Church Administration, June 1977, pp. 13-16.

DeWaal, Sidney C. J. "The Minister as Colleague: A Pastoral Care Concern." Calvin Theological Journal 8 (November 1973): 158-71.

Dickson, Robert G. "Ministering to the Minister: Formulating a Program." Reformed Review 31 (Winter 1978):88-90.

Drucker, Peter. "Martyrs Unlimited." Harper's Magazine, July 1964, pp. 12-16.

Dudley, Roger L. "How Churches Grow." Ministry, July 1981, pp. 4-7.

Eggers, Oscar R. "Seminar for Ministers: A University-Sponsored Approach to Self-exploration." Pastoral Psychology 23 (October 1972):19-23.

"Everyone Who Makes It Has a Mentor." Inteviews with F. J. Lunding, G. L. Clements, and D. S. Perkins. Harvard Business Review 56 (July-August 1978):89-101.

Faulkner, Brooks R. "What's Going On in Pastoral Support?" Church Administration 19 (October 1976):8-9.

Fitzgerald, C. G. "Ordination Plus Six." Journal of Pastoral Care 21 (March 1967):15-23.

Fletcher, John C., and Edwards, Tilden H., Jr. "Inter-met: On-the-Job Theological Education." Pastoral Psychology 22 (March 1971):21-30.

Flowers, Ron. "Journey Toward Intimacy." Ministry, April 1981, pp. 12-13.

Frazier, Richard. "The Role of 'Need' in Pastoral Care." The Journal of Pastoral Care 27 (March 1973):35-39.

Frerichs, Robert T. "A History of the Continuing Education Movement." The Drew Gateway 47/1, 1976-77, pp. 1-9.

Friesen, DeLoss D. "Confidentiality and the Pastoral Counselor." Pastoral Psychology 22 (January 1971):48-53.

Gamble, Connolly C. "Continuing Education and Creative Leisure." The Christian Ministry, January 1978, pp. 4-7.

Glasse, James. "What Will It Take?" The Christian Ministry, January 1971, pp. 20-27.

Gleason, John J. "Perception of Stress among Clergy and Their Spouses." Journal of Pastoral Care 31 (December 1977): 248-51.

Golden, Edward S. "Management and Support of Church Personnel." Ministry Studies 3 (May 1969):26-28.

Griffin, Dan L. "The Pastor and His Humanity." Leadership 1 (Summer 1980):28-32.

Griffin, Emory A. "Self-disclosure: How Far Should a Leader Go?" Leadership 1 (Spring 1980):125-32.

Hahn, Celia Allison. "'The Madness of God'--Is It Catching?" Action Information, April 1980, pp. 1-3.

_____. "'Strung Out, Harried, Overextended'; How Can You Practice the Spiritual Life in a Busy Church." Action Information, March 1979, pp. 8-10.

"Halfway Houses for Clergy Dropouts." Christianity Today, July 18, 1969, pp. 34-35.

Harris, J. C. "New Trends in Pastoral Care for Pastors." Pastoral Psychology 22 (March 1971):5-8.

Hart, Travis. "We Pastor Each Other." Church Administration, June 1977, pp. 3-6.

Hartung, Bruce M. "Identity, the Pastor, and the Pastor's Spouse." Currents in Theology and Mission 3 (October 1976):307-11.

Henson, Mitchell F. "How to Be Yourself and a Pastor." Ministry, October 1979, p. 11.

Hester, Richard L. "Transference and Covenant in Pastoral Care." Pastoral Psychology 28 (Summer 1980):223-31.

Higgens, Paul S., and Dittes, James E. "Change in Laymen's Expectations of the Minister's Roles." Ministry Studies 2 (February 1968):4-23.

Holbrook, Gary. "Benefits of a Support Group." Church Administration, October 1979, pp. 16-19.

Holifield, E. Brooks. "The Hero and the Minister in American Culture." Theology Today 33 (January 1977):370-79.

Holmes, Thomas H., and Rahe, Ricahrd H. "The Social Readjustment Scale." Journal of Psychosomatic Research 11 (1967):213-18.

Houts, Donald C. "Pastoral Care for Pastors: Toward a Church Strategy." Pastoral Psychology 25 (Spring 1977):186-96.

Howse, Kevin J. "When the Pastor Burns Out." Ministry, April 1981, pp. 28-29.

Hulme, W. E. "Pastoral Care of the Pastor." Pastoral Psychology 14 (September 1963):31-37.

Johnson, James L. "The Ministry Can Be Hazardous to Your Health." Leadership 1 (Winter 1980):33-38.

Johnson, Paul E. "Emotional Health of the Clergy." Journal of Religion and Health 9 (January 1970):50-59.

Judy, Marvin T. "Professional Ministry: The Call, Performance, Morale, and Authority." Perkins School of Theology Journal 30 (Winter 1977):5-65.

Karschner, Randy. "How to Be a Minister's Minister." Church Administration, April 1981, pp. 29-30.

Kemper, Robert Graham. "A Professional Association for Parish Ministers." The Christian Ministry, January 1971, pp. 5-7.

Klink, T. W. "Ministry as Career and Crisis." Pastoral Psychology 20 (June 1969):13-19.

Kobasa, Suzanne C.; Hilker, Robert R. J.; and Maddi, Salvatore R. "Who Stays Healthy under Stress?" Journal of Occupational Medicine 21 (1979):595-98.

Leyden, Stuart G. "Coping with Stress." Church Management: The Clergy Journal, January 1981, pp. 14-15.

Lowery, James L. "Three Types of Professional Associations for the Clergy." The Christian Ministry, January 1971, pp. 14-15.

Lyon, W. H., and Riggs, M. D. "Experience of Group Psychotherapy for the Parish Minister." Journal of Pastoral Care 18 (Autumn 1964):166-69.

McBurney, Louis. "A Psychiatrist Looks at Troubled Pastors." Leadership 1 (Spring 1980):107-20.

McClellan, Albert. "Support Systems for SBC Ministers." Church Administration, October 1976, pp. 2-7.

MacDonald, Gordon. "Dear Church, I Quit." Christianity Today, June 27, 1980, pp. 16-19.

McGinnis, T. C. "Clergymen in Conflict." Pastoral Psychology 20 (October 1969):13-20.

McKenna, David. "Recycling Pastors." Leadership 1 (Fall 1980): 24-30.

Mahon, Robert. "An Example of the Use of Professional Development Groups in Support of New Ministers." Pastoral Psychology 22 (March 1971):31-38.

Malony, H. Newton, and Falkenberg, Donald. "Ministerial Burn Out." Leadership 1 (Fall 1980):71-74.

Marney, Carlyle, and Rouch, Mark. "Continuing Education: for Selfhood or Competence?" The Drew Gateway 47/1, 1976-77, pp. 30-36.

Mead, Loren. "Mission Statement." Action Information, May-June 1981, pp. 5-6.

Mehl, Louis G. "Occupational Rehabilitation of Psychiatrically Hospitalized Clergymen." Journal of Pastoral Care 31 (December 1977):243-47.

Mills, Edgar W. "Intentionality and the Ministry." Journal of Pastoral Care 28 (June 1974):74-83.

"Ministers Are Not Quitters" (editorial). The Christian Century, December 5, 1962, p. 1471.

Myra, Harold L. "Trauma and Betrayal." Leadership 2 (Winter 1981):43-53.

Nauss, Allen H. "The Ministerial Personality: Myth or Reality?" Journal of Religion and Health 12 (January 1973):77-96.

Osterhaven, M. Eugene, ed. "Ministering to the Minister." Reformed Review 31 (Winter 1978):71-90.

Oswald, Roy M. "Your Next Job May Kill You." Action Information, November 1979, pp. 12-14.

"Pastoral Confidentiality and Privileged Communication." (Multiple authors.) Pastoral Psychology 17 (March 1966):3-46.

Patrick, Russell A. "What the Executive Leadership Course Did for Me." Church Administration, October 1976, pp. 10-12.

Patton, John. "The Pastoral Care of Pastors." The Christian Ministry, July 1980, pp. 15-18.

Pearson, Roy. "Why I Quit the Ministry." The Christian Century, December 1962, p. 1558.

Petri, Fred. "Career Counseling for Professional Church Leaders." Pastoral Psychology 22 (February 1971):49-55.

Pines, Maya. "Psychological Hardiness: The Role of Challenge in Health." Psychology Today, December 1980, pp. 34-44.

Pohl, David C. "Ministerial Sabbaticals." Christian Ministry, January 1978, pp. 8-10.

Presnell, William B. "Minister's Own Marriage." Pastoral Psychology 25 (Summer 1977):272-81.

"Psychotherapeutic Help for the Minister." (Anonymous letter with reply from A. J. Twerski.) Pastoral Psychology 16 (March 1965):50-54.

Rabior, William. "Ministerial Burnout." Ministry, March 1979, p. 25.

Rassieur, Charles L. "How Will Stress Affect Your Ministry?" Seminary Quarterly, Fall 1980, pp. 1-2.

Rediger, G. Lloyd. "Energy." Church Management: The Clergy Journal, March 1981, pp. 12-14.

_____. "Failure." Church Management: The Clergy Journal, February 1981, pp. 16-17.

Rhem, R. A. "Staff Ministries: Advantages, Challenges, and Problems." Reformed Review 31 (Winter 1978):78-81.

Robbins, Paul D. "The Ministers of Minneapolis: A Study in Paradox." Leadership 1 (Winter 1980):118-22.

Rockland, Lawrence H. "Psychiatric Consultation to the Clergy." Pastoral Psychology 21 (January 1970):51-53.

"Role Conflict among Clergy." Ministry Studies 2/3-4, December 1968, pp. 13-82.

Rouch, Mark. "What Is Continuing Education?" The Christian Ministry, May 1974, pp. 4-5.

_____. "Young Pastors Pilot Project: An Experiment in Continuing Education for Ministry." Journal of Pastoral Care 25 (March 1971):3-11.

Sawin, Margaret M. "Congregations and Families: Building Support Systems through Family Clusters." Action Information, June 1980, pp. 5-6.

Scheuer, Garry and Carolyn. "A 'Normal' Life--The Clergy Family." The Christian Ministry, March 1981, pp. 5-9.

Seamands, David A. "Perfectionism: Fraught with Fruits of Self-Destruction." Christianity Today, April 10, 1981, pp. 24-26.

Simpson, John H. "Precarious Enterprise of Ministry." Pastoral Psychology 25 (Winter 1976):108-14.

Sims, Bennet J. "Continuing Education as a Peer Support Experience in the Dynamics of Change." Pastoral Psychology 22 (March 1971):39-43.

Sims, Edward R. "WECA--A Response to Passivity and Isolation among Parish Ministers." Pastoral Psychology 22 (March 1971): 44-49.

256

Smith, Fred. "Dissecting Sense from Nonsense." Leadership 1 (Winter 1980):101-17.

Switzer, David K. "Minister as Pastor and Person." Pastoral Psychology 24 (Fall 1975):52-64.

Troost, Donald P. "The Minister's Family--People without a Pastor." Reformed Review 31 (Winter 1978):75-78.

Twyman, Louis. "Whom Can You Trust?" Church Administration, October 1978, pp. 24-25.

Wadsworth, Allen P., Jr. "Drop-out From the Pastorate: Why?" The Journal of Pastoral Care 25 (June 1971):124-27.

Wagner, Joseph M. "Parish Dynamics; Stress as the Opportunity for Supportive Teamwork in the Congregation." Lutheran Quarterly 23 (May 1971):165-77.

White, Ellen G. "Christian Work." Review and Herald, October 10, 1882, p. 625.

_____. "Help for our Scandinavian Institutions." Review and Herald, March 19, 1901, p. 177.

_____. "If Ye Know These Things, Happy Are Ye If Ye Do Them." Review and Herald, November 4, 1902, p. 9.

Wiebe, Katie Funk. "Passing Along the Faith." Today's Christian Woman, Winter 1980-81, pp. 64-66.

Wimberly, Edward P. "Pastoral Care and Support Systems." Journal of the Interdenominational Theological Center 5 (Spring 1978):67-75.

Wolf, C. Umhau. "Do Pastors Trust Their Synod Presidents?" Dialog 11 (Winter 1972):58-60.

Wolf, Sidney. "Counseling--for Better or Worse." Alcohol Health and Research World, Winter 1974-75, pp. 27-29.

Yancey, Philip. "You Gotta Serve Somebody." Leadership 1 (Summer 1980):119-26.

Zacks, Hanna. "Self-Actualization: A Midlife Problem." Social Casework: The Journal of Contemporary Social Work 61 (April 1980):223-33.

Zaleznik, Abraham. "Managers and Leaders: Are They Different." Harvard Business Review 55 (May-June 1977):77.

3. Unpublished Materials

Beavers, Jay Lane. "Building a Support Community for People in
        Crisis." D.Min. dissertation, Southern Methodist University,
        1975.

Blanchard, Dallas Anthony. "Some Social and Orientative Correlates
        of Career Change and Continuity as Revealed among United
        Methodist Pastors of the Alabama-West Florida Conference,
        1960-1970." Ph.D. dissertation, Boston University, 1973.

Burnett, Thomas Stevens. "Ministerial Roles and Institutional
        Restraints: The Mississippi Conference of the United
        Methodist Church." D.Min. dissertation, The School of
        Theology at Claremont, 1976.

Clarke, David Beach. "Burn-out: The Problem of Overextension in
        the Unitarian Universalist Ministry." Ph.D. dissertation,
        Meadville/Lombard Theological School, 1977.

Coody, Arnold Aswell. "Factors Motivating Established Ministers
        of the Church of God (Anderson, Indiana) to Leave Its
        Ministry," Th.D. dissertation, Boston University School
        of Theology, 1974.

Dickens, Douglas Melton. "Pastoral Care of Ministers in the Southern
        Baptist Convention." Th.D. dissertation, Southwestern
        Baptist Theological Seminary, 1978.

Doyle, Dennis Lee. "Annual Study Leave as a Means of Reducing
        Pastoral Dysfunction." D.Min. dissertation, The Southern
        Baptist Theological Seminary, 1977.

Dudley, Roger L.; Cummings, Des; and Clark, Greg. "The Pastor
        as Person and Husband: A Study of Pastoral Morale." The
        Institute of Church Ministry, Berrien Springs, Michigan,
        May 1981. (Photocopied.)

"Emphasis on Pastoral Ministries," Reports from the March 4-6,
        1981, meeting in Washington, D.C., with pastors. Office
        of the vice president of the General Conference for the
        North American Division. (Photocopied.)

Forney, John Craig. "Transition: A Study of United Methodist
        Clergy of the Southern California-Arizona Conference Who
        Have Left the Parish Ministry." Rel.D. dissertation,
        School of Theology at Claremont, 1975.

Fulcher, Thomas Otis. "Factors Related to Attrition of Parish
        Ministers in the North Carolina Conference of the United
        Methodist Church, 1966-1970." Ed.D. dissertation, North
        Carolina State University at Raleigh, 1971.

Gears, Judson Oscar. "Leadership Design and Positive Job Satisfaction in Staff Ministry in United Methodist Town and Country Cooperative Parishes." D.Min. dissertation, Lancaster Theological Seminary, 1976.

Graham, Jerry Boyd. "The Development of a Support Ministry for Ministers in the Susquehanna Baptist Association." D.Min. dissertation, The Southern Baptist Theological Seminary, 1975.

Graham, Larry Kent. "Ministers and Friendship: An Examination of the Friendships Established by a Selected Group of Protestant Parish Clergymen in the Light of a Working Understanding and Theological Analysis of the Nature of Friendship." 2 vol. Ph.D. dissertation, Princeton Theological Seminary, 1978.

Henzlik, William Charles. "The Isolation of the United Methodist Pastor and Some Resources for Collegiality." Ph.D. dissertation, Meadville/Lombard Theological School, 1977.

Hunter, James Elmo III. "Ministry Seminar." D.Min. dissertation, Emory University, 1975.

Johnson, Kenneth E. "Personal Religious Growth through Small Group Participation: A Psychological Study of Personality Changes and Shifts in Religious Attitudes Which Result from Participation in a Spiritual Growth Group." Th.D. dissertation, Pacific School of Religion, 1963.

Kidney, Timothy James. "A Supervision Program Including Both the Individual Pastoral Care and the Social Ministry of Roman Catholic Seminarians." D.Min. dissertation, The Catholic University of America, 1979.

McVay, William Hinton. "An Analysis and Role Description of the Seventh-day Adventist Conference Ministerial Secretary in North America." D.Min. project, Andrews University, 1978.

Manley, Wilford Clinton, Jr. "Stress among Selected Pastors in Industrial Settings." D.Min. dissertation, The Southern Baptist Theological Seminary, 1974.

Marney, Carlyle. "Interpreters' House; A Way Station for Understanding." Thesis Theological Cassettes series, March 1972.

Melo, Luiz. "A Rationale and Suggested Program for Ministerial Support Groups for Seventh-day Adventist Pastors in Brazil." D.Min. project report, Andrews University, 1981.

Meyer, Duane. "A Study of Professional Support Systems for Clergy." D.Min. thesis, Eden Theological Seminary, 1975.

259

_____. "Group Support Tape." Minneapolis: Minister's Life Resources, 1974. (Four cassette recordings.)

_____. "How to Set Up Your Own Local Support Group." Minneapolis: Ministers Life Resources, 1974. (Cassette recording.)

Mills, E. W. "Clergy Career Stress." Thesis Theological Cassettes series, 1971, No. 6.

Nouwen, H. J. M. "The Wounded Healer." Thesis Theological Cassettes series, September 1973.

Osborne, Cecil G. "Overcoming Guilt." Thesis Theological Cassettes series, December 1974.

Paul, Ricahrd Daniel. "An Investigation and an Analysis, Leading to a Reassessment of the Minister's Attitudes toward and Time Spent in Leisure Activities." D.Min. dissertation, Drew University, 1980.

Robberson, Paul W. "Report on Organization and Management Effectiveness Study for the Ohio Conference of Seventh-day Adventists." Towers, Perrin, Forster, & Crosby, February 1981.

Robinson, Frank A. "Career Development." Thesis Theological Cassettes series, July 1975.

Rouch, Mark A. "Competent Ministry." Thesis Theological Cassettes series, July 1974.

Stewart, Charles W. "Person and Profession." Thesis Theological Cassettes series, April 1975.

Till, George A. "A Career Guidance Manual for Christian Ministry." D.Min. dissertation, Western Conservative Baptist Theological Seminary, 1976.

United Church of Christ, Office for Church Life and Leadership. "For The Renewal of Our Pastors." 1979 Family Thank Offering Project: A Final Report Presented to the Special Appeals Committee of the Executive Council, project manager, Ralph C. Quellhorst, New York, New York, December 1980.

Wolf, C. Umhau. "Clergy Support Groups." Thesis Theological Cassettes series, May 1975.